T   ve

Your   ewing

The Sew & Save Source Book

Your Guide to Supplies for Creative Sewing

by Margaret A. Boyd

Betterway Publications, Inc.
White Hall, Virginia

About the Author

Over a period of years, from the time of mock-pedaling her grandmother's ancient Singer, as a child, or "preaching" under the quilting frame rolled out to accommodate the nimble fingers of The Ladies Aid Society, Margaret A. Boyd has had a love-hate relationship with sewing and her machine — through most of her five children's outfits. ("I came to love A-line dresses and hate gussets," she declared. "By the fourth addition to our family, I was re-covering grandma's baby gift-quilts on that sewing machine.") She also worked in a variety of other fiber-crafts — as student, instructor, fair participant; and as mailorder supplies dealer; later she began writing how-to articles and source books for publication, too.

Since June of 1981, she has published *Catalog Sources —News & Updates*, an ongoing source-journal that now helps update this book (and others) while it informs of new sources, trends and news for sewing and all other fiber and general crafts. She is also guest columnist for other publications.

The Sew & Save Source Book is her sixth directory.

First Printing: February, 1984
Published by Betterway Publications, Inc.
       White Hall, VA 22987
Cover design by Marion Reynolds
Cover photographs courtesy of Sunrise Industries, Inc. and Ann Breaud
Typography by East Coast Typography, Inc.

© 1984 by Margaret A. Boyd

Library of Congress Cataloging in Publication Data

Boyd, Margaret Ann,
    The sew & save source book.

    Includes index.
        1. Sewing — Equipment and supplies — Catalogs.
    2. Sewing — Equipment and supplies — Directories.
    I. Title.   II. Title: The sew and save source book.
    TT716.B69   1984   646'.1'029473   83-11888
    ISBN 0-932620-23-X (pbk.)

Printed in the United States of America

This book is dedicated to my parents,
Beatrice J. and Henry O. Probst,
with love,
and in appreciation for their encouragement
and support of creative expression.

Contents

Guide to Listings in this Book

This book is organized in sixteen sections, with suppliers, associations, and other groups listed according to their principal product or service activity. The listings begin with companies that provide basic supplies and a fascinating variety of tools, aids, and equipment, continue with detailed information on every kind of sewing specialty and material, and conclude with scores of booksellers, publications, and resources (home study courses, for example).

Each individual listing contains company name and address, followed by literature offered and cost, if any ("send SASE" means to include a self-addressed, stamped envelope). Next, the company's products and services are presented. Note of specials or sale prices or discounts follows, where applicable. (Additional wholesale data is given for those readers with business interests.)

Some listings appear less comprehensive than others. Even where only meager data was available on the products carried, it was felt that the source may well be valuable to some readers, and the listings were included with the hope of updating them in the future.

While the book is structured through sections, quick and easy access is also available for specifics through use of the INDEX at the back of the book. Use it to find company names, categories, products, services, publications, resources, etc.

Note

This book is published as a service and is not to be considered an endorsement of any company, product or service listed herein. Neither the author nor publisher can be held responsible for any unfavorable transaction that might occur as a result of information published herein.

Acknowledgments

A special thanks to:

ALL the company people who provided valuable material for this source-book, and especially to Anne Marie Soto and others of The American Home Sewing Assn. ... and The American Sewing Guild ... Ruth Perry Livesey of Society of Craft Designers ... and Joni Pascoe of Custom Sewing Guild, and to Denise Dreher of Madhatter Press, Jerry Zarbaugh of Aardvark Adventures in Handcrafts, and others who provided professional tips and hints for home sewers — the extras that helped us present a better book. And to Barbara Brabec of Artisan Crafts, whose middle name must be "Give" — she does it so often!

My appreciation also goes to those on the "keyboards" — Michael Gurrero (Mike, did you save it?) and Steve Mangham, without whom I'd have had to fold up my computer-instrument and leave the stage. And to my Frank, and the rest of the family — you are the greatest. You never fail to pitch in.

Last, thanks to the thoughtful and energetic owners of Betterway Publications, Jackie and Bob Hostage, for the attractive book you see.

Betterway and I also would like to acknowledge Dover Publications, Inc. for some of the artwork found in this source-book. Design illustrations shown *without copyright notice* are mostly taken from their Pictorial Archives Series Books, and may be used by readers without permission.

Reader Comments and Materials

Send your comments and/or listing material for future editions or for the ongoing sequel newsletter, to Margaret Boyd c/o the publisher, or write: Margaret A. Boyd, P.O. Box 6232, Augusta, GA 30906.

Introduction

When an editor friend of mine reported the enthusiastic response she had received to her lecture on sewing for fun *and* for profit, a few years ago, and told how she was overwhelmed with inquiries from consumers for sewing supplies — pleadings for new sources, more reasonable prices, and/or wholesale discounts, and the suggestion that a source-book was needed; it didn't take long to rev-up my thinking machine for a directory of sewing materials.

But there the machine idled, while I launched what I felt to be an important sequel publication to keep directory books updated, and while situations shifted in complicated ways (as they do in the publishing world). Yet I began to take a closer look at trends in crafts and needlecrafts business — indications of important changes for sewing.

Craft stores, for instance, meeting the demand of their customers for **needlecraft** supplies, were adding those items to inventories, to the extent that wholesalers jumped in as middlemen between manufacturer and supplier — a first for the rather independent manufacturers of needlecraft materials. And in with these needlecraft supplies were included many items in the realm of **"home sewing"** materials — an area previously considered separate from needlecrafts!

Then, as I did my research for the book, I saw many more how-to articles of a general sewing nature (as opposed to strictly decorative sewing/needlecraft projects) appearing in **craft and needlework** publications.

I realized that sewing is now to be considered — along with knitting, crocheting, etc. — a **needlecraft**: This means that both hand *and* machine sewing are accepted by most everyone as creative forms of expression.

Where, we may add, sewing has always belonged. Even when the sew-ER sews more from necessity than inclination. Even when she never consciously views herself as "creative", the general public sees her that way.

That acceptance of sewing into the creative realm merges with another factor — **economics** — adding more yardage to this fabric of change. More sewing machines are tuned, oiled and threaded, proportionally, as the cost of readymade clothing, accessories, furniture and home decorating items are priced out of reach and/or as more people feel the satisfaction of creating items from fabric and know-how, while they save money.

Meanwhile, the general media — that powerful vehicle of change, have picked up on this, bannering the advantages of home sewing. They point out that we can ease our budgets and please our creative urges by sewing-it-ourselves, *while* maintaining (or surpassing!) the quality we expect from readymade. (*Newsweek* says so. *The Today Show* says so.)

The media are right.

Those in television recognize this revitalized interest in home sewing. This past spring, a network presented sewing segments in prime time programs. A cable network now airs sewing instructional programs by satellite. More is planned.

This acknowledgement, this greatly intensified attention, is gratifying to those of us who always have considered ourselves to be sewing craftspeople. And I am proud to have the opportunity to help satisfy our increasing needs for source data on materials, equipment, services, and resources, as we explore the realms of creative sewing in times ahead.

Margaret A. Boyd

1
Basic Supplies & Supply Houses

This section presents company listings of supply sources for general, basic materials, and those that handle a variety of supplies, tools, equipment, etc. under one company roof.

Aardvark Adventures in Handicraft
1191 Bannock St., P.O. Box 2449
Livermore, CA 94550
415-447-1306

Catalog, $ .50.
Natesh **embroidery threads** (for sewing machine and hand work) — 336 shades, Viscose rayon (colorfast, hand washable in warm water). **Trims:** Shisha mirrors (3 sizes); camel teeth (drilled), beads ("trader" types —of horn, Mother-of-pearl; odd shapes). (And a full line of acrylic stamps for fabric, etc.). May run sales. Allows 10% discount to teachers/institutions and professionals. In business since 1976.
(Also sells wholesale to businesses — inquire for information.)

American Handicrafts/Merribee Needle-arts
P.O. Box 2934
Ft. Worth, TX 76113
817-921-6191

Free Catalog.
Kits (and thread kits): pillows, hangings, table cloths, placemats, table runners, guest towels, potholders, quilt tops (adult, baby —for embroidery, applique). **Quilting frames** (oval hoop, adjustable with stand) embroidery hoops, quilting notions, batting and "baby batting". Soft sculpture kits, patterns. Handbag handles, snaps, graph paper, threaders, markers, others. Books. (Other needlecraft supplies.) Has quantity discounts; Mastercard, Visa. May run special sales.

American Needlewoman, Inc.
P.O. Box 6472
Ft. Worth, TX 76115

Free Catalog.
Kits: candlewicking, cross stitch pillows, quilts, soft boxes, tablecloths (and thread kits), placemats, others. **Fabrics:** linens, aida, hardanger, Fiddler's cloth, Monza (polyacrylic sheer), Davosa — all by yard. **Supplies:** floss, threads, Ribband™ ribbon. Cotton and polyester batting, fiberfill, fat batts. Organizer. Hoops (wood, plastic) templates, markers. **Frames:** scroll, rotating, sit-on floor, quilting; potpourri, fabric glues, fray check, magnifier lamps. Scissors. Books. (Other needlecraft supplies.) Runs sales specials. Has quantity prices; Mastercard, Visa.

American Thread Co. Consumer Division
High Ridge Park
Stamford, CT 06905

See your fabric or needlecraft outlet.
Cotton **embroidery floss** (100% mercerized, 6 strand) in 9 yard pull skeins, full line of graduated shades. Manufacturer.

Aristera, The Left Hand People
9 Rice's Lane
Westport, CT 06880

Catalog, $1.00.
Aids for left-handed people: scissors — 21 kinds, "Third hand", rulers, zipper-pull set; left-handed instruction manuals including for embroidery (and other needlecrafts.

Give It the Needle: "Sewing machine needles do wear out. Change them often. Use only the type recommended by the manufacturer. Spending time and money on a project is wasted if you've neglected to use a good needle. Even a new needle is sometimes faulty." — Courtesy of **Gail Kibiger,** of SewCraft.

Armstrong Products, Inc.

P.O. Box 979
Guthurie, OK 73044
405-282-7584

Write for catalog.
Luxo lamps — Magnifier lamp with 36" adjustable arm, with mount; 75 watt rating. Others.

Artistry in Thread, Inc.

10746 S.E. 28th Ave.
Milwaukie, OR 97222
503-653-5744

Send SASE with inquiry (specify).
Sewing machines — domestic and commercial brands. Supplies for machine embroidery. (Also custom monogramming service, embroidered emblems.) Mastercard, Visa. Has basic specialty and instructor's classes.

Louise Bane

3010 Santa Monica Blvd. #221
Santa Monica, CA 90404

Send SASE for prices.
Extra large **tracing carbon** (washable) in black and colors; plain pattern paper.

Bee Lee Co.

Box 36108
Dallas, TX 75235

Free Catalog.
"Western" sewing supplies: thread, trims, buttons, lace, pearl and other snap fasteners (complete line).

Better Homes and Gardens Family Shopping Service

Box 6 BA, Locust at 17th
Des Moines, IA 50336

Catalog, $1.00.
"Stitch and Stuff" kits: pillows, toys, dolls, Christmas accessories; cross stitch and other embroidery, clothing (women's, baby). **Aids:** embroidery hoops, markers, pillow forms. **Frames** (blocker, quilting). And other needlecraft supplies. Has toll free number for orders; Mastercard, Visa.

Dick Blick/Horton

P.O. Box 1267
Galesburg, IL 61401
309-343-6181

Box 26
Allentown, PA 18105
215-965-6051

Box 521
Henderson, NV 89015
702-451-7662

Brochure, flyers, and supplements, $2.00.
Fabrics: cotton bunting (patriotic stripes). Felt (wool/rayon, Rhun Fhelt™ polyester, by package, yard, scraps; full range of colors. Burlap (17 shades; even-weave, natural). Leather scraps, suede scraps; by lb. Nylon net. **Dyes:** Dylon, Fibrec, Putnam; batik (batik supplies). **Paints:** Dylon, Deka, Versatex, Pentel, Prang, Paint Puffer™; markers, ball point. **Trims:** sequins, beads (seed, tile, wood, asst'd.). **Scissors/shears** (trimmers, all-purpose, heavy, bent). Complete screen printing and stenciling supplies. Fabric adhesives. Cloth strippers. **Magnifiers** (fold up, gooseneck, Optipak™ for eyeglasses). Light tables, tracing boxes. Quilting and needlecraft frames. Books. Plain and protective clothing: denim apron, wrap smock, gloves. Storage cabinets and other supportive items. (And full lines of arts/crafts and drafting supplies.) Has quantity prices. Has toll free number for orders; Mastercard, Visa. Business established in 1911.

Loop Rug Needle and yarn cutter, © Dick Blick

Boin Arts and Crafts

87 Morris St.
Morristown, NJ 07960

Catalog, $1.00.
Leathers, leather findings, stamping tools. **Threads** — embroidery and other types. Felt remnants, pieces, assortments. Burlap (10 shades). Beads (seed, wood, others), feathers, buckles. **Silk screen** supplies, tools. **Group packs:** felt projects, puppets, leather, others. (And many other craft supplies, tools, and equipment.) Has quantity prices, Bank Americard, Mastercard, Visa.

Boycan's Craft and Art Supplies

P.O. Box 897
Sharon, PA 16146
412-346-5534

Catalog, $2.00.
Kits/supplies: soft sculpture, quilting, embroidery, trapunto, candlewicking, cross-stitch, "Tint-N-Stitch" and others. **Stencils** (pre-cut mylar, others) by Plaid, Stencil Magic, Country Colors, others. **Trims** — ribbons (satins, decorator types, plaids, florals and mini prints). Laces. "Feel-O-Fleece" craft fiber (Mock wool top roving). Felt, craft fur, foam. Potpourri supplies. Extensive books and supplies — all needle and general crafts; tools/equipment, finishes and paints. Has quantity prices, discounts. (Sells wholesale to businesses — inquire for application form.) In business since 1965.

Boye Needle

4343 North Ravenswood Ave.
Chicago, IL 60613

See your dealer or send $2.00 for catalog.
Notions/aids: hand sewing needles (assortments include sharps, quilting, embroidery, darner, tapestry, beading, leather), machine needles and accessories. Pins, thimbles, hem gauge, tracing wheel, pom-pom makers, tape measures, liquid thread. Purse handles (10 styles/sizes). **Quilting frames** and stands (hoops, rotating scroll, floor, lap, blocker frames). **Hoops** — wood, plastic, metal; 3" to 18" sizes. Tapestry and yarn needles, threaders, markers. Booklets, leaflets (quilting, handbags making). Other needlecraft supplies. Allows discounts to teachers/institutions and professionals "in pack" quantities. (Also sells wholesale to businesses.) Manufacturer in business since 1907.

Braid-Aid

466 Washington St., Rt. 53
Pembroke, MA 02359

Catalog, $2.00.
Fabrics: wool (by yard, remnants, strips), burlap — Scottish, others; Monk's cloth, wrap cloth. **Aids:** shears, wool cutter units. **Threads:** heavy linen, cotton. Perfection dyes. Over 200 patterns (for rugs, others). (And complete line of rug making and weaving supplies.)

Buffalo Batt and Felt Corp.

3307 Walden Ave.
Depew, NY 14043
716-683-4100

Brochure, swatches and price list, $1.00 (Refundable).
Super Fluff™ 100" **polyester stuffing** (20 lb. per case), pillow inserts, bonded quilt batts (batts packed 10 per case). Minimum order 2 cases. "Save 30, 40, 50%." In business since 1919.
(Also sells wholesale to businesses.)

The Button Shop

951 Garfield, P.O. Box 1065
Oak Park, IL 60304
312-383-3875

Free catalog.
Sewing zippers (jacket separating - brass, trouser - brass, heavyweight with reversible slides; 2-way jacket separating; lightweight separating, extra long separating, skirt and neck types, long closed bottom, others — variety of colors, sizes.) Velcro tape fasteners (white, black); 2 widths. **Threads:** polyester long fiber Suisse, mercerized cotton (2 size spools), metallic, elastic, button and carpet, heavy duty, others. **Interfacings** (nonwoven, flexible, Hairoflex canvas), pressing cloth, twill tapes (3 sizes), cable cord, snap fastener tape, hem facing, seam bindings, bias tape, pleater tape (drapes) and hooks. Trouser pockets, Stitch Witchery. Knitted cuffs, leather elbow patches. **Elastics** — regular braid, polyesters, no-roll waistband, heavy ribbed no-roll, pj, corset repair; sew-on garters, bra-backs, elastic cords. **Mending fabrics,** iron-ons. Marking pencils, chalk, paper, wheels, Beeswax. Sewing machine **needles,** hand needles, leather needles. **Pins** — dressmaker, brass, glass head, safety. **Scissors/shears** (American, imported); Fiskars, Gingher. Gripper plier kits, snap fasteners and snaps. Assorted button bag. **Laces** — cotton, nylon, polyester, blends; braids, metallic braids. Gauges — hem, dressmakers, sew/knit. Buckle assortment (metals, plastics, slides; 15). Frogs (13 colors). Hooks, snaps, Prims buttons (you-cover), buckles, belt backing. **Buttons** — over 55 types/variety of sizes, colors (plain, decorative, fancy; metal, leather, plastics). Sewing machine shranks, bobbins, shuttle, belts, motor attachments, light bulbs, other parts, accessories. Has quantity prices. Three generations in the same business, since 1900.

Button Savvy: "The **more buttons** you use, **the smaller** they should be; **less buttons,** if **larger.** To **sew** on **buttons** a little **quicker,** thread the needle with four strands instead of two. Takes less strokes in and out of the button eyes." — Courtesy of **Artefabas;** lawyer, teacher, and author of *Super Quick Sewing Tips.*

ES 15

... ght Ave.
... 31005

...00 (refundable).
Threads: DMC, metallics, others. Felt, beads. Quilting **frames,** embroidery **hoops.** Books. (And dollmaking and other needlecraft supplies.)

Calico Junction
R.F.D. #3
Milton, VT 05468

Catalog, $2.00.
Patterns (full size — for machine embroidery, applique, quilting); **kits,** hoops.

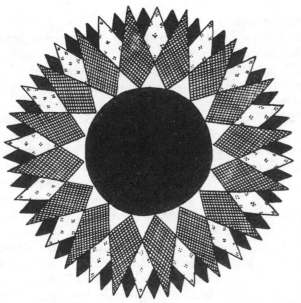

Applique design

Campau Co.
Box 20632
Dallas, TX 75220

Free Catalog.
Snap fasteners: fancy western pearl and metal snaps, variety of designs and colors.

Coats and Clark, Inc.
Consumer and Education Affairs Dept.
P.O. Box 1966
Stamford, CT 06904

See your dealer.
Sewing supplies/aids: Threads-Dual Duty Plus™, "Finesse", others. Zippers (polyester, metal, polyester invisible). Tapes, piping (and metallics) soutache, bias tape, stretch and other laces, Hem facing, seam binding, others. Stitch in Time™ educational leaflets (including "Quilted Fabrics"). Manufacturer.

Conso Products Co.
261 Fifth Ave.
New York, NY 10016
and:
Union, SC 29379

See your dealer.
FabriCraft™ **fabrics, trims,** threads, piping cords, tapes, notions. Craft project books, others.

Cornucopia
Box 362
Enterprise, KS 67441

Send SASE for price list.
Threads/yards: silk, crewel wool, tapestry, Persian, others. Folkwear **patterns.**

Corticelli
P.O. Box 261, 963 Newark Ave.
Elizabeth, NJ 07207

See your dealer or write for details.
Full line of sewing **notions and threads.**

The Craft Basket
Colchester, CT 06415

Free catalog.
Needlecraft kits: soft sculpture and others for sewing, quilts, stuffed, toys, kitchen accessories, pillows, Bermuda bags. **Supplies:** beads, ribbons. Naturals. (Other craft kits and supplies.) Has quantity prices; Mastercard, Visa.

The Craft Bug
3220 W. Florida Ave.
Hemet, CA 92343

Catalog, $2.00 (refundable).
Supplies: doll parts, beads, feathers, flowers, pearls.

The Craft Gallery
P.O. Box 541
New City, NY 10956

Catalog, $1.00.
Supplies: Monks cloth, Aida, Hardanger, evenweave; hoops, frames. Threads — linen, wool, cottons, silks including silk gauge; smocking and quilting supplies. Books (and other needlecraft supplies).

Craft Universe
2881 Clark Rd.
Sarasota, FL 33581

Catalog, $ .50 (refundable).
Supplies: beads, craft fur, cross-stitch fabric, floss, materials. (Other needlecraft supplies.)

Applique design

Craftsman Supply House
35 Browns Ave.
Scottsville, NY 14546

Catalog, $ .50.
Fabrics — burlap, Phun Phelt™, craft fur, Pellon™, metallic lame. Waxed linen thread. **Ribbons** — over 20 styles/ sizes. **Trims:** feathers, bells, sequins, pom-poms. Books. (Many other craft supplies.) Has some quantity prices.

Craftways Corporation
1465 4th St.
Berkeley, CA 94710
415-527-4561

See your local store, or write for information.
Iron-on transfer books: seven-book-in-one series; or for seasonals, "friendship", Country-home, children's and Americana, Christmas, nature (meadows, forests, seashores) and nature combo-book; embroidery transfer motifs. Transfers for cross-stitch (8 books — country, wildflowers, alphabets, birds, Christmas, children's). Transfer designs for fabric frames (all types), Country and western motifs; miniatures designs. (Other items.)
(Also sells wholesale to businesses.)

Creative Craft House
Box 1386
Santa Barbara, CA 93102

Catalog, $1.00.
Trims: sequins, metallic braids, ribbons, rhinestones, bells, beads (plastic, trading, metallics, bone, gemstones, abalone, glass). Dried naturals, shells. Potpourri supplies, novelties. Books. (Other craft supplies.) Has quantity prices, discount for large orders.

D & G Associates
67 Baldwin Rd.
Warwick, RI 02886

Free catalog.
Snap fasteners; "all types".

Decorating and Craft Ideas Patt
P.O. Box 2522
Birmingham, AL 35201

Write for list.
Patterns for variety of needlecrafts: sewing, quilting, applique, others.
(Also publishes a magazine.)

Denim Accents
1801 N.E. 134th St.
Vancouver, WA 98665
206-573-2178

Catalog, $ .50.
Denim/T-shirt: fabrics, notions (fasteners, needles, others), threads, woven labels, others.

Do-Do Sales, Inc.
Box 98
Seffner, FL 33584
813-689-7134

Free catalog.
Beads: faceted, ferris wheel, rosebud, rice, pearls, metallics, others. **Supplies:** purse handles, hardware. Craft fur, felt, art foam. (Other craft and needlecraft supplies, kits.) Has some quantity prices. Allows foreign orders.

Dritz
(see Risdon Corporation)

The Fabric Carr
381 First St., Suite 5124
Los Altos, CA 94022

Write for catalog.
Aids: Buttonhole form, button spacer, bias maker, pocket form. French curve set, Magnistitch, sewing bird and clamp (like "third hand"), "Grabbit" magnet. "Multipress", iron stand, needleboard, seam roll, clapper, sleeve and grain board. **Books.** Has Mastercard, Visa.

> **The Story on Storage:** "I am limited on storage space, but have lots of fabric!! I solved the problem by purchasing a plastic trash container and storing my 'scraps' of fabric in it. It will hold your yards of fabric, also. I decorated the outside of the can with pretty decals and set it in a corner in my sewing room. I also store my thread in a see-through old-fashioned cookie jar — the type with a metal lid on the top. You can see quickly what color you want and it looks pretty sitting on your sewing table!!" — Courtesy of **Nanci Cowles** of The Calico Candlestick.

ber Conversion, Inc.
Box 145
Broadalbin, NY 12025

Send SASE for prices.
Polyester **fiber filling,** quilt batting, fiber filled pillow forms. (Sales to continental U.S. only.)

Florida Supply House
P.O. Box 847
Bradenton, FL 33506

Catalog, $1.00.
Beads: plastic faceted, rice, oat, spacer, mushroom, heart, rosebud, bugle, rondells, wood shapes. **Fabrics:** felt, craft fur, art foam, nylon net. **Threads:** metallics, nylon, others. Purse handles. **Doll** heads, eyes, parts. **Trims:** metallic braids, sequins, ribbons, pins. **Support:** paperweights, novelties, shells (cut, drilled, etc.), adhesives, plastic and cardboard boxes. Books. (And supplies for other crafts and needlecrafts.) Has Mastercard, Visa.

French Handsewing
Rt. 2, Box 315
Montgomery, AL 36108

Send SASE for details.
French laces, ribbons, trims, imported fabrics, others. Book: *French Handsewing,* by Sarah Howard Stone — illustrated guide to the art of tucking, intricate embroidery, lace work; creating handsewn clothing; reference with artisan techniques, designs, basics to complex tucking (illustrated).

Frieda's Arts and Crafts
P.O. Box 6037
Columbus, GA 31907

Catalog, $1.00 (refundable).
Cross stitch supplies. **Trims:** silk flowers, ribbons, beads, cords. Purse handles. (And macrame supplies.) Has Mastercard, Visa.

G Street Remnant Shop
805 G St., N.W.
Washington, DC 20001
202-393-7897

Send SASE for brochure, or $1.00 for 2 garment swatches (specify), or call for information.
Fabrics — full line of imported and designer types, leathers. Trims: variety of types, sizes, colors. Antique buttons. Patterns. Notions. Books.

Gohn Bros.
Box 111
Middlebury, IN 46546
219-825-2400

Free catalog.
Over 75 fabrics (by yard) — cottons, blends, wools, crepes, denims, man's suiting, dacron, knits, cheesecloth, 7 cotton quilting prints, white huck, muslins, 80" and 90" bed sheeting, quilt sheeting, pillow ticking, drill, duck cloth, blanket, 7 fake fur linings, haircloth, interfacings, buckram, bonnet wire. Threads, **notions** (machine and hand needles, closures, elastics, pins). Shoulder pads, ribbons, tapes, zippers. Manufacturer, since 1900.

Stencil design

Goodhousekeeping Needlecraft Kits
P.O. Box 1250
West Englewood, NJ 07666

Catalog, $ .50 (U.S.); Canadians send $1.00.
Needlecraft kits: quilting, embroidery pillows, hangings, cross stitch, fashion sewing, toys, others.

The Guildcraft Co. of Buffalo, Inc.
3158 Main St.
Buffalo, NY 14214

Catalog, $2.00.
Fabric decorating: paints, dyes, batik, block printing, screen process items. **Fabrics:** burlap, nylon net, felt, foam. Trims: sequins, feathers, braids, beads (wood, plastic, bamboo, tile). Doll faces, parts. (Supplies for other crafts.)

Herrschners, Inc.
Hoover Rd.
Stevens Point, WI 54481

Free catalog.
Kits: dolls (sock, cloth), crewel, candlewicking, cross stitch, others; for home accessories; over 12 quilts and thread kits. Over 30 stamped table linens with thread kits, over 30 stamped pillow cases, placemats, others. Holiday kits. **Tools/equipment:** needlework frames (tapestry, 3-way hoop, rotating scroll, sit-on, adjustable). Fiskars scissors, clipper, sharpener. Hand-held sewing machine, 5 magnifiers, reflector/copier, adjustable dressmaker form (DuPont Neophrene). **Supplies:** fiberfill, ball point pens, glitter tubes, threads, DMC and Star floss. **Fabrics:** pillow tubing, flour sacking, gull glass toweling, cotton flannel, cream linen, Hardanger, Aida, linen toweling. Readymade towels, pillowcases. Canvases. Laces. Has some quantity prices; American Express, Mastercard, Visa.

S. R. Harris Industries, Inc.
5100 N. County Rd. 18
Minneapolis, MN 55428

Thread catalog and color chart, $3.00. Notion catalog ("save 20% to 50%"), $4.00.
Full line notions. Threads — poly-core (#50, #70) on 1,100 yard spools. **Fabrics** — (designer and mill surplus) denim, cotton/poly prints and solids, t-shirt and other knits, stretch terry, others.

Home-Sew
Bethlehem 83, PA 18018

Catalog, $ .25.
Supplies/trims: appliques, laces (eyelet and others), ribbons and other trims, ric-rac; zippers, buttons and other closures, "at reduced prices".

House of Crafts and Stuff
409 No. Gall Blvd., Hwy. 301
Zephrhills, FL 33599

Catalog, $2.00 (refundable).
Trims: sequins, ribbons (velvet, satin), metallic threads, bells, honeycomb ribbons, others. Plastic **beads:** starflake, cartwheel, faceted, frosted, metallic, aurora, pearls, glass seed, rocailles. **Fabrics:** felt, nylon net. **Support:** music box movements, wreath frames, novelties. Full line of doll and animal parts — see index. (And other craft and needlecraft supplies.)

Huning's Needlework
201 N. Main St.
St. Charles, MO 63301

Send SASE for lists.
Kits: embroidery, quilts, quilt block sets (children's geometrics, flowers), quilt tops. **Fabrics:** broadcloth blend, quilt sheeting blend (90" wide). **Supplies:** floss, other threads, fiberfill, threads, others. Has Mastercard, Visa.

Imports by Clotilde
11 S. Limestone St.
Jamestown, OH 45335
513-675-2287

Catalog, $1.00 (refundable).
Sewing notions/aids: Cutting tools (Olfa cutters and mat), "touch knife", buttonable cutter. **Iron and pressing aids** (hams, 5 cloths, presser and clapper, seam roll, point presser). **Quilting aids:** stencil plastic, graphs, grids, stripper, seamer, finger guard, leather thimble, angle and curve shapes, starmakers. Thread nippers, needles. Over 12 scissors (Gingher, others). Bodkin, bias marker bars, collar point, weights, pocket template, pin holders. Pins (all purpose, quilting, silk, glass head). **Interfacing** (knit, "pel-aire" pellon, tailor, fusible). **Ultra Suede™** fabric undercollars, scrap pieces (assorted colors). **Book:** *Sew Smart*, by Judy Lawrence and Clotilde (sewing techniques, including designers/manufacturers methods can serve as text for sewing classes); professional guide to working with knit and woven fabrics; covers facings, collar and cuff construction, pockets, neckline finishes, others; 272 pages, over 900 illustrations. (A teachers guide is also available.) In business since 1971, Clotilde brings a lifetime experience in the industry to choices of sewing supplies.
(Also sells wholesale to businesses.)

Dare the Double Needle! It makes perfectly spaced felled seams, or other decoration ... follow your machine instructions for use. Needles come in different space-widths. Experiment!

Jacquart's
505 McLeod
Ironwood, MI 49938

Free list.
Zippers: Long and short; two-way type, reversible types, others.

JerryCo., Inc.
601 Linden Pl.
Evanston, IL 60202
312-475-8440

Catalog, $ .50.
Surplus bargains/oddities, to utilize for sewing — recent listings included orange parachutes (5' diameter), military silk ribbon, webbing, elastics, elastic terrycloth tubing, camera strap braid, beltings, threads (silk suture, fiberglass, industrial rayon), disposable smocks, aprons. Military fabrics, items with fabric (canvas pole carrying case, others) and many non-sewing items. **Support items:** Plastic boxes, pull-out drawers, odd poly bags, others. "We will negotiate price and terms for any quantity buyer." Their slogan: "Remember the 'plus' in sur'-plus'." In business since 1946.

Kirchen Bros.
Box 1016
Skokie, IL 60076

Catalog, $1.00.
Kits: Holiday accessories, ornaments (soft, sculpture, felt, others), art foam. **Supplies:** Art foam, burlap, craft furs, felt pieces, handbag handles. **Trims:** Jingle bells, tassels, feathers, ribbons, sequins, threads. Naturals, magnets, craft drape solution, others. **Dollmaking** heads, hands, feet, faces, eyes; animal eyes, noses; novelties. (And other craft and needlecraft supplies.) Has quantity prices; Mastercard, Visa.

Lakeland Arts
2435 North 116th St.
Wauwatosa, WI 53226

"Discount" catalog, $1.50.
Kits: gingham/calicos oven mitts, pot holders, bibs, fabric frames. **Aids:** self-stick mounting board, Lo-ran carrying case, thread organizer, marker, line keepers. **Supplies:** DMC cotton metallic thread, synthetic embroidery thread, plastic hoops, Ribband ribbons, frames, bell pulls, wood rings, others. Scissors, needles, magnets, key rings, other **accessories. Fabrics** — Aida, Americana cloth, heritage cloth, polyester pieces (skin shades). Candlewicking kits, frames. Full line of needlecraft booklets: Christmas designs, inspirational country designs, potpourri, mini-designs; floral and animal motifs, Victoriana. Allows foreign orders.

Lansdale Discount House
816 W. Second St.
Lansdale, PA 19446
215-855-7162

Send SASE with specific inquiry.
Altra sewing kits. Complete line of fabrics, notions, patterns. (Also yarns.) In business since 1958.

Love and Money Crafts
P.O. Box 987
Ann Arbor, MI 48106

Catalog, $1.00.
Kits: counted cross stitch, patchwork pillow, candlewicking pillow; scissors, embroidery hoops; (other needlecraft items).

Manasian Mill
140 Kemble St.
Boston, MA 02119

Send SASE for prices.
Polyester fiberfill by carton (20 one pound bags). Foam pillows — knife edge, 12", 14" square and round (by carton).

Mari-Lu's Crafts
703 N. Main
Akron, OH 44310

Catalog, $2.00 (refundable).
Full line of supplies for **dollmaking** (parts — hands, feet, bodies, heads, others), bead crafts (including variety of beads), boutique **trims** (and other needle and general crafts).

Mary Maxim
2001 Holland Ave.
Port Huron, MI 48060
and: Paris, Ontario, Canada

Free Catalog.
Kits: Quilting, embroidery, cross-stitch, candlewicking, crewel; stamped goods, craft fur, cloth dolls/toys, holiday items, others. **Notions:** threads, closures, sets, zippers, others. **Aids:** Measures, stencils, quilting frames/stands. Batting, fiberfill, forms. (Other needlecraft supplies.) Has some quantity prices, runs sales; Mastercard, Visa.

Material Pleasures Fiber Arts
6606 West North Ave.
Wanwatosa, WI 53213

Catalog, $1.50.
Variety of **supplies:** stitching accessories, threads, fabrics. Books.

Nancy's Notions

Box 683
Beaver Dam, WI 53916

Send large SASE for catalog.

Notions: Gauges, rulers, bobbins, bias tape maker. Sewing machine parts: Overcast guide foot, zipper guide, buttonhole foot. Pins, needles (6 styles), adhesives, transfer paper, pencil, threads (on cones, sampler box, metallics, rayon embroidery). "Stitch witchery", and other by-yard aids. "Seams great", "Sta-tape", "Fray Check". Gingher scissors, Olfa cutters. Quilting notions: seamer, graphs, others. Elastics. Pressing aids. Adjustable dressform. Books, patterns; including *Fitting Without Guessing*, by Nancy Zieman (on slacks pivot and slide fitting, with pattern — multisized). Has very small discount on very large orders.

Natural Fiber Fabric Club

521 Fifth Ave.
New York, NY 10175

Send SASE for brochure.

Sewing aids, tailoring aids, scissors, linings, natural buttons collections. Natural fabrics (see under fabrics). Members of this fiber club receive a sewing aids catalog and handbook (with items mentioned above), and fabric swatches. They "guarantee members a saving of at least 20% from the manufacturer's recommended retail price on all items we sell. No exceptions."

The Needle People News Sewing Club

P.O. Box 115
Syosset, NY 11791

Send SASE for details.

Club members receive a newsletter, special discounts on fabrics, notions, patterns; consulting service; wardrobe and figure analysis.

Newark Dressmaker Supply

6473 Ruch Rd., P.O. Box 2448
Lehigh Valley, PA 18001

Free catalog.

Notions: Pins, needles (all kinds), sewing machine needles and accessories, zippers, snaps, buttons, others. Elastics, elastic thread. Cords, fringes, tassels, appliques, floss. **Interfacings:** Non-woven, stretch, fusible, silky. **Fabrics:** pillow tubing, muslin, crinoline, cottons, blends, lace, teal ticking, buckram, others. Knit cuffs, collars. Buttons. **Trims:** rhinestones, banding, sequins, ribbons, over 20 laces, tapes, Velcro. Threads, 15 scissors, rippers. Upholstery/tailor's materials. **Tools/aids:** sleeve board, pressers, turners, measures, bodkin, tracing items, leather stitcher, needles, rhinestone setter, templates, patterns. Has some quantity prices; Mastercard, Visa.

North Shore Farmhouse

Greenhurst, NY 14742

Catalog, $1.00.

Sewing kits: calico and other old-time, applique in variety of country designs, others. **Cottons** (calico, others —by yard). Potpourri mixtures. (And other non-sewing craft items, old-time general items.)

Oregon Tailor Supply Co.

2123 S.E. Division St.
Portland, OR 97202
503-232-6191

Free catalog.

Supplies: linings and interfacings. notions (including hard-to-find), threads (American Thread, Coats & Clark) dressmaking supplies, tailor's trimmings, buttons — full line, zippers (all sizes, types; nylon, plastic, metal and cut-to-fit sizes).

The Ossipee Owl Craft Center

Rt. 16
Ossipee, NH 03684

Catalog, $3.50.

Doll parts: heads, feet, hands, sets, noses, eyes, animal voice boxes (cat, cow, lamb), others. Accessories. **Purse handles. Trims:** sequins, metallic braids and trims, beads, ribbons, fringes. **Cloth doll/animal patterns. Bells** (16 shapes/sizes). Books. (And many other non-sewing craft supplies.)

Shanking Around: "Sewing Machine feet are somewhat interchangeable if you know what shank you have. The shanks are low (or short), high (or long) for most machines, super-hi for some Kenmore machines, and slant for some Singer machines. Once you determine which ones you want, you can get almost any foot you want. Look at these feet [see illustration] to help."

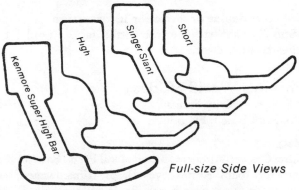

Full-size Side Views

— Courtesy of **Janet Stocker,** publisher of *Treadle-art,* from Vol. 4, #6.

COVERED BRIDGE

Summer		Winter	
⊠	medium green	⊠	black
⊙	red	⧄	black
■	black	■	black
⊡	dark green	⊙	red
⧄	light blue	⊡	dark green
⊡	brown	⊡	white
◪	medium green	◪	light grey
☐	light green	☐	white

Cross-stitch embroidery design

Pieceful Pleasures
566 30th Ave.
San Mateo, CA 94403

Catalog, $ .50.
Natesh embroidery thread (in 336 colors), dyes, shisha mirrors; textile arts books. Others.

The Porcupine Pincushion
(See The Silver Thimble)

Posi-Bender
Box 2173
Westminster, CA 92683

See your dealer or write for information.
"Stiff 'N Fab" stiffener for cotton fabrics (and cotton threads) dries clear.

Poston's World of Ideas
300 S. Prosperity Farms
No. Palm Beach, FL 33408

Catalog, $1.00.
Kits: Crewel, stitchery, others. Doll Parts. **Fabrics:** Felt, craft fur, foam. Animal eyes. Beads/trims: faceted, seed, others; sequins, pom-poms, jingle bells, pearls. **Equipment:** Embroidery hoops (plastic, metal, wood), quilting frames. Books. Has Mastercard, Visa.

William Prym, Inc.
Dayville, CT 06241
800-243-1832

See your dealer.
Prym™ sewing notions — cover-your-own button kits (including with simple-to-use 2-part tool); many other notions.

Pure Silk China Co.
Rt. 2, Box 70
Holdrege, NE 68949
308-995-4755

Color card, $2.00 ppd.
Silk embroidery threads (single 14 yd. skins) in 64 colors; reasonable.

Putnam Company
(See The Frugal Fox)

Rando
Box L — The Commons
Macedon, NY 14502
315-986-3324

Contact your dealer, or distributor.
Randofluff™ polyester fiberfill (2 size bags). Manufacturer.

Rhode Island Textile Co.

P.O. Box 999
Pawtucket, RI 02862
401-722-3700

See your fabric dealer, or distributor.
Stretchrites™ elastics — woven, knitted, and braided types; for all applications.

Risdon Corp.

P.O. Box 5028
Spartanburg, SC 29304

See your dealer.
Dritz™ line of sewing **aids/notions:** Trace-B-Gone™ colored tracing papers, Mark-B-Gone™ wash-out pen, kits, sets, pincushions, needles, pins, other notions; machine covers. 14 candlewicking kits (muslin). Buttons-to-cover, buckles-to-cover, Fray Check™ and Seams Great™ finish. Elastics, bras and swim bras and parts. Maternity panels, patching cloth, pockets; others.
Manufacturer.

Ron's Craft Supply House

177 Main St.
Greenville, PA 16125

176 page catalog, $3.00 (refundable).
Complete supplies for: dollmaking, cross-stitch (and non-sewing crafts). Art foam, beads (variety of plastic kinds), others.

S & S Arts & Crafts

Mill St.
Colchester, CT 06415
203-537-3451

Free catalog.
Sewing group/bulk packs (children's, adult's) soft sculpture, felt (puppets, dolls, boutique items), tote bags, hangings, boxes, calico flowers, padded clothes hangers, leather items. **Supplies:** Beads (most kinds), linen thread, ribbon, fabrics (felt, burlap, gingham, calico; scrap leather, felt. Unbleached muslin). Batting. (Packs for other crafts.)

Sax Arts and Crafts

P.O. Box 2002, 316 Milwaukee St.
Milwaukee, WI 53202

Catalog, $3.00.
Complete supplies for: leathercrafts (garment leathers, others, threads, needles, dyes; tools/equipment, needlecrafts (embroidery, cross-stitch, and others). **Kits:** groups and classroom needlecraft packs, others. **Fabrics: velveteen, felt, cotton canvas, muslin, burlap. Supplies:** stencil and graph papers, boutique trims, adhesives. Fabric paints, dyes, screen supplies. (And full lines of most all other general and needlecrafts.)

Seams Great

12710 Via Felino
Del Mar, CA 92014

See at your notions counter.
Seams Great™ seam maker/reinforcer/finisher (1¼" wide tape) used when altering knitted/crochet garments — makes seams, and also seams for sleeves when shoulders are too wide, etc.

Sew Craft

Box 6146
South Bend, IN 46660
219-256-6866

Free catalog. Natesh color card, $2.00 and SASE.
Machine sewing: Threads — Natesh rayon, Mexican rayon, metallics. **Aids:** Hoops, thread holders, needles, transfer items, stabilizer, pen, Gingher and Wiss scissors. Transfer paper, markers. Patterns, books. May have sale items. Has quantity discounts.
(Also sells wholesale to businesses.)

Sew It Up

Box 3293
Marion, IN 46952

Catalog, $ .75 ('83 — '84), $1.00 ('85).
Sewing aids/notions: Biar marker bars, bodkins, "Third hand", lubricant, weights, markers, Dritz Trace-B-Gone™, seamripper, folding scissors, magnetic strip, Schemtz needles. Presser feet, guide feet (overcast, blindstitch, buttonhole) button foot, roller feet (high and low shank), ringer (zigzag machine attachment, makes circular designs — 3 sizes). Simflex expanding gauge, "handi-bob" bobbin holder, thread clip. Magnistitch™ magnifier, Dream Seamer™ seam marker, safety stitcher guard, iron cleaner, Japanese nipper, pattern marker, Olfa cutter, Marks pinking shears, fabric paint, fabric crayons. Buckles, elastic, pellon, embroidery hoops (wood, spring), velcro, knitted collars, cuffs, transfer designs. Interfacings: Stitch Witchery, Fure-Fuse, Easy-Knit, pellon, Easy-Shaper (2 weights). Fabric glues. Gingher scissors (left/right hand) 8", 4", 5", 6" applique knife edged; Marks buttonhole. Fray Check™. Books: *Sew/Fit* and others, how-to's. Master patterns. Marilyn Bardsley is a certified Sew/Fit counselor.

A Melted Nylon Finish: "Instead of cutting and then searing nylon taffeta or rip-stop where seared notches are required (such as clipping a curve), try heating a sharp knife and melting notches into the nylon fabric. In one step this sears the fabric to prevent fraying, makes the notch, and lessens the chance of burning the material in this area that is small to work with, and hence, more difficult to sear." — Courtesy of **Fuzz Freese** of Timberline Sewing Kits.

Sew Nice
8675 Reitz
Perrysburg, OH 43551

Catalog, $1.00.
Sewing: full lines; sewing notions, dressmaker aids, snaps and other attacher tools. Over 300 buttons. Complete line trims (braids, appliques, tapes, ruffles, facing, transfers, buckles, beltings). Full line threads including embroidery, silk, metallics, Swiss, long staple. Interfacings, elastics. Quilting — templates, 7 frames, batting. Marking aids. Over 30 scissors, cutters. Boxes. Books. Needlepunch, fabrics, hoops. Counted cross-stitch fabrics. Transfers, plastic canvas. Books. Has quantity prices, discounts on larger quantities.

The Silver Thimble
311 Valley Brook Rd.
McMurray, PA 15317

Catalog, $1.00.
Aids/tools: "Great Grid" ¼" scale tracing paper — sheets. Scissors, rotary cutter, measuring items, marking items, fabric glues, fusible pattern reinforcer. **Machine items:** magnifier, seam guide, ripper, hoops. **Pressing:** cloths, mitt, pad, clapper, ham, seam roll, Elnapress, multipresser, steam iron. Interfacings. Books. Has Mastercard, Visa.

Staple Sewing Aids Corp.
141 Lanza Ave.
Garfield, NJ 07026
201-546-2222

See your dealer or write for information.
"Fix Velours" self-gripping fastener/closure — ¾" wide in light and regular weights, 3 colors, (for sew, staple, glue). "Gibby Fuse" polyester iron-on fabric joiner (¾" tape, by yard or in wide sheets). Manufacturer.

Stitches and Stuff
1212 72nd Ave., N.
Minneapolis, MN 55430

Send $1.00 and SASE for details.
Fabrics (huge selection) — cottons, silks, polyester, linens, wools, blends. **Supplies:** threads, needles, quilting notions, others.

The Stitchin' Post
161 Elm, P.O. Box 280
Sisters, OR 97759

Catalog, $1.00.
Fabrics: cottons, silks; and **Trims.** Patterns including for patchwork/applique, others.

Talon America Consumers Products Division
High Ridge Park
Stanford, CT 06905

See your distributor or dealer.
Supplies/aids: machine and other needles, bodkin, snaps, Velcro™, coordinated threads, zippers (polyester), appliques laces (variety of widths, styles), other trims and braids. (And other needlecraft supplies.)

Taylor Bedding Mfg. Co.
P.O. Box 979
Taylor, TX 76574

See your dealer or write for information.
Morning Glory™ poly/cotton fiberfill, Dacron™ batting and layer built batting, cotton batts. Infant and other bed pads. Pillow forms. Manufacturer, since 1903.

Taylor's Cutaways & Stuff
2802 S. Washington St.
Urbana, IL 61801

Brochure, $1.00 (refundable); leather thimble kit, $1.50 ppd.
Fabrics: (by pound or quarter yard): Satin, velvet, cotton (calico, gingham, solids, quilt-pack, corduroy), blends, satin knit, felt, others. Fabric squares. Christmas pack prints. Soft sculpture doll patterns. Books. (Other needlecraft items.)
(Also sells wholesale to businesses.)

Thimbleweed
2975 College Ave.
Berkeley, CA 94705

Send SASE for brochure.
Fabrics (cottons, silks, linens, others), notions.

Cella Totus Enterprises

P.O. Box 539
Toppenish, WA 98848
509-865-2480

Catalog, $2.50 (refundable).
Designs (printed on pellon — 3 sizes) — over 1,000 authentic American Indian motifs, full range of subjects; for appliques, patches, medallions, pictures and other decoratives.

Traditions

8010 Cessna Ave.
Gaithersburg, MD 20879
and:
3095 Presidential Dr., E.
Atlanta, GA 30340

Free Catalog.
Stencils and supplies. Fabrics, candlewicking and other needlecraft items, lampshade supplies. Folk art and American designs. (Other craft supplies.)

Treadleart Studio

25834 Narbonne Ave.
Lomita, CA 90717
213-534-5122

Catalog, $1.00.
Sewing machine accessories (Elna, Bernina, others), "The Walking foot" for quilting. Stabilizers, fusible interfacings. Machine embroidery threads (DMC, nylon, metallics). Transfer items. Needles, hoops, scissors, Olfa cutter, patterns. Books (includes Ordori — Japanese). Other items. (Publishes *Treadleart* magazine).

Two Brothers

1602 Locust St.
St. Louis, MO 63103

Send SASE for prices.
Zipper assortment — nylon and metal types; lace assortments — variety of sizes, colors, types.

V & E Creative Expressions

6 Gregory Dr.
Ronkonkoma, NY 11779
516-981-9298

Catalog, $1.00.
DMC embroidery floss, threads (quilting, sewing). Quilting — needles, leather thimble, marker, quilt batting (2 cut sizes, or by yard). Cross-stitch fabrics (Aida, Hardanger — by yard). Embroidery hoops (spring, wood, plastic). Fiberfill, pillow forms. Stencil designs, fabric paints, brushes. Needles. Olfa cutter sets. Has quantity prices. Holds specials periodically. Owner Ellen Nardozza is a recreation therapist, certified needlework teacher and scout craft advisor.

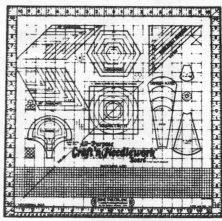

Craft 'n Needlework board, © Lee Wards

Lee Wards

1200 St. Charles Rd.
Elgin, IL 60120

Free catalog.
Kits: embroidery (dining accessories, pillows, others), cross-stitch, crewel accessories, holiday accessories and ornaments; stitchery, felt. **Trims:** ribbons (gingham, velvet, lace, bandana, prints, others), beads, others. Frames: quilting, lap types. **Supplies:** quilt batting, cotton fabric, pillow forms, transfers, markers. Books. Has some quantity prices, may have sales specials. Has Mastercard, Visa; toll free number for orders.

Wilson's Fashions in Fabrics

RD #2, Box 355
Kuntztown, PA 19530

Catalog and swatches, $2.00.
Quilting supplies: threads, notions, wood hoops. **Fabrics:** calicos, broad cloth. Cross-stitch and candlewicking supplies. Has quantity prices.

Needle Numbers: The **higher** the number on the package, the **heavier** the sewing machine needle.

For woven fabrics, use these sewing machine needles: Lightweight — size 11, mediumweight — size 14, heavyweight — size 16.

For Knit fabrics, use these sewing machine needles: Lightweight — size 9 to 11 ballpoint needle, mediumweight — size 11 ballpoint needle, heavyweight — size 24 ballpoint needle.

Purchase a special sewing machine needle for **leather.** If you can't, try using a size 14 on a **scrap** of garment weight leather, or size 18 on a heavier weight leather (vary the stitches, too, when experimenting, to see if the needle will work on the leather scrap. If the needle doesn't break, you know it will work.)

For Quiana fabric, a number 7 machine needle does well. — Courtesy of Margaret A. Boyd.

Weaving Design

The World in Stitches
82 South St.
Milford, NH 03055
603-673-6616

Catalog, $1.50. Send SASE for Quilt Kits List (specify).
Kits: Brazilian, French; stitchery (unicorn, others).
Threads: 12 metallics, linens, over 18 cotton, 11 wools, velvet, 17 silks, 16 rayons, Charted designs, Shisha mirrors. **Aids/tools:** Rulers, magnifier, tweezers, organizers, 8 paperweights. **Fabrics:** Ramie, Glenshee, 22 linens, raw silk, evenweave, Fiddler's, cottons, jute, homespun, silks, others. Colored metallic kidskin. **Quilting items.**
Frames: rollers, stretchers, sit-on, fanny style, Quandra needlework. Books. In business since 1976. (Publishes *Fancy-Work*, quarterly.)

YLI (Yarn Loft International)
742 Genevieve, Suite L
Solana Beach, CA 92075
714-755-4818

See your fabric or craft store; or get catalog, $1.00.
Olfa rotary cutters and cutting base mat (cutters with straight or wavy edge, and heavyduty model, with/without guide arm). Base is plastic, double sided. **Sewing supplies:** bias seam tape in 22 colors (in plastic cartridge that affixes to sewing machine), silk batting. Threads, variety of types. Others.

Yarn 'N Shuttle
199 So. Highland at Poplar
Memphis, TN 38111

Catalog, $ .50.
Trims/accessories: bells, shells, feathers, ribbons, dry naturals, others. Over 75 **handbag handles. Beads:** ceramic, wood, plastic types, glass. Needles, threads. **Needlecraft supplies:** floss, threads, Persian wools. Fabrics: count cloth, burlap, stiff scrim lace weaving net. (And complete line of yarns, weaving materials/equipment, other needlecrafts.) Has quantity discounts.

Zippers Unlimited
505 McLeod
Ironwood, MI 49938

Free catalog.
Zippers — all types, "discounts to 40%".

2
Tools, Aids & Equipment

The companies shown in this section provide sewing machines and other multipurpose aids for home sewing, as their only products. (Other company-sources throughout the book may also carry these items. Locate specific products here, or in the index.)

Adsco Inc.
P.O. Box 2391
Anderson, IN 46018

Send for information.
"Zook" **quilting frames** — folding, 3 rails for independent tension, disassembles.
(Also sells wholesale to dealers.)

Ain't It Ducky
P.O. Box 2278
Edmond, OK 73083

Send SASE for brochure.
See-Square™ **measuring tool** (transparent orange acrylic) — makes any size square or rectangle directly onto fabric, makes bias and strips.

Allyn International
1224 Broadway
Denver, CO 80203

See your dealer or write for information.
Necchi **Sewing Machine** including free-arm model W2-Sp. motor; 15 selectable stitches (smocking, scrolls, ribbon, ducks, tulips, others); and "Necchi-lock" serger in 3-thread and 4-thread models.

Baby Lock
(See Tacony Corp)

Baby Lock, Spa Inc.
P.O. Box 31715
Seattle, WA 98103
206-783-8087

Brochures and price list, $1.00.
Baby Lock **overlockers/sergers** — 4 models (overlocks edge, makes seam, trims fabric — in one operation), "at wholesale prices". Table for machines. Ships U.S., accepts C.O.D.'s.

Dorothy H. Becker
1378 E. 8th St.
Brooklyn, NY 11230

Send SASE for prices.
Dressmaker **graph papers** (2", 1", and ½" rules), for reducing/enlarging.

Bernina Sewing Center
3625 Weston Rd., Unit 8
Weston, Ontario M9L 1V9, Canada

See your dealer or write for information.
Sewing Machines, including Electronic model 930 (does 28 stitches — utility and decorative, including seven locked, one inch long basting), others. Has automatic buttonholer, five needle positions with self-adjusting tension for all materials; open arm; nine clamp-on presser feet. Other machines. Manufacturer.

Blossoming Softly
895 N. Calle Circulo
Camarillo, CA 93010

Send SASE with inquiry.
Background stabilizers, transfer paper (wash out type), transfer pencils.

> **Puckering Seams?** First try shortening the length of stitches, before adjusting machine tension. — Courtesy of **Margaret A. Boyd.**

...eather Products, Inc.
...en Dr., P.O. Box 2
...land, OR 97520

See your retailer or write for information.
Grabbit™ **magnetic pincushion** (plastic, 4½" diameter, with glasshead pins).
(Wholesale information available to retailers.)

Rush A Bowman and Associates
3723 Oakley
Memphis, TN 38111

See your dealer or write for information.
"Pandora Products" needlework **frames** — rotating rug, hand, floor and table frames for all fabrics and all sewing/needle purposes.

Boyd Associates
6634 Summerfield Rd.
Temperance, MI 48182
312-847-0065

Send SASE for details.
Omni-Kolor **artist's lamp** — blends flourescent and incandescent light sources to produce a naturallike daylight for color evaluation, etc., with adjustable stand (2½' to 5') swivel lamp (vertically, horizontally). Colorect Lamp — North White bulb lamp that emits constant north daylight spectrum for color matching and blending; adjusts as other lamp.

Bruin International
2265 Westwood Blvd. #462
Los Angeles, CA 90064

Send SASE for price list.
Japanese palm scissors (lightweight, eliminates finger strain) for sewing, etc.

Bruna
Box 3161
Ventura, CA 93006

Send SASE for prices.
Square hoop/frame (5" x 7" plastic, 5 colors) snaps in place to hold fabric or canvas; other side provides frame for finished work.

Calico Patch Leather Thimble
Box 47
Rosemount, MN 55068

Sample, $2.00.
Leather thimbles (flexible finger/thumb cover with wide elastic-hold).
(Sells at wholesale to businesses.)

Calico Patches
P.O. Box 3446
Longwood, FL 32750

See your dealer or write for information.
Aluminum **quilting frame**, quilter's scale, mylar sheet for templates.

Carradus Gifts
Box 88, Rt. 1
Dundee, IA 52038

Descriptive price list and photo, $ .50.
Thimbles (wood, unpainted, ringed with a rim; painted, plain, tapered shape) in 30 common woods, 12 unusual woods; in fancy grained and burl woods; adults, child's size, doll sizes (in exotic woods, vegetable ivory or buffalo horn). **Thimble tree** (wood holder with spool spacers — to hold 12 thimbles, up to 50 thimbles; miniature size holds 12 doll-size thimbles. Limited edition thimbles (Christmas designs, birds or plants designs).
(Also sells wholesale to businesses. Inquire on letterhead with resale number.)

Clancy Enterprises
P.O. Box 772
Amityville, NY 11701
516-957-7639

Send SASE for details.
"Northlite" **color corrected lamps** (with mix required for color evaluation, etc.) on 2' - 7' telescope stand, foldable legs; with 10" reflector; with bulb.

Comar Lap Frames
P.O. Box 337
Lomita, CA 90717
213-548-3524

Write for information.
Needlecraft lap frames (fabric sewn onto wood) adjustable tensions (for quilting, needlepoint, embroidery).

Consew
(See Consolidated Sewing Machine Co.)

Consolidated Sewing Machine Co.

1115 Broadway
New York, NY 10010
212-929-6900

See your dealer or write information.
Consew machines: "Tuffylock" overlock model (heavy duty, portable single needle-three thread model 93) over-edges, trims light to heavyweight fabrics; cross and plain seams, pintucks, braids (also in two-needle, 4-thread model). New all purpose compound feed machine with walking foot lockstitch, for lightweight fabrics and also for leather, vinyl, canvas, upholstery coated materials, others; features an oversized bobbin. Others include: a single needle monograming/embroidery zig-zag lockstitch machine. Single needle chainstitch/blindstitch machine (with swing down arm and work plate, skip/non-skip stitch lever) for home sewing of most materials. Single needle dropfeed zig-zag lockstitch model (and same type in high speed model). (Also has some measuring tools.) Manufacturer. In business since 1950.
(Also sells wholesale to distributors and retailers.)

"Tuffylock", Consew Model 93, Consolidated Sewing Machine Co.

Cosmic Constrictions

Box 554
Auburn, ME 04210

Send SASE for list.
Metal rulers (with 1/12th scale markings) — singly or by dozen.

Cotton Patch

6512 N. Greeley
Portland, OR 97217

Send SASE for details.
Fabric **strip cutter** (cuts ¼" to ½" for Seminole work, bias tape, string patchwork, other). Has Mastercard, Visa.

Craft Accessories

P.O. Box 367
Stillwater, MN 55082

See your dealer or write for information.
Magnifier Lamps — 2 head styles, variety of base styles/colors.

Craftistic Basic Board
(Quilts, Et Ceteria)

3208 W. 111th St.
Cleveland, OH 44111

See your dealer or write for information.
"Basic Board" 11" x 15" non-skid **work surface** (holds fabric without pins) — water resistant, masonite backed; for dressmaking, quilting (and other needlecrafts).

Cynthia's Sewing Room

2229 E. Burnside, Suite 109
Gresham, OR 97030
503-661-2102

Send SASE for information, specify item.
Bias tape maker (2 sizes, ½" and 1" folded tape) "a 36" square makes 36 yards of ½" folded bias tape." "Thread tree" **spool holder** (for up to 8) in horizontal position for machine embroidery, applique, double needle (fits vertical spool pins only).

The Dan-Sig Co.

P.O. Box 2141
Memphis, TN 38101
901-525-8464

Send SASE for information.
DAZOR **Magnifying lamps:** floating arm pedestal, and floating arm model (on rollers).

Quick and Easy Shoulder Pads — You-Make:
"Use ¼ yard Pellon fleece, ¼ yard fusible webbing.
   1. Cut three circles of pellon fleece, decreasing size by one inch — for example 9", 8", 7".
   2. Cut two circles of fusible webbing in the two smallest sizes — for example 8", 7".
   3. Stack the circles with the fusible webbing between and press lightly.
   4. Cut circle in half and shape for armseye by cutting a curve along straight edge.
   5. Shape on ham with steam and moisture.
   6. Place in garment so that largest circle is on top next to garment, extending ½" over seam line. Baste into place.
   7. The shoulder pads can be covered with lining for a designer touch." — Courtesy of **Dorothy Stringer,** of Bishop Method of Clothing Construction Council, Inc.

DeMonia's Gallery
12421 York R.
North Royalton, OH 44133

Complete information, $1.00.
Framing kit with shadow box mat (for finished quilting, others) — wood with plastic "glass" and materials, instructions; variety of sizes, colors. Has Mastercard, Visa.
(Also sells wholesale to retailers).

Design Aline
101 Pickard Dr.
Syracuse, NY 13211
315-454-3887

Free brochure.
Service: customized **dressforms** — to personal contour

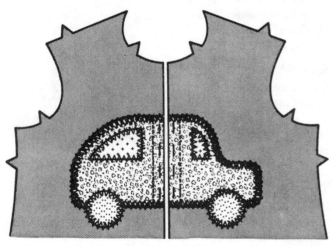

© Ginger Designs

J. M. Devrey, Inc.
210 Hanse Ave.
Freeport, NY 11520

Send SASE for details.
Ultra-Fit® **dressmaker form system** — leotard, for blouses, dresses, and jackets; tights for pants and skirts; a stretch suit with marked, padded lines strategically placed for personal fit; with instructions. Has toll free number for orders, Mastercard, Visa.

Betty Donahue Enterprises
2624 W. 155th St.
Gardena, CA 90249

Send $1.75 for samples.
Grid sheets kits (and tracing sheet) for designs (enlarging, reducing) in ½" to 3" grid markings.

Elna
(See White Sewing Machine Co.)

Fancyfree Enterprises
Star Rt., Box 26
Malin, OR 97632

Send SASE for prices.
Spool storage rack ("Spoolaway") walnut stained, louvered — 2 sizes.

Farr Manufacturing Co.
P.O. Box 1098
New Bedford, MA 02746
800-343-8090

See your dealer or write for information.
Line of **scissors/shears:** leather shears, 6" sewing, 8" bent trimmer, 7" long nose snips, 8" curved blade, 6½" knit/craft, 3½" embroidery, 7" straight, 4½" U-set thread clips, 5" applique/curved. "Nearly a century of cutlery experience."

Fashion Able
Box S
Rocky Hill, NJ 08553

Brochure, $ .50.
Self-help items/aids: Wood Clamp-on embroidery hoop (clamps to table, chair, lapboard, etc., for one-hand embroidery; swivel-adjusts, tilts). Magnifiers (around neck, wide angle mirror, prism glasses, illuminated reader/-magnifier, recliner viewer, illuminated adjustable arm, purse size lighted type, headband type with easy-grasp knob). Self-opening scissors (Swedish, with stainless steel blades, non-slip plastic handles, for easy-cutting by squeeze action of either hand), 5 types (lightweights, safety tipped, nail scissors, lightweight pruners). Locking pliers (holds even pins). (And other self-help aids of non-sewing but helpful/supportive uses); for cleanup, dressing, reaching, wheelchair maneuvering, therapy, etc. Has Mastercard, Visa.

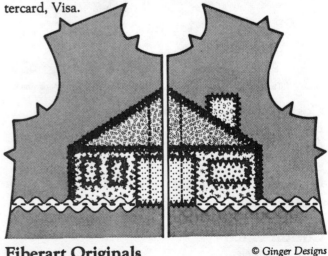

© Ginger Designs

Fiberart Originals
11831 Kokomo
Franktown, CO 80116

Send long SASE for prices.
Magnifier lamps — desk, bracket and pedestal models.

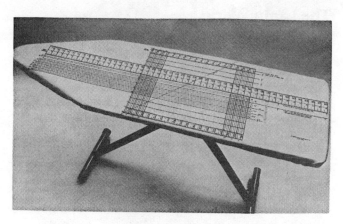

"Press-a-Magic" cover, © Golden Hands Corp.

Fibercraft Company, Ltd.
115 Maple Court Crescent, S.E.
Calgary, Alberta, Canada 52J 1V9
403-271-0762

See your dealer, or write for free brochure.
Freehand® **clamp base** — crafts system (portable, interchangeable). The Base supports quilt block frame, embroidery hoop holder, primitive loom or drawing board. "Dealer inquiries welcome."

Finger-Booties
Rt. 5, Box 228
Chapel Hill, NC 27514

Sample, $2.50.
Finger-Booties™ leather **thimbles** with sewn seams; 3 sizes.

First State Sew 'N Vac
82 E. Main St.
Newark, DE 19711

Free catalog.
Imported **sewing machines** below cost — Elna, White, New Home, others. Holds sales.

Fiskars
10261 Yellow Circle Dr.
Minnetonka, MN 55343
612-935-9222

See your dealer.
Scissors: full line, including 8" (with and without, a scissor sheath and sharpener unit). Manufacturer.

Gingher
P.O. Box 8865
Greensboro, NC 27410

See your fabricshop or department store.
Scissors/shears — lightweight 8" bent trimmers (1.8 oz.), 4" embroidery.

Golden Hands Industries, Inc.
P.O. Box 110
White Plains, NY 10602
914-723-3633

See your retailer or send SASE for information.
Ironing board cover: Press-a-Magic™ multipurpose measuring guide (premeasured guidelines — in inches and metrics — are printed on standard size ironing board covers with graph, for smocking, templates, quilt blocks, reducing/enlarging, patternmaking, etc., a ⅝" and ⅜" guideline, short guidelines for hemming, etc., horizontal guidelines for large items.

GraphiCraft
Box 509
Westport, CT 06880

Send SASE for details.
Pantograph redrawing aid — resizes work up to 72" by tracing, with reductions to 1/10 and enlargements to 10:1. Hardwood bars (21") assembled, with instructions; also in resizing/reproportioning/reversing "regraph" model.

Tom Hansen
P.O. Box 6996
Bellevue, WA 98008
206-641-8222

Write or call for information/prices.
Bernina **sewing machines** "at the **lowest** prices possible", all models. Ships anywhere in U.S.

Import/Export Emporium
122 Spanish Village Center
Dallas, TX 75248

Send SASE for prices.
Singer sewing machines, including multistitch model.

Industrial Machines
6750 Odana Rd.
Madison, WI 53719

Catalog, $1.00.
Industrial sewing machines for upholstery, drapery, leather and others specialized uses. Buys/sells/rents.

Helpful Hint: "To save rethreading your sewing machine when changing thread colors, cut the thread at spool, change spool and tie the new color to the old thread. Remove the thread from eye of needle and simply pull the new thread down through the machine. Snip off the knot and just thread the needle with the new color." — Courtesy of **Fuzz Freese** of Timberline Sewing Kits.

Johnson Enterprises

8303 Mount Vernon St.
Lemon Grove, CA 92045

Send $1.50 ppd.
The **Needle Nabber**™ **holder,** pins to work material or clothing, holds needle magnetically, when not in use. (Also sells wholesale to dealers.)

Juki Industries of America, Inc.

421 N. Midland Ave.
Saddle Brook, NJ 07662
201-796-8800
and:
20437 S. Western Ave.
Torrance, CA 90501
213-320-9001

Send for details.
Juki **Lock**™ **sewing machine** — one needle, 4-thread model (for three stitch types while trims excess fabric) and single-needle, 3-thread model (for overedging and trimming); for silks and taffetas through to heavy wools and denim.

L & M Adjustable Dress Form Co., Inc.

380 Throop Ave.
Brooklyn, NY 11221

Send SASE for complete details.
Adjustable **dressmaking forms** (cloth covered wire); variety of sizes, deluxe and regular models.

The Lamp Works

Box 1467
Sumter, SC 29150

Free brochure.
"Quilter's Lamp" in two styles (bridge or standard) in black wrought iron stand, adjustable (height to 68" and 360 degrees around), light swings around close to work area; with three-way socket and opaque shade.

Lieba, Inc.

405 W. Franklin St.
Baltimore, MD 21201

Send SASE for prices.
"Shag" loop/tufts maker tool (for sewing machine use) makes yarn loops for trims, etc.; with pattern booklet.

Lin & Mary Needlework

372 31st St.
Lindenhurst, NY 11757
516-226-1175

See your needlecraft store or write for information.
Light switch plates (clear acrylic with insert cover — protects fabric with applique, needlework, etc.) with instructions — single or double types.
(Also sells wholesale to businesses.)

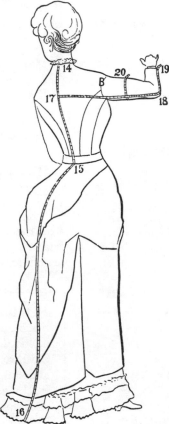

Measurements, as taken for garments at the turn-of-the-century © Past Patterns

Magna-Lite
79-20 108th St.
Forest Hills, NY 11375
212-261-1243

Write for details.
Magna-Lite™ multi-purpose magnifier lamps with three diopter glass lens; three cool circline fluorescent models with 5" diameter lens, adjustable arm reach; clamp, base or floor stand. "Magna Lux" incandescent magnifier lamp, lightweight (3 lbs.) with adjustable arm reach; clamp or optional base.
Shop owners inquiries accepted.

Magnifier Lamps
Dept. of Optics
P.O. Box 1261
Midland, MI 48640

Send SASE for prices.
Magnifier lamps: Fluorescent, with 5" diameter convex lenses, 3 diopter power, (4 models for floor and desk, with/without clamps).
(Also sells wholesale to dealers.)

Magnistitch, Inc.
P.O. Box 2424
Birmingham, AL 35223

Write for information.
Magnifiers — with adhesive pad, or clamp-on model, rectangular with arm (for sewing machine, hoops, etc.); optional stand kit.
(Also sells wholesale to businesses.)

Marie Products
P.O. Box 5863
Tucson, AZ 85703

See your dealer or write for information.
Frames/stands — quilting square frame with stand, sampler stand (18 x 27 oval, mini-scroll frames 6" sq.) on 3-way clamp-all or with table stand; 3-way clamp-all stand (for hoops), adjustable clamp-all floor stand; others; "American Heritage" hoops in rounds — 8 sizes to 23", ovals — 3 sizes), "Princess" hoops for embroidery and framing, etc.; others. Manufacturer.

Marks International, Inc.
60 Wells Ave.
Newton, MA 02159
617-965-4000

See your fabric store or distributor.
Full line of Marks® Sewlite® stainless scissors/shears — dressmaker shears, sewing scissors (fine point), others. Manufacturer.

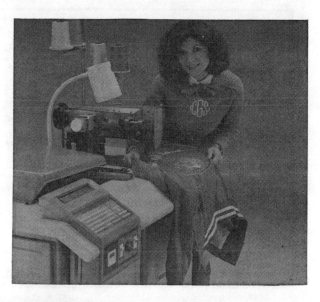

The Meistergram model M700 XL brings advanced computerization to monogramming and embroidery. © Meistergram

Meistergram
310 Lakeside Ave., W.
Cleveland, OH 44113
216-621-8731

Write above, or call toll free 800-321-0486 for details.
Monogramming/embroidery equipment including model with adjustable pantograph, template to produce eight sizes (for most fabrics/garments). Computerized/automatic model features computer/cassette system that "reads" alphabet styles, etc.; sews 1500 stitches per minute, automatically repeats, recalls, adjusts, spaces; with optional 3-line lettering, upside down and backward lettering use. Supplies: hoops, templates and cassettes — full line "Insta-Patch" patches, supply kits, parts kits, needles, threads, backing materials, measuring and other aids. Business established in 1933.

Mini Lock®
Division of King Distributors, Inc.
599 Industrial Ave.
Paramus, NJ 07652
201-967-0777

Call or write for additional information.
Mini Lock™ **sewing machine** (single and 2-needle models) with "over-lock" stitch, a "safety" stitch, and a single needle chainstitch for home sewing of clothing, towels, linens, spreads, etc.); with carbide cutting knife; runs up to 1700 stitches per minute with contoured, swing-out cloth plate, calibrated adjustment dials.

> **What is a Serger?** A serger is a machine that sews, trims, and overcasts a seam in one step at twice the speed of a "regular" sewing machine.

Butterfly, © *Vea Prints*

Montavilla Sewing Machine & Vacuum Center
8326 S.E. Stark
Portland, OR 97216
503-254-7317

Send SASE for details.
Buttonmatic self-sizing buttonhole attachment (for most all machines — hi shank, low shank, snap on and slant needle).

Necchi
(See Allyn International)

The New Home Sewing Machine Co.
171 Commerce St.
Carlstadt, NJ 07072

See your dealer or write for information.
New Home **Sewing Machines** including also the "Combi" model machine: a combination sewing machine and 2-thread serger.

What Direction, Topstitching? "Directional **topstitching** means you do not topstitch in one continuous stitching all around a neckline and down the front of a vest or dress; rather you will do it in parallel directions, much like stay-stitching. Sometimes you can backstitch; other times it's better to pull threads to wrong side & tie; then thread ends through large-eyed needle and sandwich about 1-inch of threads between the two layers of fabric before emerging." — Courtesy of **Phyllis Eifler** of Phyllis Eifler's Sewing Seminars, from *Sewing Is Getting Easier All The Time.*

P.E.P. Company
Box 340
Redfield, IA 50233

Send SASE for prices.
Graph paper in 1" and 2" grids (for enlarging/reducing) in 1122 sq. in. piece.

Pacific Button Co., Inc.
P.O. Box 2125
La Habra, CA 90631

See your fabric store or write for information.
Full line of buttons. "Spool-It" spool holder for sewing machine use. (for other than usual spools.) Manufacturer.

Pantograms Manufacturing Co., Inc.
6807 S. MacDill
Tampa, FL 33611
813-839-5697

Write or call for information.
Home **Monogramming** System (embroidered) equipment 2 template-tracing models. Pantograms II model combines embroidered monogrammer with standard, straight-stitch sewing machine — converts for tailoring, alterations, general sewing. As monogrammer, it features adjustable pantograph used on other models; as sewing machine it also has a zig-zag capability, variable stitch length, changeable presser feed and feed dogs, and forward/reverse variable speed fabric feed. (Conversions from one operation to the other should take only minutes.)

Patchwork Plus
35847 Highway 58, P.O. Box 687
Pleasant Hill, OR 97455
503-747-2414

Send SASE for details.
Readymade scrap **catcher/caddy** for sewing machine (catches trimmings, holds scissors; with removable metal plate for washing, detachable pin cushion. Has Mastercard, Visa.
("Dealer inquiries welcome").

Pfaff American Sales Corp.
610 Winter Ave.
Paramus, NJ 07652
201-262-7211

See your dealer, or write for information.
Sewing Machines including Tiptronic® microprocessor controlled model, with stitch programs, free-arm conversions, other. Tipmatic® and other models, some with free-arm; zig-zag, decorative stitches and other features.

PO Instrument Co., Inc.
13 Lehigh Ave.
Paterson, NJ 07503

Free Catalog.
"Extra Hands" clamps on stand, with and without magnifier — (other tools).
(Also sells wholesale to businesses.)

Quest International
2067 Broadway, Suite 276
New York, NY 10023

Send SASE for details.
Swiss electric scissors (for fabrics, plastic, paper).

The Quilt Basket
Box 471
Mill City, OR 97360

Send SASE for details.
Opaque Projector (enlarges patterns, clippings, drawings) — projects onto wall.

Seasons, © Vea Prints

Quiltcraft
Waycroft Dr., Rt. 7
Salisbury, MD 21801

Sample pencil $1.50 ppd., specify color.
Washout pencil (sponges out in cold water) in blue, red, green. Masking tape (¼" — by 60 yard roll).
(Also sells wholesale to dealers.)

Rivers Import-Export Co.
P.O. Box 1422
Omaha, NE 68101

Send SASE for details.
Swiss electric scissors (for fabrics, light plastics); with front guide light, 2-speed.

H. Russell Designs
5730 Kirkwood Pl., No.
Seattle, WA 98103

Send SASE for details.
Sewing Box: hardwood box with peg spool holders and holders for scissors, bobbins, etc.; stands open on end.

Salem Industries, Inc.
P.O. Box 43027
Atlanta, GA 30336
800-241-4998

See your dealer or write for information.
"Salem Quik Stripper" (patent pending) slits quilt strips, bias tape; of nylon with rotating blades, 1" — 6" measure-spacer for straight or curved cuts.

Sergers
P.O. Box 168
Panguitch, UT 84759
801-676-8027

Send SASE for brochure.
Sewing Machines: Bernina, Viking models, "save"; model usage lessons on tape for each model. Accepts mail order by phone, ships in U.S., "credit terms available".

Sew Fit Company
905 Hillgrove #6
La Grange, IL 60525

Free catalog.
Sewing aids: Olfa cutter and mat, magnetic pinholder, buttonhole cutter set, metal gauge (expandable), pattern weights. Sewing machine guide foot (feet?) for all types. "Seamstress" ironers; Simflex gauge, "Seams Great" seam finish (by roll), glue stick, "Clover" bias tape maker, "Ringer" tubing turner, adhesive, instant vinyl, markers, Others. Books: Sew/Fit how to's for slacks, dresses, suits, tailoring, etc. Sew/Fit Manual. Holds sales, allows discount to teachers/instructors.
(Also sells wholesale to businesses.)

Threading Up Rayon: "When machine sewing with rayon threads, reduce top tension slightly to handle the delicate thread. If thread tends to slip off spool and wind around base of thread holder, place a small, shallow dish immediately behind the sewing machine and lay the spool of rayon thread in the dish, then thread the machine in the normal manner. Thread will unreel with no problems." — Courtesy of **Jerry Zarbaugh** of Aardvark Adventures in Handcrafts.

Shereo
Box 7666
Colorado Springs, CO 80933

Send SASE for information.
"Super snip" scissors: powerful heavy duty shears, cuts heaviest materials "never need sharpening", developed by paramedics.
(Also sell wholesale to businesses.)

The Singer Co.
135 Raritan Center Pkwy.
Edison, NJ 08837
(with distributors throughout the U.S.)

See your dealer or write for information.
Full line of sewing machines, including: A flat bed model that flips to free-arm, electronic and electronic sewing system — Touch-tronic™ (with "Touch" change of stitches, in-place bobbin rewind, sew buttonholes with foot pedal, other features). Serger model machine. Others.
Parts/aids/accessories: Needles, cutting board, tape measures and gauges, rulers, french curves, tracing materials; bobbins, zipper foot, light bulbs and other machine items. "Select-O-Pack" needle organizer/application guide (to dial correct needle), others.

Sew 'N Vac
(See First State Sew 'N Vac)

Sewin' in Vermont
84 Concord Ave.
St. Johnsbury, VT 05819

Send SASE for list.
Sewing Machines: all major European brands, Singer, Pfaff, Viking; other new/current models, "save 25% to 30% from list price". Has free shipping.

Pattern Preservation: "Clear Contact Paper is the cheapest, easiest method of use to preserve a tissue pattern. Nothing to trace, and you do not have "copies" plus the original to store!! But contact paper can be very sticky and hard to handle. To make contact paper 'behave', simply put the whole roll into the freezer for a day or two! When removed, the backing paper is easily separated, and most of the adhesive seems to be gone. Lay the clear contact paper on a table, adhesive side up. After dry pressing your tissue pattern (steam pressing can shrink the paper), roll each piece into a tube shape, then simply unroll onto the clear contact paper. Allow to set completely before handling. This needs to be applied on one side only, and on some 'favorite and well-worn' patterns, I use it only in spots for reinforcement." — Courtesy of **Irene M. James** of I. M. James Enterprises, from her book, *Sewing Specialties.*

Applique design

Speed Stitch
P.O. Box 3472
Port Charlotte, FL 33949

Send SASE for brochure.
Speed Stitch™ designs: free-notion machine embroidery "thread sketching" — a stitch and "tear-away" design technique for fabrics; in Beginner's Kit, Plant Series, Shell Series (of designs).

The Sewing Emporium
1087 Third Ave.
Chula Vista, CA 92010

Lessons on machine embroidery (specify) $1.00 or send SASE for information.
Ruffler sewing machine attachment (ruffles, gathers, pleats) for high shank, low shank, slanted shank, left or center needle positions (most all machines). Cutting mat surface (for rotary cutters) — sizes to 4' x 8', (will custom cut). Other sewing aids. Has Mastercard, Visa.

Sewing Machine Consultants
P.O. Box 1027
Newark, DE 19715

Catalog, $3.00 (refundable).
Sewing machines, "up to 50% off list": Household and industrial types, major brands. Machine parts, supplies, cabinets, accessories.

The Sewing Workshop
2010 Balboa St.
San Francisco, CA 94121

Sewing tips and ideas booklet, $3.00; send SASE for prices.
Double tracing wheel (for seam allowances, making facings, patternmaking, and as single wheel). Pattern weights sets. Other sewing aids.

Sudberry House

P.O. Box 895
Old Lyme, CT 06371
203-739-6951

Catalog, $2.50.
Needlework accessories: trays, Small furniture, mirrors
— accepts needlework inserts.

Mary Francis Tackett

10041 Ashworth North,
Seattle, WA 98133
206-524-5912

Send SASE for details.
Custom dress forms "to order", "easy to clean", table
top model with no stand, and floor model and stand.

Tacony Corp.

4421 Ridgewood Ave.
St. Louis, MO 63116
800-325-3912,

450 Oehler Place
Carlstadt, NJ 07072
800-526-6211

6635 Highway Ave.
Jacksonville, FL 32236
800-342-5853

121 Lulu
Wichita, KS 67211
800-835-2002

1415 San Mateo Ave., S.
San Francisco, CA 94080
415-871-5411

See your dealer or write for information.
Baby Lock® (sewing) serging Machine (sews, overlocks and trims in one operation).

June Tailor, Inc.

P.O. Box 208
Richfield, WI 53076

Free catalog.
Finishing aids: Hams, point pressers, Velvaboard™
pressing board, pressing cloths. **Blocker/frame:** cush-
ioned, with ruled markings; holds moisture. Manufacturer.

Total Sewing, Inc.

P.O. Box 438
Brookfield, IL 60513

80 page catalog, $3.00 (refundable).
Sewing machines — household and industrial types
(known brands including industrial blindstitch, straight
stitch and other models), machine **supplies,** parts, motor
stands; sewing cabinets. Olfa cutters and guide, Gingher
scissors. Notions: full lines of items.

Tuffylock
(See Consolidated Sewing Machine Corp.)

United Cutlery, Inc.

108 E. 16th St.
New York City, NY 10003
212-473-7745

See your dealer or write for catalog.
Shears/scissors: trimmers, dressmaker set (3), embroid-
ery/needlepoint, applique/silhouette, folding scissors,
pull-twist-snips, stork scissors, others.

Viking Sewing Machine Co., Inc.

2300 Louisiana Ave., North
Minneapolis, MN 55427
612-544-2700

See your dealer or write for information.
Sewing Machines including models with computer-
controlled functions (regulates speed), with stitch by
stitch control; sews any material; controls stitch selection
and formation with "press button" with dual lights;
"jamproof bobbin", offers mirror image of pattern. Others. Manufacturer.

Straight Through a Zipper: "When to the point
of turning fabric to the right side to stitch a zipper in,
by hand or machine, "TO HELP YOU STITCH
STRAIGHT, tape a straight pin to zipper foot and
position pin so that head of pin rides in well of seam.
Sewing machine needle should be in groove at edge
of ZIPPER FOOT. (Ladies at seminars love this
one!)" — Courtesy of **Phyllis Eifler** of Phyllis
Eifler's Sewing Seminars, from *Sewing Is Getting Easier All The Time.*

White Sewing Machine Co.
11750 Berea Rd.
Cleveland, OH 44111

Elna Sewing machines including new electronic models with 14 built-in stitches; available as portable free-arm, and as convertible (installs in machine cabinet, or table). Aids: Elnapress ironer, with Vap-O-Jet™ vaporizers, **Elna accessory set for machines, (designed for handicapped sewers):** adapters to fit over control knobs and dials, strips of flexible material to shape user's personal needs, dial adapters for ease of turning, extension for cloth presser bar lever to reduce effort needed to raise the foot and release upper tension, bobbin extension with one end for problem-free removal of bobbin from rotary hook (other end with hole in which needle can be held for inserting into needle clamp) — for all Elna machines.

Yo's Needlecraft
P.O. Box 4735
Carson, CA 90749

See your dealer or write for information.
"Clover" tape maker (makes folding tapes — no moving parts) in 1" and ½' sizes.

3
Fabrics & Leathers

❦❦❦❦❦❦❦❦❦❦❦❦

While most of the listings in this section present source-materials for garments, others provide materials for draperies, upholstery, fabric panels, etc. (and see the index, or other categories of sewing throughout the directory, for specific fabrics).

❦❦❦❦❦❦❦❦❦❦

Allied Felt Group
Division of Central Shippee, Inc.
P.O. Box 134
Bloomingdale, NJ 07403

See your local store, or distributor.
Craft felt (40% virgin wool, 60% viscose rayon) in 72" width bolts, or squares; 36 colors. Manufacturer. (Also sells wholesale to businesses.)

Ameritex
533 Seventh Ave.
New York, NY 10018

See your dealer, or write for information.
"Country Coordinates" line of eight, 100% cotton prints (stencil-look and other designs in muted shades), others.

Architex International, Inc.
625 W. Jackson Blvd.
Chicago, IL 60606
312-454-1333

Send SASE with specific inquiry.
Flame retardant fabrics.

Art's Trims and Textiles
3306-83rd St., P.O. Box 6722
Lubbock, TX 79413

See your dealer or write for brochure.
Specialty stretch fabrics, sequin material, others. Rhinestone motifs, other trims.

Laura Ashley Catalog
Box 5308
Melville, NY 11747

Catalog, $3.00.
"English country" prints (and accessories — coordinated wallpapers, paints. Other non-sewing items.)

Bazaar Cloth
P.O. Box 7281
Santa Cruz, CA 95061
408-425-7239

Brochure and samples, $2.00.
Handwoven all-cotton cloth from Guatemala, in 36" width, machine washable; some are ikat (tyed, dyed to specific design before weaving); in brilliant stripes and plaids; multicolors, or in color groups (browns, reds/violets, greens; others). Natural fabrics from other countries sometimes available. Has quantity prices.

Bead Different
1627 S. Tejon
Colorado Springs, CO 80906
303-473-2188

Call or write for special prices on 10 and 25 yard bundles. Send SASE with inquiry.
Stretch fabrics for dancers, skaters, gymnasts: Lycra-Spandex prints and solids, cotton Lycra, Glitterskin, stretch satin, super stretch, Glisenette, others.

Yardage Conversion Guide		
FABRIC 60"	**45"**	**36" Wide**
1 yard	= 1⅜ yards	= 1¾ yards
1¾ yards	= 2¼ yards	= 2⅞ yards
2 yards	= 2¾ yards	= 3⅜ yards
2⅜ yards	= 3⅛ yards	= 4¼ yards
3 yards	= 4 yards	= 5 yards

Berman Leathercraft
147 South St.
Boston, MA 02111
617-426-0870

Catalog and garment samples, $2.00. ($1.00 refundable.)
Garment leather — variety of types, (smooth grain, sueded pigskin and unusuals). Belts, dyes and tools, kits (other leathercrafting supplies). In business since 1905.

Big Apple Textiles
300 Canal St.
Lawrence, MA 01840

Sew With Fakefur™ idea book, $ .25.

Brewer Fabric Shop
Twin City Plaza
Brewer, ME 04412

Send $3.50 for 600 swatches.
Fabrics (100% cotton) Calicos, solids, chintz by: V.I.P., Concord, Fiesta, R.J.R., Peter Pan, Ely Walker, Rusticana, Jinny Beyer Collection, others.

Britex-By-Mail
146 Geary St.
San Francisco, CA 94108

Write for information.
Fabrics (domestics/imported): woolens, silks, cottons, linens, knits, synthetics; designer fabrics. Personalized swatch service.
(Also sells wholesale to fabric shops.)

Sally Buell Handwoven Textiles
P.O. Box 45277
Seattle, WA 98105

Samples, $2.00.
Handwoven Fabrics from an American studio — seasonal collections; silks and cottons.

C. T. Textiles
340 E. 57th St.
New York, NY 10022
212-486-1299

Send $1.00 and SASE for indicated color choice.
Garment leathers — smooth grain, (full color range, large skin sizes), suede pigskin, metallic leathers, pearlescents; by sq. foot. Minimum order, $25.00.

> **The Better the Quality of Cotton Fabric, the Fewer the Wrinkles When Washed.** — Courtesy of **Margaret A. Boyd.**

Calico 'N Things
P.O. Box 265
Marquette, MI 49855

Catalog and 250 swatches of fabric, $3.25.
Jinny Beyer fabrics (color-coordinated) including "Amish Special" ¼ yard assortment of 16 colors with traditional Amish patterns and instructions, others. (And quilting kits.)

Calico Stocking
1600 North St.
Suffield, CT 06078

Samples, $1.00.
Calico ribbons, fabrics: holiday prints.

California Peninsula Textiles
P.O. Box 7000-14
Rolling Hills Estates, CA 90274
213-515-7001

Send SASE for prices.
Nylon ripstop fabric (1.5 ounce) in 8 colors, 41" width, by yard (for kites, etc.).

Cara
4508-19th St.
San Francisco, CA 94114
415-864-5624

Complete samples $3.00 (refundable on order).
Garment Leathers and Suedes — variety of colors (for designers, individuals and manufacturers).

Caro Creations, Inc.
P.O. Box 3262
Forest City, FL 32751

See your dealer or write for information.
Vaida™ **Cloth** (Vinyl Aida in 14 and 18 count) an "all environment" indoor/outdoor material (machine washable and colorfast, fire resistant; in 60" width, vanilla or white, pastels). Also pre-cut place mats.

Carolina Mills Factory Outlet
Box V, Hwy. 76 West
Branson, MO 65616
417-334-2291

Sample swatches, $2.00 (gets future mailings).
Fashion Designer fabrics (including season overruns, leftovers, etc. from Butte Knit, Jantzen, Jonathon Logan, Quoram, Act III, Leslie Fay, Long Fog, others) — some factory coordinated or color matched with others; "about 30% — 50% **below ... ordinary "yard goods"** (most first quality unless identified as "seconds" or "irregulars".)

Carriage House Antiques
2 Lincoln Way West
New Oxford, PA 17350

Brochure, $1.00 and long SASE (refundable).
Old-style fabrics: Ginghams (tiny checks, larger checks), Imported Batiste, lawn, nainsook, organdy, voiles, Moire taffetas, satins, others. (And doll notions, fabric.)

Central Shippee, Inc.
The Felt People
46 Star Lake Rd.
Bloomingdale, NJ 07403
201-838-1100

Free leaflets.
Felts: Mead, Tempora, craft and wallcovering (wools or blends, 54" to 72" widths), 72 colors. Willi-cloth for pool tables.

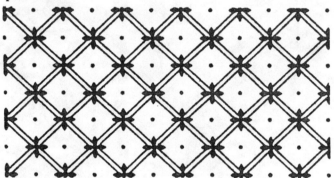

Fabric samples in this section courtesy The Second Yard

Cloth to Quilts
224 Quincy St.
Port Townsend, WA 98368
206-385-3890

Send SASE with inquiry — specify.
Specialty fabrics (imported/domestic): silks, woolens, linens, cottons; Folkwear and Vogue patterns; specializes "in personalized service and mail order". Notions, including unusuals.

Commonwealth Felt Co.
211 Congress St.
Boston, MA 02110

See your dealer, or send SASE for prices.
"Perfection" Felt (by yard or pieces), felt letters and shapes. Snug'N Comfy™ **filler** (polyester needle punched quilting-fill, 90" wide, doubled and rolled.

Continental Felt Co.
22 W. 15th St.
New York, NY 10011

See your dealer or write for information.
Felt — by the yard, squares; full line of colors. Manufacturer, since 1905.

Crompton's Fabric Shop
12th St. and Arch Ave.
Waynesboro, VA 22980

Send SASE for list.
Fabrics including corduroy, cottons, others. "Reasonable prices".

Dan River, Inc.
111 W. 40th St.
New York, NY 10018

See your dealer.
Full line of fashion fabrics including "Oxford" and Westport Chambray™ stripes; plaids, others; in cotton/Fortrell and other blends.

David-Harvey, Inc.
1224 E. Olympic Blvd.
Los Angeles, CA 90021
213-622-6544

See your dealer, or send SASE for information.
Fabric remnants: quilteds, knitted suede, Velour, T-shirts; prints (tropicals, flanelettes, calico, etc.) jogging fleece, Corduroy, denim, linens, Velvet, Velveteen, poly/-cotton Lycra, swimwear, voile, others. Manufacturer.

Dazians, Inc.
40 E. 29th St.
New York, NY 10016
212-686-5300
(also in Beverly Hills, Boston, Chicago, Dallas, Miami).

Free catalog.
Theatrical fabrics: nylon (organdy, Georgette, sheers, crepe, others) satins (slipper, cotton-back, stretch super, others), flameproofed twill, polyesters, taffetas, velveteen, metallics (13 solids, textured, "nugget cloth", opalescent, "tissue **lahm**", stripes, multi-dotted) metallic highlighted fabrics; brilliant/flourescent colors and patterns; tubular springweave, lace and metallic lace fabrics. **Basic plain Fabrics:** satins, sheers, nets, taffetas, crepe, nylon organdy, stretch fabrics, velvet, vinyl, coated patent leatherette, felt, unbleached muslin, buckram, permafirm crinoline, polyesters China silk, others; full range of colors on most. (And full line of boutique trims, readymade dancewear, hats and hat frames.) Manufacturer, in business since 1842. Their slogan reads: "The World's largest and oldest theatrical fabric organization".

Wooling Down: "Wools may be preshrunk by placing them in your dryer with a damp towel and tumbling for 5-10 minutes at a medium temperature." — Courtesy of **Bethany Reynolds** of Union River Fabrics.

Dell Fabrics/Mail Order Dept.
6130 Olson Hwy.
Minneapolis, MN 55422
612-544-1477

Send SASE with inquiry (specify interest).
Complete line of **fabrics**, fabric-craft items, aids; notions (for hand and machine sewing).

Denim Accents
180 N.E. 134th St.
Vancouver, WA 98665
206-573-2178

Catalog, $ .50.
Denim and T-shirt fabrics variety of colors and weights (and notions, threads, labels), others.

Designers Choice
P.O. Box 687
Manchester, NH 03105
603-622-6134

Brochure and samples, $1.50.
Silk fabrics (for fibercrafts, etc.) including degummed, Services: custom color dyeing; unusual silks.

Direct Mills Div.
Box 10
Wills Point, TX 75169

Send SASE for prices.
Fabrics — variety of types, prints and solids; sewing aids.

Discount Fabrics
3 W. Broad St.
Palmyra, NJ 08065

Send SASE for prices.
Calico fabric pieces (cotton blends) — light or dark assortments.

Earthtone Interiors
P.O. Box 188
St. Joseph, MI 49085

Send $2.00 and color scheme and use description, for sample swatches.
Decorator fabrics: upholstery, drapery, covers and spread types — velvets, tapestry, Jacquard, antique satin, textured, leather, vinyl; prints.

J. Edwards Glove Co.
P.O. Box 112
Appleton, WI 54912

Send SASE for price list.
Glove leather scraps — elkskin; by 10 pound bag.

Elegance Paris Fabric Collection
272 N. Rodeo Dr.
Beverly Hills, CA 90210

Fashion magazine, $10.00; catalog and complete swatches (over 300) $35.00.
Designer fabrics: international selections. Has Mastercard, Visa; has toll free number for orders.

Ellsworth Cascade Fabrics
(See Union River Fabrics)

Executive Button Corp.
239 W. 39th St.
New York, NY 10018

Send SASE for list.
Novelty Buttons: Hearts, bows, stars, other shapes; variety of colors.

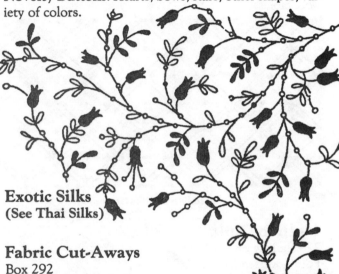

Exotic Silks
(See Thai Silks)

Fabric Cut-Aways
Box 292
Glendale, SC 29346
803-579-2033

Catalog, $ .50.
Fabrics (factory remnants, irregulars, seconds) — velvets, upholstery velvet, knit velour, wool, cottons and cotton blends (quilters, prints, flannel), and denim, knit satin, other knits. Lycra Spandex knit, others; by pound, piece or yardage. Mill end seams fabric for rag weavers. Batting. Quilting threads, templates, patterns. "Up to 80% savings off first quality." In business since 1973. The business has moved to become an outlet shop, and welcomes visitors.

Fabric of the Month Club
P.O. Box 402098
Miami Beach, FL 33140

Send SASE for details.
Fabric swatches are mailed to members of this **club**, on payment of annual fee; offering monthly selections and savings — fabrics include designer styles, and may include upholstery offerings.

Fabrics
138 Main
Gloucester, MA 01930

Swatches and discount coupon, $6.00.
Over 600 **cotton calicos; and fabrics** of Cranston, Concord, others.

Fabrics
Box 515
Sharon, MA 02067
617-784-3910

Send SASE for details.
Fabric assortments (15 yards and up, "at wholesale"): Calicos, solid cottons, prints, Christmas prints, permpress unbleached muslin, sailcloth, denim, corduroy, velveteen, others. Linings, interfacings; button and zipper assortments.

Fabrics by Melissa
P.O. Box 404
Leonia, NJ 07605

Catalog and coordinated swatches, $4.00.
Fabric Collection: Naturals (cottons, linens, silks, wools), blends; prints, solids, textures.

Fabrics in Vogue, Ltd.
200 Park Ave., Suite 303 E
New York, NY 10017

Send large SASE for complete information.
Membership in this **service** insures a 6 times yearly selection of fabric swatches (coordinated with Vogue Patterns) and notions, buttons, other patterns, linings, other sewing supplies. Has Mastercard, Visa.

Fabrics Unlimited
5015 Columbia Pike
Arlington, VA 22204

Send large SASE for sample request sheets.
Designer fabrics from: Calvin Klein, Adele Simpson, others, including exclusive; Ultrasuede™ in over 30 colors. Has sales periodically; Mastercard, Visa.

Fashion Fabrics Club
122 Cutter Mill Rd.
Great Neck, NY 11022

Send SASE for complete details.
Club members get monthly swatch folders on dress designer closeouts, others; Vogue patterns, sewing supplies. Has Mastercard.

Feathered Star Calicos
P.O. Box 426
Columbia, MD 21045

Send SASE for swatches and prices.
Fabrics: Ecology cloth, V.I.P.'s "Indigo", others; by yard.

The Felters Co.
22 West Street
Milbury, MA 01527
617-865-4401

See your local store, or write for information.
Felts: Acrylic felt (machine washable) in 24 colors; pieces or put-ups (15 yd., D & R, 50 yds. D & R, 72" full width rolls) and "Craft 2001" felt (60% rayon, 40% wool). (Also sells wholesale to businesses.)

Fiber Designs
P.O. Box 51
Bricelyn, MN 56014

Send SASE with inquiry (specify).
Wool blanket remnants. (Also weaving supplies.)

Filmax Textile Corp.
250 W. 39th St.
New York, NY 10018

See your dealer or write for information.
Pile fabrics: Velvet, Velveteen, corduroy (solids and prints).

Frankel Associates
321 S. Robertson Blvd.
Los Angeles, CA 90048
213-878-1421

Send SASE with specific inquiry.
Flame retardant **fabrics.**

Pre-doing for Fabrics: "Always wash fabric after buying and **before** using! Test fabric patches for color fastness, too, by wetting with hot water and blotting. If color bleeds, soak all of fabric in water, then blot dry. Repeat, if needed, until water is clear." — Courtesy of **Margaret A. Boyd.**

Genesis Production Co.
Rt. 1, Box J12
Kalona, MI 52247

Samples and Idea List, $2.00.
Lambskin pieces.

Gill Imports
P.O. Box 73
Ridgefield, CT 06877

Catalog, $ .50.
Handcrafted crewel designed material, in over 20 designs - by yard.

Grandma's Attic
2055 Alamar
Medford, OR 97501

Brochure, $ .50 (refundable).
Handprinted/screened "Country" fabric pieces: Feedsack and flour, Victorian designs, Teddy bears, chickens, cows, pigs, wheat, other motifs.
(Also sells wholesale to businesses.)

Greenwood Mills, Inc.
111 W. 40th St.
New York, NY 10018
212-398-9200

See your dealer or write for information.
Polyester/cotton **blends,** solids and patterns.
Manufacturer.

Hallie Greer, Inc.
Cushing Corners Rd., P.O. Box 165
Freedom, NH 03836
603-539-6007

Catalog and Swatch, $2.00 (refundable).
Country/decorator fabrics, 54" wide, 100% cotton (and home furnishings).

Gurian's
276 Fifth Ave.
New York, NY 10001

Catalog, $ .50.
Multi-color crewel fabric (wool flowers on handloomed cotton) — by yard.

Gutcheon Patchworks
611 Broadway
New York, NY 10012

Newsletter and Swatches $1.00.
Fabrics assortments: florals, calicos, polished cottons, solids, others. Quilting books. Has discount program for teachers.

Hearthside Mail Order
P.O. Box 19112B
Charlotte, VT 05445

Catalog and Swatches, $2.00.
Fabrics: Die-cut patches, calico prints and solids, 108" wide, muslin; by yard.
(Also has quilt supplies.)

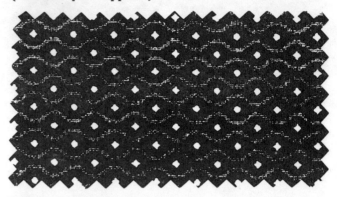

Hi-Fashion Fabrics, Inc.
483 Broadway
New York, NY 10013

See your retailer.
Fashion fabrics collection — full line of styles; prints, solids, textures.

Hi-Pro-Form Fabrics, Inc.
962 Devon Dr.
Newark, DE 19711

Send SASE with specific inquiry.
"Kelvar 49" fabric (lightweight, strong material used in modelmaking, etc.).

Homespun Weavers
530 State Ave.
Emmaus, PA 18049

Free Brochure with Swatches.
Homespun Tablecloth fabric in authentic patterns (diamond, original) in 100% cotton; white with 7 color combinations; 52" to 72" widths, by yard. Reversible, "no ironing". (Also has readymade cloths.)

Imaginations
51 Marble St.
Framingham, MA 01701
617-620-1411

A year's catalogs with swatches $10.00 (and get $5.00 credit).
"Haute Couture" fabrics collections from name manufacturers (John Kaldo, Skinner Ultra Suede®, Maygashel linens, Cantoni cottons, Ralph Lauren tweeds, Toyaba polyesters, Jonathan Logan knits; others), "at savings". Coordinating **notions** (threads, buttons, linings, others). Fashion **patterns.** (all major lines). Has seasonal offers.

Importadores Del Mundo
P.O. Box 300
Ridgeway, CO 81432

Send SASE for fabric samples and prices.
Handloomed Guatemalan cottons, by yard.

Iowa Pigskin Sales Co.
RR 2,
West Branch, IA 52358

Sample swatches, $2.00.
Soft sueded pigskin (by square foot) in 7 colors, (for vests, blazer, outerwear, dresses, etc.).

J & J
Box 46665
West Hollywood, CA 90046

Send SASE for prices.
Scrap suede garments — assorted, by 15 lb. or 50 lb. lots. (also has **used kimonos** for fabric, 15 lbs. up lots).

Jack's Fabrics
33 S. Main
Port Chester, NY 10573

Samples of all-cottons and calicos, $1.00.
Fabrics: dress and decorator types; calicos, others. In business since 1946.

Jalinda Creations
Craft Dept., P.O. Box 2389
Santa Cruz, CA 95063

Free catalog.
Decorator squares (8", 16" hand screened cotton with quilted design) in 20 original designs (for you-sew pillows, quilts, others).

Janknits
Box 315
Ingomar, MT 59039
406-354-6621

Complete catalog (pattern/kits) $1.00 or send SASE for prices (specify).
Sheepskin — mouton and garment types, in natural, limited colors. (Also complete line of knitting kits, yarns.) Owner Janet Mysee is author of *Affordable Furs* released fall of '83, gives instruction on furs and leathers garment construction (with knitting).

Jehlor Fantasy Fabrics
17900 Southcenter Pkwy.
Seattle, WA 98188
206-575-8250

Write for details.
Over 1500 **specialty fabrics** and trims ("sparkly, glimmering, silky, flashy", etc.)

Joann
P.O. Box 1171
Taylors, SC 29687

Send SASE for list.
Fabrics (by 3 lb. bundles) calicos, small prints — ¼ to 1 yard pieces.

Jolley Farms
Dresden, TN 38225

Send SASE for price list.
Cotton quilting fabric (by piece; variety of solids, prints) in pound lots or piece assortments.

John Kaldor Fabricmaker U.S.A., Ltd.
500 7th Ave.
New York, NY 10018
212-221-8270

See your fabric store.
Sofrina™ fabric "looks like leather and sews like fabric", in 25 colors.

Kap-Pee Fabrics, Inc.
P.O. Box 19939, 1026 Broadway
Kansas City, MO 64141

See your dealer or send SASE for information.
"Quilting" Fabrics: Unbleached muslin, "drip dry" muslin, broadcloth solids, calicos and matching solids.

Kasturi Dyeworks
1959 Shattuck Ave.
Berkeley, CA 94701
415-841-4509

Catalog, $5.00 (U.S.) refundable with initial order of $25.00.
Fabrics from Japan: Tsumugi (plain, striped), ikat (hand or machine woven), Indigo cotton, others. **Fabric dyes** from Japan — natural, Mijako, yuzan and shibori supplies, (Also has weaving supplies and folkcrafted gifts.)

Leather, the Indian Way: "For sewing leather in Indian style garments, use a glovers needle with an overcast stitch." — Courtesy of **J. Rex Reddick,** of Crazy Crow Trading Post.

Kenyon Consumer Products

200 Main St.
Kenyon, RI 02836

See your dealer or send SASE for list.
Nylon fabrics (water resistant) of downproof taffeta and ripstop; coated fabrics (pack cloth, ripstop, taffeta. "K-Tape" repair tape, reflective tape and patches (for outer-wear, bags, etc.).

Kieffer's Lingerie Fabrics and Supplies

1625 Hennepin Ave.
Minneapolis, MN 55403

Free catalog.
"Kwik-Sew" patterns catalog, $2.75. Full line of **fabrics,** including lingerie, swimwear, etc.: nylons (tricot, crepe, lace, brushed tricot, suede, terry, sheers, novelties; blends), polyester and blends, Qiana, lycra blends. Tubular acrylic knits, nylon knits. Stretchable fabrics. Thermal prints, sweat shirt fleece prints, knits (acrylic), jersies, brushed types; full assortments of colors, prints, laces, solids Sewing patterns. Bra closures. Patterns. Full line of trims —laces, braids, novelties. Has sales periodically.

S. H. Kunin Felt Co., Inc.

Brussels St.
Worcester, MA 01610
617-755-1241

See your local dealer, or write for information.
Felts: Polyfelt,™ premium **felts** — Felt on bolts, 1 and 2 yard packaged, pieces, Presto-Felt™ peel and stick pieces or by yard. Feltie™ shapes, frame kits, felt magnet kits, 3-d felt frame kits, others. Manufacturer.

Las Manos

Box 515
Lower Lake, CA 95457
707-994-0461

Send $2.00 for samples and prices.
Handwoven fabric from Guatemala: contemporary, traditional and designer patterns; 100% Guatemalan cotton, German dyes.
(Also sells wholesale to businesses.)

A Silk Whitewash: "Keep white washable silks white by occasionally putting a drop or two of ammonia and hydrogen peroxide into warm sudsy water; to remove yellowing add three tablespoons of white vinegar to a basin of cool water; perspiration and sticky deodorant stains can be a problem with any fabric — they are not removable, and you should use small shields." — Courtesy of **G. D. Morgan** of Thai Silks.

Emma P. Lawless

Rt. 2
Coulterville, IL 62237

Send SASE for fabric price information.
Three yard **assortments** of Velours, and heavy velvets. **Laces** to 6" wide.

The Leachman Friesen Co.

P.O. Box 668
Oakley, KS 67748

Send SASE for price list.
Glove leather assortments of scrap pieces, variety of colors.

The Leather Factory

P.O. Box 2430
Chattanooga, TN 37409

Catalog, $1.00 (refundable).
Leather skins including for garment making, others; lacing, tools, books (also kits, others).

Leather Unlimited Corp.

R.R. 1, Box 236, 7155 County Hwy. "B"
Belgium, WI 53004

Catalog, $2.00 (refundable).
Leathers including garment types; deerskin, deerskin splits, sheepskin; leather pieces. Belt blanks. **Accessories/parts;** snaps, rivets, snap/rivet setters, zippers, pulls, buckles (over 200). **Supplies:** finishes, dyes, adhesives, threads, tools/aids; cutters, punches, stamping tools and designs, snap/rivet setter machine. (Other leathers and supplies.) Has quantity prices; Mastercard, Visa.

The Leather Warehouse

3134 S. Division
Grand Rapids, MI 49508

Free mailers.
Complete line of **leather,** leather craft products.
(Also sells wholesale to businesses.)

Left Bank Fabric Co.

8354 W. 3rd St.
Los Angeles, CA 90048

Send SASE for brochures (specify fabric interest).
Designer fabrics: (from St. Laurent, Blass, Klein, Simpson, Dior, Halston and other houses); cottons, silks, wools; blends; one-of-a-kinds. Has Mastercard, Visa.

Samuel Lehrer & Co.
100 Research Dr.
Stamford, CT 06906
203-323-9999

Swatch Book (over 70 samples), $15.00.
"Classic" fabrics for suits and coats, etc.; wool worsteds and blends, Donegal tweeds, wool velour, others.

Leiters Designer Fabrics
P.O. Box 978
Kansas City, MO 64141

Write for information.*
Leiters designer fabrics collection (imported wool, silks, cottons, knits, lambskin and pigskin suedes (designer colors) and synthetic leathers (smooth and suede).
*Or write for information on becoming a Leiters sales representative.

Louise A. Lew
108 Fifth Ave.
New York, NY 10011
212-242-1475

Send SASE for current prices. (Specify fabric).
Tailoring fabrics: Fusible interfacings, linings, hair canvas (60" — 3 grades); velvets, others.

Libra International, Inc.
259 W. 30th
New York, NY 10001
212-695-3114

Garment Leather skins (textured, smooth grain; glittery, other unusuals) by square foot; "couture" quality.

Lore Lingerie, Inc.
2228 Cotner Ave.
Los Angeles, CA 90064

Send SASE for price list.
Silk satin fabric remnants: Solids/prints assortments, in pound and up bags.

Louise's Fabrics and Quiltworks
13972 Riverside Dr.
Sherman Oaks, CA 91423

Send SASE for list.
Fabrics including Mettler Swiss cotton "Soraya" others. Has Mastercard, Visa.

MacPherson Brothers
P.O. Box 99442
San Francisco, CA 94109

Catalog, $1.00 (refundable).
Leathers, leather tools, saddle stamps, dyes, buckles, others.

The Mail Train
5401 Dashwood, Suite 2A
Bellaire, TX 77401

See your dealer or write for information.
"Huckaback" cotton fabric (for Swedish weaving, etc.) with linen feel; 36" width, 5 colors, by yard.
(Also sells wholesale to businesses.)

Marushka
Box 723
Spring Lake, MI 49456

Catalog, $2.00.
Fabric **prints/panels: over** 200 hand-screened designs. Has Mastercharge, Visa.

Maxine Fabrics
417 Fifth Ave.
New York, NY 10036

Send $3.00 and SASE for swatches, prices (specify interest).
Fabrics: chiffon (polyester), Imported Swiss shirting materials, wool coatings, ultra suede, others.

Mid-West Scenic and Stage Equipment Co.
224 W. Bruce St.
Milwaukee, WI 53204
424-276-2707

Send SASE with inquiry.
Flame-retardant fabrics, retardant compounds.

Threading Up for Silk: "Use natural cotton 60's (cotton 50's for heavier weight silks). Silk thread is ideal for basting thread but too strong for the finished garment; cotton thread has more 'give'.

To avoid puckering, tension should be loose, about a #2 or #3 tension; for file silks 10-12 stitches per inch and 8-10 stitches for heavier." — Courtesy of **G. D. Morgan** of Thai Silks.

Mill End Store

8300 S.E. McLoughlin Blvd.
Portland, OR 97202
503-236-1234

Send SASE for current offerings.
Fabric — nylons (assorted weights), stretch ski pant material; Drisilk rainwear, nylon faced fleece, polyesters, cottons, taffeta, satin, Georgette, failes, velvet and velveteen organza. Altra kits. Green Pepper patterns. Laces, lace collars, medallions. Ribbons (all widths/colors). And has Bridal fabrics, accessories.

Mills Division

Box 10
Wills Point, TX 75169

Send SASE for listings.
Fabrics ("under half price"): cottons, blends, others.

Monterey Mills Outlet Store

1725 E. Delavar Dr.
Jamesville, WI 53545
608-754-8309

Send SASE for prices. Sample package $4.00 ppd.
Complete line of **Fur-like fabric** — by yard, scrap, remnants; first quality, second quality, closeouts, overruns, discontinued; 60" width; assorted patterns and solids, crushed velvet look, novelties, pastels, animal-like furs. (Use for home accessories, bedding, toys, clothing, draperies, other.) Half-yard minimums per item. "Savings up to 50% and better."

Muffy's Boutique

1516 Oakhurst Ave.
Winter Park, FL 32789

Send SASE for prices.
Fabric assortments of all cotton, or cotton/polyester prints.

Natural Fiber Fabric Club

521 Fifth Ave.
New York, NY 10175

Send SASE for brochure.
Fabric Club — members get a Sewing aids catalog, 4 scheduled (seasonal) mailings of swatches of fashion fabrics (from worldwide). Portfolio of basic fabrics swatches (cotton, sateen, wool gabardeen, silk crepe de Chine and broadcloth, others). Also unscheduled specials periodically. "Guarantee members a savings of at least 20% from the manufacturer's recommended retail price on all items we sell. No Exceptions." Allows foreign orders. Has Mastercard, Visa.

New Jersey Tanning Co.

410 Frelinghausen
Newark, NJ 07114

Send SASE for swatches.
Leather for garment sewing (smooth grain skins, "nude" by square foot).

Dan Newman Co.

57 Lakeview Ave.
Clifton, NJ 07011
201-340-1165

Write for sample swatches.
"Logo" or "Name" cloth — 60" wide flame retardant fabric with ¼" names or logos woven in — polyester; custom names to 15 letters; for 5 yards minimum order (names in repeated herringbone effect, 7 base fabric colors with names in white or contrasting color). Also readymade drapes, tablecloths, etc. Has Mastercard, Visa. Has quantity prices, and allows discount to teachers/institutions and professionals. In business since 1955.

Nizonie Fabrics, Inc.

East Highway 160, P.O. Box 729
Cortez, CO 81321
303-565-7079

Send large SASE for brochure.
Handprinted textiles (for draperies, clothing, others) in variety of Navajo and other American Indian design, overall motifs and border prints, by yard.

Norton Candle and Handwork House

1836 Country Store Village
Wilmington, VT 05363

Catalog and 200 swatches, $2.00.
Calico fabrics by the yard or assortment.

Oriental Silk Co.

8377 Beverly Blvd.
Los Angeles, CA 90048

Samples (specify type). $1.00.
Chinese silks: jerseys, Tussah, silk satin, brocades, Pongees; blends.

Palmser/Pletsch Associates

P.O. Box 8422
Portland, OR 97207

Send SASE for details.
Book: *Sensational Silk*, by Gail Brown (handbook for sewing on silk or silk-like materials — and seam and edge finishing techniques, trouble free zippers and button-hole making.

Patti
63 Starmond
Clifton, NJ 07013

Catalog with swatches, $1.00 and large SASE.
Fabrics: calicos, ginghams, solids; by V.I.P., Concord, Springmaid; "below retail price".

Pellon Corp.
119 W. 40th St.
New York, NY 10018

See your dealer or distributor.
Pellon™ **non-woven interfacing:** Fuse'N Fold™ pre-cut band-widths with perforated fold lines (3 widths, 75 yd. rolls). Pellon™ **Phun Phelt™ non-woven polyester craft fabric** (firm, retains shape, can be washed and painted or written on) full line of colors by 36" or 72" wide bolts, or pieces. Manufacturer.

Pennywise Fabrics
R.R. 1, Box 305
Harrisburg, MO 65256

Send large SASE and $1.00 for swatches.
Natural fabrics (by yard): Cottons (denims, muslin, batiste, etc.), wools, others.

Peters Fabrics
1412 Broadway, 10th Floor
New York, NY 10018
212-944-0440

See your dealer or write for information.
Fashion Fabrics: Wool blends, tartans and mini-tartans, tweeds, plaids, stripes, flannels, heather solids.

Piira Prints
P.O. Box 1592
Ogden, UT 84402

See your dealer, or send $8.50 for informative catalog ($8.95 in '85).
Uncommon threads™ country designer prints on hand-screened cotton: in 18" x 44" panels of designs on ten-yard bolts (country checks, Christmas cat, Fantasy, florals, hearts, travel motifs, sheep, folk design); and in 6" wide rolls (with instruction sheets attached for home accessories projects). Nanny Patches™ screened 6" squares, with project instructions. Manufacturers, since 1982.
(Also sells wholesale to distributors, retailers, teachers/institutions; informative catalog available, $4.25, $4.50 in '85).

Portfolio Fabrics
4984 Manor St.
Vancouver, BC, Canada V5R 3Y2

Send SASE for details.
Subscribers/fabrics: Bimonthly portfolios of imported fine fabrics swatches; newsletter of tips and treats. Has Mastercard, Visa.

Portland Textile Co.
P.O. Box 84
Portland, ME 04112

Send SASE for price list.
Fabrics: Cotton chamois, "Country Slicker" poplin, others; by yard.

Product Supply Co.
Rt. 3, Box 503
Raleigh, NC 27603

Send SASE for prices.
Aida cloth (cotton 14 and 18 count, white and ecru; 48" width, by yard), "save 30%".

Deby Radstrom
12237 Hartsook St.
N. Hollywood, CA 91607
213-508-0209

Send SASE for details.
Color swatch guide — 32 true color fabric swatches in palettes for coordinating wardrobes, etc.; (2" sq. swatches in plastic fan-out holder); in 4 separate seasonal guides.

"Uncommon Borders", © Piira Prints

Regency Mills, Inc.
259 Center St., P.O. Box 677
Phillipsburg, NJ 08865
201-454-1112

See your dealer or write for information.
Specialty fabrics: Fiddler's cloth (by roll goods, or pieces), dolly cloth (soft sculpture 62" wide goods, or pieces, 4 skin shades), unbleached muslin, Aida, Hardanger. 'Peel-N-Pat' velour sheets (8 colors), "Swiss Micro" cotton velour paper (16 colors, sheets).

> **Slick Sewing on Silk:** "Place slippery silks on lightweight shelf paper and cut through pattern, fabric and shelf paper." — Courtesy of **G. D. Morgan** of Thai Silks.

Arthur Muray Rein Furs

32 New York Ave.
Freeport, NY 11520
516-379-6421

Free literature.
Mink fur sections/trimmings (about ½" — 2½" wide, by 2" to 6" long) in assorted natural browns, greys, tans, pastels, by pound (includes fur sewing needle for assembling and sewing sections into pieces for projects). Also has new fur skins, 9" promotional mink Teddy bears (and fur coats). Has quantity prices.
(Also sells wholesale to retailers, professionals, and teachers/institutions. Provides sales literature at cost.)

Rockland Industries, Inc.

Falls Rd. near Ruxton
Brooklandville, MD 21022

See your local store or call 800-638-6390 for nearest dealer and about sewing instructions booklet.
Rock-lon® Warm Window™ **quilted fabric** (four-layer insulated, with magnetic seal edge) "reduces heat loss through single-glazed window up to 81%" while "solar heat gain is reduced up to 79% ...", to be covered with selected fabric for mounting to window, etc. Mounting hardware.

Rosari's Fabrics

400 No. Canon Dr.
Beverly Hills, CA 90210

Send SASE for information (specify interest).
Fashion Fabrics (by yard): Silks, printed silks, linens, cottons, woolens, others. Has Mastercard, Visa.

Rose Brand Textile Fabrics

517 W. 35th St.
New York, NY 10001
212-594-7424

Flame retardant fabrics.

Royal Arts and Crafts

650 Ethel St., N.W.
Atlanta, GA 30318

See your dealer or write for information.
Colored muslin (in 5-yard rolls), in 5 muted shades, coordinated with Wrights Berlin framing hoops. Others.

Royal Creations, Ltd.

Box 3201, W. End Station
West End, NJ 07740

Send SASE for price list.
Acetate satin patches: assortment of colors, 8" sq. (for patchwork, etc.).

The San Francisco Pattern Company

821 Market St.
San Francisco, CA 94103
415-982-6585

See your dealer or write for information.
Imported fabric panels — 12 Kissenkinder™ designs printed on 100% cotton (for pillows, quilts, clothing, hangings, etc.).

Sawyer Brook Distinctive Fabrics

Heritage Place
Amherst, NH 03031

Swatch portfolio, $5.00.
Fabrics (imported/domestic): natural cottons and blends, silks, linens, denims, outing flannel; batik fabrics. Has Mastercard, Visa.

Schwartzchild Textiles
Division of Mayar Silk, Inc.
1040 Ave. of the Americas
New York, NY 10018

See your fabric store or send SASE for fact sheet.
"E.T.T." fabric — 100% spun bonded olefin; lightweight, waterproof (for ski-wear, etc.), in 54"/56" widths (hand washable). Others.

Selwyn Textile Co., Inc.

15 W. 38th St.
New York, NY 10018
212-921-9355

Free samples and price list.
Fabrics (for framing, etc.): linens, cottons, silks, suedes, velveteens, burlaps, grasscloths; linen/cotton canvases; widths up to 120 inches; "discounts for quantity".

Serotex, Ltd.

P.O. Box 11176
Charlotte, NC 28220
704-523-8033

Denim fabrics — 100% cotton, "neon" 6 oz., washed 100% cotton; by bolts.

Seventh Ave Fabric Club
450 Seventh Ave., Suite 602
New York, NY 10123

Send SASE for details.
Fabrics subscription service: annual membership fee assures a four-times-yearly mailing of swatch books of seasonal fashion ("at savings"); overruns, etc. from garment manufacturers.

Sew What Fabrics
2431 Eastern Ave., S.E.
Grand Rapids, MI 49507

Swatches, $5.00.
Natural fabrics (by the yard): cottons, linens, silks (crepe de chine, silk noil, silk linen), lamb suede skins (in colors), others. Gingher shears.

Shepherd Estates of New Zealand
1368 Washington
Eugene, OR 97401
503-485-4515

Unsheared sheepskin in colors, by skin.

Silver Thimble Quilt Shop
249 High St.
Ipswich, MA 01938

Over 400 swatches, $3.00.
100% cotton mini-prints: holiday prints and solids.

Something Special
616 W. Church St.
Champaign, IL 61820
217-359-8342

Send SASE with specific inquiry.
Handwoven fabrics (for historic reproductions) and handcrafted laces (also other fibercraft supplies).

Stacy Fabrics Corp.
38 Passaic St.
Wood Ridge, NJ 07075
201-779-1121

Interfacings: "Easy Shaper" fuse and sew-in (four shades). Appli-Quik™ **support backing** for applique (36" x 24" sheets). **Quilting fleece** (polyester — precut sheets, for machine and hand work). Others.

Street Fabrics
1143 E. Garvey, N. #27
W. Covina, CA 91790

Samples, $1.00.
Specialty fabrics: upholstering, quilt and pillow prints.

Carol Strickler
1690 Wilson Ct.
Boulder, CO 80302

Send SASE for details.
Handwoven fabrics including of 19th century designs, others and exclusive designs (for scale miniatures and other uses).

Sunflower Studio
2851 Road B½
Grand Junction, CO 81503
303-242-3883

Catalog, $2.50. Sample swatches, $ .50 each (specify).
Handwoven, hand-dyed traditional/natural fibre fabrics (for clothing and home decorating): 18th and 19th century adaptations; wools — flannel baize, upholstery worsted and serge, shalloon, croise serge, calamanco, camlet, sabanilla, homespun broadcloth, frieze, others. **Linens and blends** — checks, stripes, cats' paw overshot, others. **Cottons** — corded, callicos, dimety, others. **Lindsey-Woolsey** — light and heavyweights, checks, "Log Cabin" weave. All 36" wide, by yard. Sunflower Studio handwoven fabrics are widely used by museums and restorations. (Has museum discounts and discounts to authorized dealers. Modest trade discounts on quantity orders.)

Fur-ther Tips: "For ease in cutting furs I recommend a single edge razor blade. You can easily cut the backing, and not the fur fibers. For ease in sewing furs, I feel ball point sewing machine needles are better than regular needles, and for heavy duty sewing the best needles to use are leather needles. Not only will you experience less breakage with leather needles, but make it easier to sew heavier furs."
—Courtesy of **Diane Babb** of By Diane — a professional craftsperson for over ten years.

Sureway Trading

826 Pine Ave. #5
Niagra Falls, NY 14301
716-282-4887

Send SASE for brochure.
Silk samples: naturals/white $8.00 per set; colors,
$12.00 per set.
Pure **silk fabrics:** China Pongee, Habotai, twill, crepe
Georgette, satin, Jacquard, taffeta, organza, Noil, Doup-
pioni, Tussah, pearl pongee, shantung, knit, basket weave,
tweed, others. Silk and wool blends (tweed, suiting). Silk
threads, French **dyes** for handpainting, silk-screening;
dye supplies, books. Business established in 1979.

Tandy Leather Co.

Box 2934
Fort Worth, TX 76113

Write for 104 page catalog.
Leather sewing: sewing and garment leathers, metallic
cowhides, "sof-suede", washable suedes, chamois, cabretta, vogue splits, others. Leather dyes, finishes. Tools:
needles, punches, grommets, other notions and sewing aids
(also has other leather craft supplies, dyes, kits, beltings,
buckles, etc.).

The Tenth House

P.O. Box 464
Deerfield, IL 60015

See your dealer or send SASE for prices.
Flour sacking toweling (prewashed, pre-shrunk cotton)
28" by 29" hemmed size; by 50 piece bundle.

Testfabrics

P.O. Drawer "O"
Middlesex, NJ 08846
201-469-6446

Free catalog.
Fabrics (for printing, dyeing, painting, etc.); cottons,
wools, silks, viscose, others. Has Mastercard, Visa.

Lambsuede by Machine: "Most new machines
(home type) and walking foot machines will sew
lambsuede with no trouble. Try your machine with a
scrap of suede before investing in a lot of skins. I use
"Barge" cement for gluing hems and facings when
needed. Avoid gluing long seams as this will make
your garment hang stiffly.

I use cotton wrapped polyester thread — size 50.
This is available on large cones. This thread is very
strong and will not break easily. You don't want
your suede to outlast your thread." — Courtesy of
Jennifer Morgan of Jennifer Morgan Designs.

Thai Silks

252 State St.
Los Altos, CA 94022
415-948-8611

Brochure, $ .35; sample sets (specify): **China silks —
$ .80, Jacquard Palace silks — $ .80, silk prints**
(Crepe de Chine) — **$1.60, silk Organzas** (for flow-
ers) — **$ .60, medium Boucles** (dress weights) —
**$ .80, silk tapestry brocades — $1.00, close out spe-
cials** — 200 item pack, **$6.00, Thai silks — $ .80,
Indian silks — $ .40, Italian silks — $ .80.**
Full line of **silk fabrics** (in 80 colors — mostly from
China; for fashion sewing, upholstery, draperies):
China, raw, organzas, boucles, Crepe de Chines, tapestry
brocades, spun "taffetas", shantung, noil, Fuji broadcloth, pongee, crepe back silk satin, palace silks, raw and
dyed silk Tussah, silk corduroy, others; (raw, colors,
prints; suit and dress and blouse weights). **Cotton fabrics**
(malay batik, Chinese, Indian, Javanese batik). Silk scarves.
Has cash discount on retail orders of 10% for $30 and up;
to 25% for $200 purchases. Allows 10% discount to
teachers/institutions. (Also sells wholesale to fabric
stores.) In business since 1964. Many fashion magazines,
including Vogue, use Thai silks.

Thimbleweed

2975 College Ave.
Berkeley, CA 94705
415-845-5081

Send SASE for brochure.
Cotton fabrics: Liberty brand and Italian pima cottons.
Quilting/smocking supplies and notions. Full line of
buttons. Books, others.

James Thompson and Company, Inc.

1133 Ave. of the Americas
New York, NY 10036
212-575-8811

See your dealer or write for details.
Fabrics: basics (muslin, ticking, toweling, cotton/
polyester, nylon net), **crafts** (muslins, quilt backing, rugs
and needlepoint canvases), burlap (supreme and decorator grades).

3M Center
St. Paul, MN 55144

See your dealer or write for information (specify).
Thinsulate™ **thermal insulation fabric** (thin — for rain-wear, windbreakers, etc.).

Triblend Mills, Inc.
4004 Anaconda Rd.
Tarboro, NC 27886

Free fabric swatches, prices, details, call toll free, 800-334-5620 or write above.
"Barrier-Lok" **drapery fabrics** (by yard) — self-lined, self-insulating, "at mill-end prices". Orders include free "How to Sew Draperies" book.

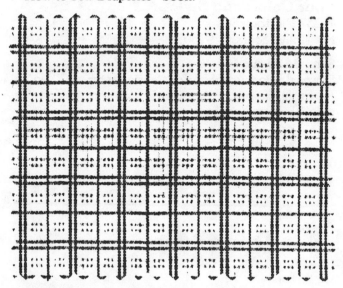

U.S. Interiors, Inc.
400 N. Main St., P.O. Box 848
Goshen, IN 46526
219-534-1441

Send SASE and $1.00 for prices/samples.
Shade cloth (vinyl backed or coated) in 12" to 20" widths, by yard or roll; can be painted on. Trims, by roll. (Also sells wholesale to businesses.)

Union River Fabrics
125 High St.
Elksworth, ME 04605
207-667-5894

Send SASE for prices (specify interest).
Designer, imported and other fabrics: woolens and worsted wools, wool blends (including Scottish, others), camel hair, cottons, batik Japanese, Guatamalan; cotton lawn, stonewashed and other denim, linette, others. Wool/poly twills. Silks. Quiana taffetas, "Country slicker" poplin, others. Patterns: Butterick, Burda, Folkwear, Vogue, Kwiksew. Guterman threads. Has quantity prices, holds sales. 10% discounts to teachers/institutions and professionals. Has "30% discount on full bolts".

Utex Trading
710 9th St., Suite 5
Niagra Falls, NY 14301
416-596-7565
and in Toronto, Canada

Send SASE for brochure; sample deposits: $35 for complete set, $20 for silk prints, $8 for white silks, $12 for colored silks.
Silk fabrics: prints, Crepe de Chine; silks from China, Thailand, Fuji, Silk doupioni, organzas. Silk knits, Jacquard, crepe satin, shantung, taffeta, twill, chiffon, boucles, tussah, others; dress and suit weights. Silk threads —embroidery and sewing.

Vea Prints
729 Heinz #2
Berkeley, CA 94710

See your dealer or write for catalog sheets.
Designs screened on fabric (pieces or patches): Country designs in one of many colors (for embroidery then sewing to pockets, potholders, etc.). Designs include flowers, scenics with quotes, animals/alphabet letters, sheep, Christmas, others. Manufacturer.
(Also sells wholesale to businesses, teachers/institutions.)

Vermont Country Store
Weston, VT 05161

Free catalog.
Extensive selection of **old time fabrics** (by yard): calicos, birds eye diaper cloth, flannel, rubber sheet, flour sack cloth, checked damask, batiste, monks cloth, silvercloth, cambric, turkish toweling; cotton batting sheet, old time linens. (Also other old time gifts, kitchen items, others.)

Veteran Leather Company, Inc.
204 25th St.
Brooklyn, NY 11232
212-768-0300

Send for catalog.
Leathers: English morocco, grained cowhide, splits, skivers, sueded cowhide splits, chrome and kip sides, others; remnants (by pound). Belt blanks. **Tools/equipment:** punches, rivets, stamps, studs, fasteners, cutters, eyelet setters, lacing and stitching tools. Others. Dyes, finishes. **Kits:** handbags, accessories, others. **Beads:** wood, horn, seed. Threads. Laces. Has quantity prices.

Naturals for Quilting: "For cathedral window designs, always use a good quality muslin — not perma press — wash, rinse with fabric softener, and then press while damp." — Courtesy of **Lorraine Braden** of Quilt Easy. She is teacher, lecturer and pattern designer.

V.I.P. Crafts and Fabrics
1412 Broadway
New York, NY 10018
212-730-4600

See your dealer or write for information.
Fashion fabrics: Calicuts™ calicos in ½ yard cuts; variety of prints/colors. Poly/cotton prints, others.

Warren of Stafford
P.O. Box 45
Stafford Springs, CT 06076

Catalog, $3.00 (refundable).
Fashion fabrics: Woolens, wool blends, cashmere, camel's hair, others; variety of weights. Allows Canadian orders, has Mastercard, Visa.

Weaving Workshop
3352 B Gakstead
Chicago, IL 60657
312-929-5776

Send $ .50 and SASE for samples and information.
Handwoven Guatemalan fabric: ethnic plaids and stripes, 36" wide, by yard.

With You in Mind, Inc.
P.O. Box 100607
Ft. Lauderdale, FL 33309

Catalog and fabric swatches, $2.00.
Home **decorator fabrics** (with coordinated home furnishings) variety of prints/solids, materials.

S. Wolf's Sons
771 Ninth Ave.
New York, NY 10019
212-265-2066

Flame retardant fabrics: flame retardant material, others.

Your Colors and Style
12237 Hartsook St.
No. Hollywood, CA 91607

Send SASE for details.
Seasonal color **swatch guide:** fabric swatches (2") in 36 colors, in fan-out holder; for each of four seasons (for wardrobe coordination).

4
Trims & Fillers

❧❧❧❧❧❧❧❧❧❧❧❧❧❧❧❧❧

This section presents companies with sources for fabric trims (for you-sew-on) and naturals-fillers for soft sculpture containers (i.e., soft boxes, baskets, sachets, etc.). Among the fillers are feathers, flowers, drilled shells, and potpourri — most of these can serve as trims, too. (And see other sections throughout, or consult the index for specific trims.)

❧❧❧❧❧❧❧❧❧❧❧❧❧❧❧❧

All the Trimmings
Box 15528
Atlanta, GA 30333

Catalog, $ .50.
Trims (full line): laces — imported and domestic (embroidered, eyelets, insertion and lace edges, lace braid, Galloon; cotton, nylon, others), elastics, braids, ric racs. **Specialty fabrics:** Organdy, dotted Swiss, Batiste, nainsook, muslin, net, others.

Alohalei Hawaii
Box 17718
Irvine, CA 91713

Catalog, $ .50 (refundable).
Pearls: full line of shapes, colors, sizes; kits, patterns, beaded holiday trims, others.

The Antlershed
12 Wynwood Dr.
Hagerstown, MD 21740
301-791-4951

Free brochure.
Antler buttons.
(Also sells wholesale to businesses.)

Aprilz Apothecary, Inc.
Box 111
Waterloo, NE 68069

Catalog, $1.00.
Potpourri/sachet supplies/kits: all scents (exotic, holiday, floral, spicy, citrus, others); blends; botanicals — full line, in ¼ lb. and up packages. Over 12 essential oils; extracts. Has some quantity prices.

Art's By De-Da
614 Coulter
Rockdale, TX 76567

Catalog, $2.00.
Silk flowers (and kits/parts — petals, leaves, stamens): daffodils, tulips, roses, carnations, poppies, daisies, dogwood, dahlias, orchids, violets, zinnias, iris, lily, poinsetta and others; variety of sizes. **Dried flowers,** fans brooks, baskets, **wedding accessories,** others.

Bead Supply House
P.O. Box 5512
Rockford, IL 61125

Catalog, $ .50.
Beads: plastic - faceted, tri, snowflake, berry, spaghetti, krackle, saucer, rosebud, fruits/leaves, flair. Pearls, metallic pearls. Rocailles, bugles. **Bells:** pearl, metal, wood. Metallic cords. Felt squares. (Other beading supplies.)

No Pocket Shadow: "To avoid pockets shadowing through light colored fabric, i.e. white, pink, yellow linen skirts or dresses: Make the pockets out of **natural** color nylon tricot sheer or poly-organza —they'll never show through. Also, to keep them from becoming 'popper' pockets, attach a stay of lining fabric from one pocket to the other, thus holding them in the correct position." — Courtesy of **Clotilde** of Imports by Clotilde, from her book, *Sew Smart*; written with Judy Lawrence.

Beader Bee's
22623 No. Black Canyon
Phoenix, AZ 85027

Price list, $ .50 and large SASE.
Beads: variety of plastic types, colors, sizes; rocailles, Indian seed. (And other trims.) Books.

Beads
Box 80053
Indianapolis, IN 46260

Catalog, $1.00.
Trims: beads, beaded appliques and trims, sew-on jewels "direct from the garment industry".

BEL
Box 182
West New York, NJ 07093

Sample assortment, $2.00.
Embroidered appliques: patches, flowers, figures, animals, others.

Berger Specialty Co.
413 E. 8th St.
Los Angeles, CA 90014

Send SASE and description or sample with inquiry.
Trims, beads: full line, most all types, colors, styles.

B. Blumenthal and Co., Inc.
Division of Belding Hemingway Co.
Industries
140 Kero Rd.
Carlstadt, NJ 07072

See your retailer.
LaMode™ buttons: full line, all sizes (and expanded big button — ¾" to 1" — line). Manufacturer, in business for over one hundred years.

Bolek's
330 N. Tuscarawas Ave., P.O. Box 184
Dover, OH 44622

Catalog, $1.00.
Beads (variety of types, colors, sizes). Plastic **doll heads.** (Other needlecraft supplies.)

A Great Iron-off: "Hot iron cleaner works will to clean fusible 'goo' off the iron; better yet ... prevent it; fusibles won't stick if an IRON-SAFE iron cover (love it) is used." — Courtesy of **Phyllis Eifler** of Phyllis Eifler's Sewing Seminars, from *Sewing Is Getting Easier All The Time.*

Boston Carpet Fringe Co.
P.O. Box 605
Needham, MA 02192

Sample book, $1.00.
Carpet fringes: variety of styles, sizes, colors.

Boutique Trims, Inc.
21200 Pontiac Trail, Drawer P
South Lyon, MI 48178

Catalog, $3.00.
Fabric **painting** supplies, doll heads, holiday ornament kits, music box movements. **Trims:** laces, sequins, spangles, ribbons, beads, rhinestones, threads, pearls, ornaments, metallic braids. (And eggeury supplies.)

B. Bucciarelli Cloisonne
P.O. Box 3240
Berkeley, CA 94703
415-655-0559

See your favorite store or send SASE for information.
Designer buttons: cloisonne buttons, variety of styles and color choices (flowers, birds, Chinese characters, others).

Button Creations
26 Meadowbrook Lane
Chalfont, PA 18914

Catalog, $2.00.
Buttons: basic types (plastics, pearls, backer buttons), heavy backs — blazer sets, woods (including shanks and toggles), ivory nut, leather types, antler crosscuts and toggles, English horn, Mother of Pearl, handmade pottery, ceramic critters, metal "Battersea" mini-masterpieces, hand-cut glass; button pins and toggles, pewter replicas, and others, button grab bags including: designers types, novelty shapes, animals, nautical designs, patriotic and Indian, toys, hearts and flowers, fruits, "Peter Rabbit" collection, zodiac reproductions; fancy and plain, complete line of sizes/shapes/styles. Has quantity prices.

The Button Shop
P.O. Box 2053
Artesia, CA 90701
213-865-6420

Catalog, $ .25 plus SASE.
Buttons: variety of styles, colors, sizes. Business established in 1957.

Buttons
P.O. Box 2381
Ft. Pierce, FL 33454

Send SASE for prices.
Button assortments (12 sizes), styles, colors.

Buttons and Things

24 Main St.
Freeport, ME 04032

Free brochure.
Buttons "thousands": variety of colors, sizes, types; from "factory outlet".

Candee's Beads-N-Things

5224 Yarmouth
Encino, CA 91316

Send SASE for list.
Beads (imported): glass and crystal types, pearls. (Other beading supplies.) Books.

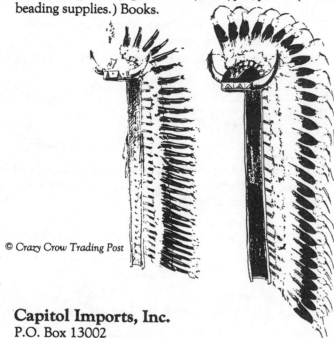

© Crazy Crow Trading Post

Capitol Imports, Inc.

P.O. Box 13002
Tallahasse, FL 32308
904-385-4665

See your dealer or send SASE for list.
Imported trims: Swiss embroideries, batistes, French Val Laces, satin ribbon (double-faced), English needles. Antique Mother-of-Pearl buttons.

Cardin Originals

15802 Sprindale St. #1-S
Huntington Beach, CA 92649

Color catalog, $2.00 (refundable).
Machine applique patterns (18 original designs by Mary Cardin), full-sized with directions and color covers; landscapes, shore scenes, nostalgia, ducks, geese, others.

Chan Imports

Box 134
Atlantic Highlands, NJ 07716

Catalog, $1.00.
Potpourri supplies: variety of herbs, spices, essential oils, others.

Christopher Book

P.O. Box 595
W. Paterson, NJ 07424

Free catalog.
Silk flowers, boutiques, plants, trees.

Crazy Crow Trading Post

Box 314
Dennison, TX 75020
214-463-1366

Catalog, $2.00.
American Indian oriented trims: beads, bells, conchos, feathers, bone items, shells, fringes, buttons (silver, antler, bone pewter), others. (And full line of other Indian kits/supplies — see section 7). Has quantity prices, discounts to teachers/institutions and professionals. In business since 1970.
(Also sells wholesale to businesses.)

Creative Heirlooms

Box 3614
Van Nuys, CA 91407

Send SASE with specific inquiry, or $1.50 for complete illustrations.
Imported beads in bulk. (And beaded needlepoint kits, supplies.)

Cinderella Flower and Feather

57 W. 38th St.
New York, NY 10018

Send SASE for price list.
Feathers: cocquil, turkey ruffs, boas (maribou, ostrich, rooster, turkey), ostrich plumed, peacock sticks; feather fringes. Hat forms, flower clusters.

Save a Feathered Friend: "Most old **ostrich feathers** can be cleaned and re-curled by a simple process. Before you begin, cut a small amount off the bottom of the feather to test it. Wash the ostrich feather in a solution of lukewarm water and a small amount of liquid dishwashing soap. Be careful not to tangle the flues. Dump the water and fill the bowl with clear water. Swish the feather back and forth again to rinse it until all the soap is gone. Hold the feather upside down and use a warm (not hot) hair blow-dryer to dry it, shaking the feather occasionally. Comb the flues straight out from the stem with a wide tooth comb. To curl, use a curling iron."
—Courtesy of **Denise Dreher** of Madhatter Press, professional hatmaker and author of the book, *From The Neck Up.*

Jeanette Crews Designs, Inc.
4 Killian Hill Rd.
Lilburn, GA 30247
Order: 1-800-241-1962

See your dealer or write for catalog.
Laces (long staple cotton): flat, gathered; variety of widths and styles on 18 yd. bolts; accessories, books.

Daisy Kingdom
598 Main St.
Boise, ID 83702

Send SASE for prices.
Lace medallions, variety of designs.

Dazian's Inc.
40 E. 29th St.
New York, NY 10016
212-686-5300
(and in Beverly Hills, Boston, Chicago, Dallas, Miami)

Free catalog.
Boutique/theatrical trims: Spangles, sequins, spangle cloths (stretch, taffeta backed), elasticized spangles, rhinestone/bead/sequin motifs, sew-on jewels, rhinestones, mirror "jewels", glass mirrors, beads, pearls, bead tassels, metallic coins, ribbon, plastic fringes, skirts, leis. Indian bells, tassels, fringes, braids, ric-rac, cords. Feathers, flowers. Theatrical fabrics. Has quantity prices by bolts; allows discount to professionals. In business since 1842.

Discount Craft Supply
6234 2nd Ave., No.
St. Petersburg, FL 33710

Free catalog, samples $1.00.
Supplies: beads, including ceramic animals, others; felt, plastic grids (other needle and general craft items), at "tremendous savings".

Discount Lace Co.
P.O. Box 2031
Norwalk, CA 90650

Free catalog.
Laces: eyelet, polyester, nylon; variety sizes; by 100 yard rolls; "wholesale prices. Save 50% or more".

The Edge of Lace — West
4650 S.W. Betts Ave.
Beaverton, OR 97005
503-643-5500

Send SASE for list.
Trims: eyelets, cluny, ribbons, braids, appliques — variety of designs (by Wrights, Offray, Lion, Embassy, others), "all at close to wholesale prices".

Eggs O' Beauty
P.O. Box 571073
Miami, FL 33157

Catalog, $1.50.
Trims: metallic braids; rhinestone ornaments, novelty miniatures (and complete eggeury supplies), rhinestone chain.

Elsie's Exquisiques
205 Elizabeth Dr.
Berrien Springs, MI 49103
616-471-3844

Write for catalog.
Trims: silk ribbon (3 widths), rosettes and rosebuds, angel lace, other narrow trims.
(Also sells wholesale to businesses.)

Enterprise Art
3860 Roosevelt Blvd.
Clearwater, FL 33520

Catalog, $1.00.
Beads (bulk): variety of plastic types, pearls, others. Beading kits, jiffy stitchery **ornament kits** (stuffed). Other needlework and craft items.

Everlasting by Agatha
5795 Phillips Dr.
Tipp City, OH 45317

Send SASE for prices.
Potpourri mixes — 5 blends, by 3 oz. packets.

Executive Button Corp.
239 W. 39th St.
New York, NY 10018

Send SASE for list.
Novelty buttons: Hearts, bows, stars, others.

Feather creations
Box 161
Pequabuck, CT 06781

Catalog, samples, $2.00.
Feathers: complete line, including natural colors; ostrich, pheasant, peacock, marabou, coque, others.

G. G.'s of Birmingham, Inc.
4137 Sharpsburg Dr.
Birmingham, AL 35213
205-871-9136

See your fabric store, or write for free brochure.
Trims including Pied Piping™ mini-piping (for children's items, smocking, etc.); 15 colors; single or double piping color combinations; by 3 yd. packages.

The Golden Egg
P.O. Box 59
Millersville, MD 21108

Catalog, $2.00.
Trims: beads, jewel chains, pearls, rhinestones, metallic braids and cords, ribbons. **Aids:** scissors, tweezers, magnifying lamp, "third hand", brass rods and tubes. Music box movements, miniatures. (And full line of eggeury supplies and equipment.) Has Mastercard, Visa.

Goodwin Creek Gardens
Box 83
Williams, OR 97544

Send large SASE for price list.
Potpourri supplies and dried flowers (baby breath, straw-flowers, others) including unusual varieties.

The Great American Sewing Factory
7 Susquehanna Rd.
Ossining, NY 10562

Catalog, $ .50 (refundable).
Laces: eyelet, cluny, cotton; flat, ruffled types; variety of sizes and designs. **Ribbons** and other trims in variety of colors, sizes, patterns.

The Greatest Sew on Earth
P.O. Box 214
Fort Tilden, NY 11695

Catalog, $1.00.
Trim bargains: Sequins, metallic glitter, embroideries, cluny and bridal laces and trims; "colossal savings".

The Green House
Rt. 4
Potsdam, NY 13676
315-265-4735

Catalog, $ .50.
Potpourri mixtures: 12 blends, home grown and collected; 29 dried herbs (whole, ground, sifted), essential oils (½ oz.).
(Also sells wholesale to businesses.)

Grey Owl/Indian Craft Mfg.
113-15 Springfield Blvd.
Queens Village, NY 11429

Catalog, $1.00.
American Indian oriented trims: Bells, lacing, mirrors, laces, drilled shells, tin cone jingles, sequins, tassels, fur trims and parts, feathers, fringes, ribbons, beadwork, buttons (shell, military metal), variety of beads. (And other sewing items.) Has quantity prices; Mastercard, Visa. (Also sells wholesale to businesses.)

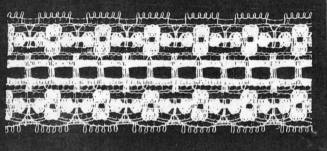

© All The Trimmings

The Hands Work
P.O. Box 386
Pecos, NM 87552
505-757-6730

Catalog, $2.00 (refundable).
Handcrafted porcelain buttons, (in shapes of, and decorated): chickens and eggs, other farm animals, pets and wild animals, fish, frogs, snail, teddy bears, cones, fruits, boats, clown faces, cars, painted geometric shapes and designs (many sizes), hearts, flowers, rounds and ovals, glazed in variety of shapes, marbled and gloss colors. Offers free shipping on large orders.
(Sells wholesale to businesses.) In business since 1979.

> **Better Buttonholes:** "Use good merchandised cotton or long-staple polyester thread for your buttonhole, and cord it (by attachment, or zig-zag over)." — Courtesy of **Margaret A. Boyd.**

Buttons, © The Hands Work

Herbal Holding Co.
Box 5164
Sherman Oaks, CA 94131

Catalog, $1.00.
Potpourri supplies, bath herbs, botanicals, others; "at discount". Manufacturer.

Herbitage Farm
Rt. 2
Richmond, NH 03470

Catalog, $1.00.
Potpourri mixtures (fillings for sachets, etc.) in ¼ cup and up lots. Has quantity prices.

Hobbs Feather Co.
P.O. Box 187
West Liberty, IA 52776

Write for prices.
Feathers (natural and dyed); pearl peacock, duck, goose, turkey, others (for hatbands, sew trims, others), "wholesale prices".

Hobby Hunting Grounds
Box 447
Sedro Woolley, WA 98284

Price list, $1.00 (specific beads).
Beads: bone, metallic, sterling, ceramic, glass, horn, plastic types, abalone, nut, seed, shell, wood. (And other supplies). "Wholesale".

Hollywood Fancy Feather Co.
512 South Broadway
Los Angeles, CA 90013
625-8453

Send SASE for price list.
Feathers (imported/domestic, natural, dyed): marabou (and fluffs), hackle, goose, turkey quills, peacock, ostrich, turkey boas; strung chicken, coque and others.
(Also sells wholesale to businesses.)

Indiana Botanic Gardens
P.O. Box 5
Hammond, IN 46325

Catalog, $ .25.
Dried herbs/spices, essential oils (also incense, others).

Janya Associates
49 Longview Rd.
Staten Island, NY 10304
212-981-9545

Send SASE for price list.
Closeouts: may include beads, doll eyes, felt pieces, potpourri (by pound), others "at wholesale prices".

Kahaner Co.
55 W. 38th St.
New York, NY 10018
212-840-3030

Write for brochure and name of distributor.
Full line of **appliques** including selection of unusuals.

Emil Katz and Company, Inc.
21 W. 38th St.
New York, NY 10018
212-221-6171

See your fabric.
Collection of **laces** (imported and domestic).

Keepsake Designs
571 North Madison
Ogden, UT 84404
801-782-6369

Send SASE for details.
How-to sewing books, including on making lace with your sewing machine (directions, illustrations, patterns) and on keepsake cutwork patterns by machine (designs for collars, cuffs, pockets; medallions, florals, others — with directions) both by Charlene Miller. Has quantity prices, large order discounts, discounts for professionals and teachers/institutions.
(Also sells wholesale to businesses.)

Kaydee Bead Supply
Box 1449
Cape Coral, FL 33910

Catalog, $1.50.
Beads: full line of plastic types/sizes/colors; pearls, others.

Ken's Craft Supply

250 E. Main St.
Midland, MI 48640

Send SASE for prices.
Trims: beads (plastic varieties), pearls, sequins, silk flowers (and supplies for general crafts). Has quantity prices. (Also sells wholesale to businesses.)

Kieffer's Lingerie Fabrics and Supplies

1625 Hennepin Ave.
Minneapolis, MN 55403

Free catalog, "Kwik-sew" pattern catalog, $2.75.
Full line of trims for lingerie, other sewing: Braids (all colors, woven, metallic, foldover; cotton, nylon, others. Embroidered edgings, all sizes, and with colored embroidery trims. **Laces** — nylon, cotton; cutout ¼" to 12" widths, most colors. "Bridal" laces, natural laces, novelties (galoons, multicolor), stretch laces — variety of sizes, styles, colors. Stretch lace medallions. Embroideries trips, embroidered medallions, nylon inserts, satin medallions. Ribbons — satin, double face satin, elastic, plush back elastic, piquot edge elastic. Has sales specials.

Kit Kraft

Box 1086
Studio City, CA 91604

Free catalog.
Beads: seed, rocailles, tile, others. Rhinestones and setter. Books. (And other craft supplies.) Has quantity discounts; Mastercard, Visa.

Lace Lady

1602 Locust St.
St. Louis, MO 63103

Send SASE for price list.
Lace assortments (bargains): edgings, insertions — selected colors, sizes, widths. Buttons assortments.

Lacis

2990 Adeline
Berkeley, CA 94703

Catalogs: Laces, $1.50. Sample bead strand, $1.25 and large SASE.
Laces — new and antique (cottons, others). **Victorian glass beads.** (Also lacemaking supplies.)

Ladish Pearl Button Co.

P.O. Box 941
Shawnee Mission, KS 66201
913-677-1244

See your fabric store.
Mother of pearl buttons: full line of sizes and colors. Manufacturer.

Lansing Co., Inc.

1701 Inverness Ave.
Baltimore, MD 21230

See your dealer, or write for information.
Buttons: Standard assortments and "Cute 'N Clever Boutique" buttons (animal shapes, bow, card suites, fish, other novelties). Manufacturer, since 1855.

Leisure Craft

Box 743
Mendota, MN 55150

Catalog and color cards of braids, $2.25.
Trims (Austrian, West German, others): Soutasch, loop and fancy braids, ric-racs, nylon and woven braids; assorted colors, widths. Metallic trims (some with woven colors) over 60 designs. Laces (30 designs). Pellon, felt pieces, jute, stretch lace and elastics.

Maison Mini

3647 44th St., Apt. #1
San Diego, CA 92105
714-281-2068

Send SASE and description or samples for quotes.
Beads (all types — full line): wood, glass, plastic, metal, stone, bone, cork, pearls, coral (all shapes/sizes/colors, and striped, irridescent, translucent). Bead needles. Has bead search service.
(Also sells wholesale to businesses — include resale number with inquiry.)

Megokla/Society for Eggeury Art

P.O. Box 18982
Oklahoma City, OK 73113

Catalog, $3.00 (refundable).
Boutique trims: Pearls, rhinestones, braids (and eggeury supplies). Has quantity prices, large order discounts. Holds sales. Allows discount to teacher/institutions.

The Mill Store

P.O. Box 366
West Warren, MA 01092

Send SASE for list.
Discontinued, irregular and overstocked **Trims:** (by yard): eyelet laces, beading and other poly/cotton trims, nylon/acetates, Venice, tatting, fold-over polyester solids.
Assortments: blanket binding, bias, seam binding, apparel ribbons, iron-on patches and fabrics, honeycomb, patches.

> **A No-Sew:** "I glue rather than sew — if possible. Useful for padded picture frames, baskets, lampshades, memory books." — Courtesy of **Aleene Eckstein** of Artis, Inc.

Miller's Craft Corner
Box 7232
Columbus, GA 31908

Catalog, $1.00.
Naturals: dried eucalyptus, ferns, baby's breath; others.
Beads, trims. Has Mastercard, Visa. (Other craft supplies.)

Mountain Mama
235 Bella Vista Lane
Watsonville, CA 95076

Price list, SASE. Sample package, $1.00.
Feathers: natural and unusual colors; quills.

Muscatine Pearl Works
P.O. Box 739
Muscatine, IA 52761

Check your fabric store or write for prices (to order in
quantity specify carded, loose or gross with inquiry).
Buttons (full line): Garment buttons, craft button
assortments (for dolls, doll clothes, stuffed animals, etc.
— toggles, eyes, hearts, small black shanks, pastel sew-
throughs, others.

C. M. Offray and Son, Inc.
261 Madison Ave.
New York, NY 10016

See your dealer or write for information.
Ribbons: novelty metallic Jacquard, gros-grain types,
feather edge satins, gingham, taffetas, Moire; Tuxedo
assortment, ribbon collectibles (satin printed with whimsical characters, quotes, etc. in rainbow colors), others.

Parradee's
1809 Manhattan Beach Blvd.
Manhattan Beach, CA 90266

Free list.
Beads: plastics (faceted, tri, berry, cartwheels) pearls;
"Bargains".

Plume Trading Sales Co.
P.O. Box 585
Monroe, NY 10950

Catalog, $1.00.
American Indian oriented trims: feathers (imitation
eagle types, dyed, plumes, pheasant tails, others), metal
bells (7 sizes), metal cones, rabbit and other fur strips,
ribbons, conchos, seed beads and bead kits. Also has
Indian clothing/craft supplies. Has quantity prices.

Promenade's Lebead Kits
P.O. Box 2092
Boulder, CO 80306

Send SASE for information.
Beading kits: florals, others for clothing, accessories, etc.
— includes beads, bead transfer, needles. Beading supplies.

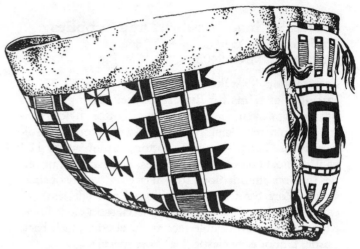

Arapaho beadwork on hide

Roberts Indian Crafts and Beading Supplies
404 W. Virginia Ave.
Anadarko, OK 73005

Send SASE for price list.
Trims (American Indian): beads, bells, shells, fringes,
feathers, horsehair, and others.

The Rose Jar
RD 1, Mountain Rd.
Hopewell, NJ 08525

Send $1.00 for list.
Potpourri, sachet, and pomander supplies: herbs, flower
spices, essential oils, fixatives.

St. Louis Trimming, Inc.

Trims: Stitch-A-Trim™ domestic and Swiss embroidery,
cluny lace (white natural and colors), ruffled, unbleached
muslin trims (natural and colors), domestic and French
Val laces, full line of venise motifs, others. In business
over 30 years.

Shamek's Buttons
709 Pine St.
Seattle, WA 98101
206-622-5350

Free circular.
Buttons: full line of colors and sizes; natural buttons
(shell, horn, wood, agate, others); covered buttons and
belts.

Sheru Enterprises
49 W. 38th St.
New York, NY 10018

Send SASE for list.
Trims: full line of beads, sequins, and others.
(Also sells wholesale to businesses.)

Spore Handicrafts, Inc.
12195 U.S. 12 West
White Pigeon, MI 49099

Catalog, $2.00 (refundable).
Trims: beads (plastic — variety of shapes/sizes, wood), sequins, pom-poms, ribbons, silk flowers. (And other craft supplies.)

Statice Gardens, Inc.
P.O. Box 609
Galesburg, IL 61401

See your dealer or write for information.
Dried flowers: variety of types, fillers, bouquets, others.

Stella Buttons
University Station, P.O. Box 5632
Seattle, WA 98105

Catalog, $1.00.
Mother-of-Pearl buttons: (Italian) variety of sizes, colors, types.

The Stitchin' Post
161 Elm, P.O. Box 280
Sisters, OR 97759

Catalog, $1.00.
Trims (for garments, quilts): laces, ribbons — variety of types, colors, widths.

Ojibway quillwork on buckskin bag

Streamline Industries, Inc.
845 Stewart Ave.
Garden City, NY 11530
and in Canada:
S.B.I. Fashion Industries, Ltd.
617 Denison St.
Marham, Ontario L3R 1B8

See your distributor or retailer. Free leaflets: "Button Talk", "Ribbon Talk", — write to Attn: Amy Arrow. Streamline **ribbons:** poly/satin, poly/grosgrain, nylon velvet. "Colorific buckles", stretch belts, "Colorific" buttons; other buckles, buttons, toggle closures, trims, appliques; fabrics, fashion accessories. In business since 1934.
(Also sells wholesale to retailers).

Susan of Newport
219 20th St., P.O. Box 3107
Newport Beach, CA 92663

Brochure and samples, $2.00.
Laces: nylon, polyester, poly/cotton, old-lace, cotton cluny; dollmaker's dainties; variety of widths; white, colors. **Ribbons:** metallic (soutache, braids), polyester satin, Offray grosgrain and satins, others. **Grab bags:** laces, ribbons, ric-rac, Christmas ric-rac. **Fabric seconds:** calicos, solid cottons — by yard or grab bag. Trims at discount prices but minimum purchase is $10; has some quantity prices, holds sales. In business since 1980.

Thimbleweed
2975 College Ave.
Berkeley, CA 94705
415-845-5081

Send SASE for brochure.
Full/extensive line of buttons: old antique glass, shell (variety of designs), horn, stone, agates, pewter and other metals; (And cotton fabric, quilting/smocking supplies.)

Twin Oaks Crafts
308 N. Dogwood
Villa Rica, GA 30180

Send SASE for price list.
"Tatties" trims (handcrafted): tats (bells, rabbits, kittens, flowers, butterflies); tatting by yard (6 designs).

A **Heady Appearance:** "If you've kept the old **foam wig head form,** place large toothpicks or sucker sticks 1¼" apart all over the head. It will be a real conversation piece when the head is covered with spools of colorful thread and bobbins." — Courtesy of **Artefabas;** lawyer, teacher and author of *Super Quick Sewing Tips.*

Va Les Bead Trailer
4333 No. 59th Ave.
Phoenix, AZ 85033

Send large SASE for prices.
Beads: Rondells, faceted types, tri, berry, cartwheels, rosebuds, alphabets, novelties, rocailles, crackles, pearls (all sizes). Beading supplies. Has quantity prices; Mastercard, Visa. In business since 1975.

W.F.R. Ribbon Corp.
115 W. 18th St.
New York, NY 10011

See your dealer or send $3.00 for catalog, and/or $2.00 for set of project sheets.
All-fabric ribbons: satins, velvets, moires, florals, plaids, calicos, checks, stripes, novelties, double-faced suede, grosgrain polyester; others. Over 30 project sheets. Manufacturer.

Wake'Da Trading Post
P.O. Box 19146
Sacramento, CA 95819

Catalog, $ .50.
Trims (American Indian oriented): Bells (sheep, sleigh — 4 sizes, brass hawk costume), conchos and silver slides. Needles (sharps, beading, glovers). **Feathers** (pheasant, turkey, imitation types) pheasant skins golden, ringneck, Reeves). **Beads:** bone, shell, trade mosaics and others, bugles. **Buttons** with slogans ("Custer had it coming","Arrow power", and others). Has quantity prices; Mastercard, Visa.

Wood Forms
Foster Hill Rd.
Henniker, NH 03242

Free catalog. All samples, $2.00. Sample buttons, $1.25.
Wood buttons/beads: Zebrawood, tulip wood, rosewood, other exotics.
(Also sells wholesale to businesses.)

The Wright Mill Store
P.O. Box 366
West Warren, MA 01092

Send for brochure.
Wright trims: variety of fabric styles, colors.

5
Fabric "Wet" Decorating

These companies provide supplies and equipment for the printing of fabric — by brush, dip or squeege — one way for original "commade" pizazz with sewing projects. Whether printing an overall pattern, or highlighting with color, your designs are personal expressions in cloth.
(In addition to these companies, check the index for other sources of fabric colors.)

Aardvark Adventures in Handicrafts
1191 Bannock St., P.O. Box 2449
Livermore, CA 94550
415-447-1306

Informative catalog, $5.00.
Deka fabric **paints** and transfer paints; marking pens. Full line of pictorial **acrylic stamps** (for fabric, etc.) including some sewing oriented motifs, other original designs (whimsical, country look, contemporary; calligraphic quotations, others. (Also has embroidery threads and trims.) Allows 10% discount to teachers/institutions and professionals. In business since 1976.
(Also sells wholesale to businesses.)

The American Quilter
P.O. Box 7455
Menlo Park, CA 94025

See your local shop, or send SASE for brochure.
Stencil design kits (turns any design into quilting or fabric stencil) with patterns, electric pen, work board, and plastic. Electric pen tips, plastic available separately. Fabric **paints,** brushes, others.

Artis, Inc.
Box 407
Solvang, CA 93463
805-688-7339

See your local outlet or write for information.
Aleene's "Tacky" **Glue** for fabric (also paper, etc.) in 2 oz. to 8 oz. squeeze bottles, 4 oz. to gallon, or 2 size tubes.
Dyes — Hi 'Dye Procion™, for natural fibers — 11 shades (use with print base for textile painting, or screen, brush batik, stencil, dip dyeing) by package. Batik wax, Tjanting pens, Plastic sheets (for stencils, templates making) — clear, opaque; 11" x 17" by 3 sheet or group project package, other craft items.
Manufacturer, in business over 40 years.

Batik Art Place
410 Boas Dr.
Santa Rosa, CA 94505

Catalog, $1.00.
Batik supplies. Procion fabric **dyes** (by lb.), beeswax (by lb.).

Adele Bishop, Inc.
Box 557
Manchester, VT 05254
802-362-3537

Catalog, $2.00.
Stencilling kits (heirloom motifs) for fabrics (and others) — beginners to advanced.

Paint & Sew: "When sewing hand painted garments always paint and steam set your fabrics before sewing it together. Avoid designs which need matching at the seams! Preplanning will pay extra dividends in the quality of the end product." — Courtesy of **Diane Tuckman** of Ivy Crafts Imports. She has been teaching silk painting for the past few years.

Boyd's

P.O. Box 6232(SS)
Augusta, GA 30906

Mini-directory, $3.75 ppd.
Rubber Stamps of Creative Kind: Sources of supplies
for creative, graphic, rubber or acrylic stamp impressions
(all subjects including children's florals, teddys, quotes,
alphabets, fantasy, Oriental, American Indian; other
whimsical, old-time or contemporary, classic; copyrighted/
uncopyrighted designs) for fabric and other printing.

Catco Manufacturing

12086 N.W. 25th St.
Coral Springs, FL 33065

Free details.
Screen print kits (single or multicolor) for fabrics, t-
shirts, other; "inexpensive".

Cerulean Blue, Ltd.

P.O. Box 21168
Seattle, WA 98111
206-634-2636

Catalog, $3.00.
Fabric dyes (Procion, Naphthols batik, other) for screen
printing, painting/dyeing, batik, photo printing, others.
Print kits. Resists, chemicals.

Colorcraft Ltd.

P.O. Box 936
Avon, CT 06001

Send SASE for list. Has toll free number "for ordering
information and personal assistance" 800-243-2712.
"Createx" fabric colors — water-based permanent pig-
ments for all fabrics. Liquid fiber reactive dyes (for hand
painting or batik, on natural fibers).

Decart, Inc.

Box 308, Lamoille Industrial Park
Morrisville, VT 05661
802-888-4217

See your dealer, or send SASE for information.
Deka™ **fabric paints** (20 shades liquid, ¾ oz. to qt. size)
for light colored natural and synthetic fabrics; machine
washable, blendable colors. Metallic fabric paints — 8
shades; machine washable. Fabric iron-on paint for synthetics (12 colors paint on non-absorbent paper and iron
onto fabric; machine washable, waterbased paint). "Series
L" powdered **dyes** for textiles; 33 colors washable (for
tie-dye, batik, etc.). (Has other paints.)

Delta Technical Coating, Inc.

P.O. Box 3584
South El Monte, CA 91733

See your dealer, or send SASE for information.
Permanent fabric **dyes** (for direct application) or Deka
Iron-on (paper painting, transfer method).

Dharma Trading Co.

Box 916
San Rafael, CA 94915

Free catalog.
Textile colors, dyes (procion cold water, disperse and
pigment types). Batik fabrics, tools. Has bulk prices.

Earth Guild

One Tingle Alley, (Lexington Park)
Asheville, NC 28801

Send SASE for price list (specify dyes).
Procion **dyes,** others (natural, chemical), mordants. Batik
items. (Also spinning/weaving supplies.)

Evening Star Farm

12621 Overbrook
Leawood, KS 66209
913-649-6820

See your dealer or send SASE for prices.
Patterns for **Stencilling** technique. Stencil sponge in tear-
off roll.

Fabdec

3553 Old Post Rd.
San Angelo, TX 76901
915-944-1031

Write for information. Fabric samples, $1.00.
Procion fiber reactive **dyes** (for direct application to
fabrics; for screen printing, batik, stamping, fold/dye,
etc.). **Fabrics** — white (grey goods for dyeing) natural
fiber material. Has quantity prices. In business since 1968.

Fibrec, Inc.
(See Flynns)

First Impressions
P.O. Box 682
Fairfield, IA 52556
515-472-2735

Catalog, $2.00.
Graphic **rubber stamps** "See-thru" (mounted on solid acrylic cube, or hollow plastic box). Designs include children's, sun faces, animals, fowl, butterflies, wildlife, scenics, holiday images, occasional; slogan combinations; alphabet set, "Valley Talk" slogans; 9 Teddy Bears, including 8 different Stamp & Sniff™ teddies with scented stamp pads (8 colors — banana yellow, etc.). Designers gold stamp pads.
(Also sells wholesale to businesses.)

Flynns
Box 985
San Francisco, CA 94101

Free catalog, "Versatex color chart", $1.50, Dye color chart, $1.50.
Fibrec cold water **dyes** (for all natural fabrics, leather, others) in pack or bulk; 23 shades. School packs. Procion dyes for natural fabrics (cold water); 16 shades. Batik supplies. "Versatex" fabric paints — 16 shades, and in school packs, starter sets. **fabrics:** cottons (sateen, pima, others) rayon, silk habuate — by yard. Books. Manufacturer since 1969.
(Also sells wholesale to businesses.)

Gatco Manufacturing
12086 N.W. 25th St.
Coral Springs, FL 33065

Free details.
Screen print kits (single or multicolor) for fabrics, t-shirts (other), "inexpensive".

Gramma's Graphics
20 Birling Gap
Fairport, NY 14450

Brochures, $1.00.
Photo prints kit for fabrics (you-sunprint photos) for heirloom quilts, portrait and other designed pillows, etc. (kit has instructions and solution mix to print 20, 9" x 12" squares).

Ivy Crafts Imports
5410 Annapolis Rd.
Bladensburg, MD 20710
301-779-7079

Color charts, catalog, and "Grapevine" Booklet, $3.00.
French colors for **fabric painting:** Tinfix, Tincoton, Super Tinfix; Batik Tintout dyes; color samplers; French color craft kits (beginner fabric, design, instruction, colors for 3 design choices). Sennelier (French Tinfax) color kits, others. Resists, solvents, wax, thickener. Tools, steamer, frames. China silk (5mm, 8mm, and 10mm white). Bleached cotton batiste. Tjaunting tools. Has quantity prices. Allows 15% discount to teachers/institutions. In business since 1977.
(Sells wholesale to businesses - inquire for specifics.)

Morilla, Inc., Stencils
21 Bowers St.
Holyoke, MA 01040

Write for information.
Stencil kits: Includes brass stencils, 12 designs. Stencil brushes (and paints for paper, stationery supplies).

New England Stencil Co.
P.O. Box 253
Old Mystic, CT 06372

Catalog, $1.50.
Precut **stencils** — variety of Early American designs, others; stencil **supplies** (brushes, paints).

Pentel of America, Ltd.
2715 Columbia St.
Torrence, CA 90503

See your dealer or send SASE for information.
Fabric crayons — in sets, markers, dyes (others, paints, supplies).
Manufacturer.

Pro Chemical and Dye, Inc.
Box 14
Somerset, MA 02726

Free catalog.
Dyes for cottons, rayon, wool, polyester, silk, nylon; auxiliary supplies. **Textile inks** (for painting, and silkscreen).

> **Print Works: Block printing** works best on smooth fabric without nap — canvas, cottons, linens, and other similiar materials. — Courtesy of **Margaret A. Boyd.**

RIT

P.O. Box 307
Coventry, CT 06238

Check your grocery, variety, or hardware store or write for information.
Fabric dyes — liquid, full range of shades.
Manufacturer.

Rollerway, Inc.

P.O. Box 757
Silver Spring, MD 20901
301-649-4422

Free catalog.
Hand roller tool with pattern embossed (paints on fabrics - curtains, upholstery, lamp shades, tablecloths; and other flat surfaces): over 100 designs — florals, geometrics, classic and contemporary motifs, Oriental, whimsical, woodgrains, textures, others.

Savoir Faire

3020 Bridgeway, Suite 305
Sausalito, CA 94965

Brochure, $2.00.
French **dyes:** tinfix, Super Tinfix, Tincoton — in liquid form — for silk, wool, cotton. Gold and silver qutta.
Equipment: brushes, steam ovens, fabric stretching frames.

Sax Arts and Crafts

P.O. Box 2002, 316 Milwaukee St.
Milwaukee, WI 53202

Catalog, $3.00.
Complete supplies, tools and equipment for: fabric **painting/dyeing,** batik, **block printing, screen process, stenciling,** (and many other needlecrafts, arts/crafts — most with complete supplies). Has quantity prices; Mastercard, Visa.

Stencil designs

Skil-Crafts Division
Box 105, 305 Virginia
Joplin, MO 64801

Catalog, $1.00.
Complete supplies for **screen process, block printing,**
fabric **painting;** boutique trims. (Complete arts/crafts
supplies, most categories.)

Stencil Ease
P.O. Box 225
New Ipswich, NH 03071

See your dealer or write for catalog, $3.00.
Quilt stencil designs — precut, in traditional and
"country" styles. "Fab-Tex" textile paints, brushes, Japanese paints in colonial colors.
(Also sells wholesale to businesses.)

Straw Into Gold
3006 San Pablo St.
Berkeley, CA 94702

Catalog, $2.00.
Complete **batik** supplies; fugitive marking crayons,
transfer pencils and tracing cloth. **Dyes:** Kiton acid,
Direct, Procion; mordants, chemicals. Fabrics (for printing): cottons, rayons, silk, polyester. Equipment: dye
pots, bags, measurers, scales, others. (And extensive supplies and equipment for spinning/weaving.) Books. Has
some quantity prices.

Strawberry Emporium
618 Aster Blvd.
Rockville, MD 20850

Catalog, $1.50.
Stencils (solid brass): American traditional designs (for
fabrics, others). Stencil **kits,** brushes, paints. **Rubber
stamps.**

Sureway Trading Ent.
111 Peter St., Suite 211
Toronto Ontario M5V 2H1, Canada

Send SASE for samples.
French **dyes. Printing fabrics:** silk Pongee, twill crepe,
others; silk scarves (25 colors).

Ethnic with Elan: "West Africans have found that
elegance, comfort and ease of construction can be
combined in the same garment. The true creative
effort can then be directed to the surface design and
embellishment of the cloth." — Courtesy of **Chris-
tine A. Rex,** of Folk Fabrics & Garments; author of
the book, *Comfort Clothes* (Easy To Make And Easy
To Wear West African Garments For Everyone).

Textile Resources

P.O. Box 34786
Los Angeles, CA 90034

Brochure, $ .50; fabric swatches, $1.50.
Photosensitizing kits (prints blue or brown on fabric
without equipment; utilizes stencil, negative or found
object); Printing chemicals, dyes (procion, Deka™ acid).
Resists. **Fabrics:** silks, linen, rayon, 9 cottons. Silk and
cotton scarves. **Equipment/acids:** scales, tjanting, mortar and pestle. Books.

The Whole Kit and Kaboodle Co., Inc.

8 W. 19th St.
New York, NY 10011

Brochure, $1.00.
Fabric stenciling: kits (for placemats, Christmas motifs,
other designs) pre-cut stencils in over 40 designs. Stencil
brushes, paper. **Paints** (acrylic colors, permanent fabric
stencil dyes, kits). Guide books.

Wild West

415 N. 5th Ave., Kerrytown
Ann Arbor, MI 48104

Send $ .50 and SASE for information (specify).
Batik dyes and fabrics. (And complete line of yarns.)
Fiber/needlecraft books.

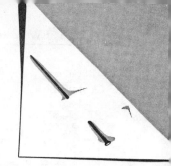

6
Specialty Sewing

This section presents sources for specialty fabric decorating — of the needle-and-thread kind. (And see HOME ACCESSORIES, PERSONAL ACCESSORIES, and the index for specific items.)

A. EMBROIDERY/CROSS STITCH

American Crewel & Canvas
Box 394
Oneida, NY 13421

Catalog, $3.00.
Fabrics — linens (Belgian, Irish, others), Aida, evenweaves, satin, others. **Specialty threads** — Brazilian, rayon, DMC, silk, wools, others. Aids/notions: needles, graphs, frames, and stands.

Susan Bates, Inc.
212 Middlesex Ave.
Chester, CT 06412
203-526-5381

See a mail order outlet, or send $3.00 for catalog.
Notions/aids — hand sewing needles, threaders, embroidery floss; other needlecraft supplies. Allows discount to teachers/institutions, sells at wholesale to businesses. Manufacturer, in business since 1873.

Betty K
Box 7024
Beaumont, TX 77706

List, $ .50.
Patterns for **alphabets** (assorted styles) for hand or machine embroidery.

Bettye's Monograms
1912 Colquitt
Albany, GA 31707

Send SASE for details.
Book: *Learn to Monogram* (with sewing machine) instruction manual.

Bluebonnet Co.
P.O. Box 10944
Houston, TX 77018

Catalog, $ .50.
Needlecraft kits: stitchery, on polyester fabric; variety of designs including birds.

The Busy Needle
4560 Winchell Rd., P.O. Box 128
Mantua, OH 44255

Catalog, $1.00.
Fabrics (by yard) — Aidas, Hardanger, huck, fiddler's, natural (11 to 22 count), Ribband evenweave/bands; variety of colors. DMC threads. Organizer, needles, scissors (stork, folding), spring hoops, others — wood and plastic. Magnifiers (magnetic for line minder, "free hands" type). (Also extensive counted cross stitch books, needlecraft accessories.)

Fabric Choices for Creative Quilting: "A good rule of thumb:
1. Large Print-dark background to "set" the color tone.
2. Small Print-dark background that echos above.
3. Predominant Color-solid or pin dot to match or blend with backgrounds 1 and 2.
4. Light Print-medium or small design with background matching a color in the prints.
5. Accent, color-solid or pin dot — matching a color in the prints." — Courtesy of **Joyce Kelly** of Patches of Joy, Inc.

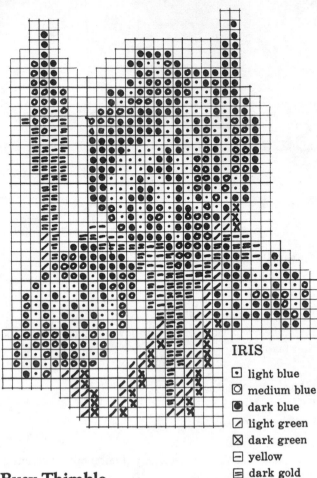

IRIS

- ⊡ light blue
- ⊙ medium blue
- ⬤ dark blue
- ⊘ light green
- ⊠ dark green
- ⊟ yellow
- ☰ dark gold

Busy Thimble
1127 N. Hondo
Anaheim, CA 92807

Catalog, $1.25.
Embroidery supplies: metallic threads, DMC floss.
Cross stitch accessories, paperweights, coasters, ashtrays,
mounting boards. Evenweave fabrics, leather, stitch find-
ers, others.

Carolina Cross Stitch, Inc.
P.O. Box 845
Laurinburg, NC 28352
919-276-4278 and 800-334-3990

See your dealer or send SASE for details.
"Sal-em" fabric — evenweave 50% polyester, 50%
rayon ("look of linen" in 60" width; 14 or 26 count) — in
1, 3, and 5 yard pieces. **Plain finished linens** (for cross
stitch, etc.) — napkins, placemats, card holders, towels,
others. Apron, bib, and tote bag inserts.

Celebrations in Needlework
P.O. Box 236
Oceanport, NJ 07757

Catalog, $1.00 (refundable).
Cross stitch - **religious, designs and patterns** (Bible,
wedding/birth, holiday, religious occasions, others),
fabrics, floss, kits, accessories.

Chaparral
3733 Westheimer
Houston, TX 77027

Free supply list.
Silk **threads,** metallic threads (all types), other embroi-
dery/tapestry threads (and other needlecraft items).

Charles Craft
Box 1169
Laurinburg, NC 28352

Send SASE for list.
Evenweave cloth ("Fiddler's" Cloth) cotton/polyester
(60" wide).

Children's Corner, Inc.
4004 Hillsboro, Suite 202
Nashville, TN 37215
615-292-2244

Brochure, $1.00.
Over 60 **designer patterns** for: smocking, French hand
sewing, traditional sewing, and cross stitch.
(Also sells wholesale to businesses.)

The Counting House
Box 155
Pawleys Island, SC 29585

Catalog, $1.00.
Embroidery: Cross stitch kits (brand names designs).
Threads, embroidery hoops, graphs. Accessories: trays,
coasters, lamps, others. Books.

Country Yarn Barn
Box 476
Lethbridge, Alberta, T1J3Z1, Canada

Catalog, $3.00.
Line of supplies for crewel **embroidery,** cross-stitch,
other needlecrafts.

Craft Barn
Box 435
Drakes Branch, VA 23937

Catalog, $1.00.
Supplies: cross-stitch and other fabrics, accessories,
DMC embroidery floss — "major discounts".

Crafts 'N Things Patterns
Box 178, Old Chelsea Station
New York, NY 10113

Send SASE for list.
Transfers and other patterns: quilting, easy designs,
embroidery butterflies, others.
(Publishes "Crafts 'N Things" magazine.)

Creative Needlework
41 Nut Plains Rd. W.
Guilford, CT 06437

Send SASE for list.
Huck weaving fabric (60" wide), huck towels, kits. Hopscotch cross-stitch fabric.

Cross-Stitch Concepts
P.O. Box 2594
La Habra, CA 90631

Send 2 stamps for catalog.
Cross-stitch — complete line of fabrics, floss, accessories.

Cross-Stitch Cupboard
Rt. 3, Box 439
Taylorsville, NC 28681

Catalog, $1.00.
Counted cross-stitch: "Country" **frames,** supplies.

Cross-Stitch Fabrics
Box 383
Eden, NC 27288

Send SASE for prices.
Cross-stitch fabrics — variety of sizes and colors.

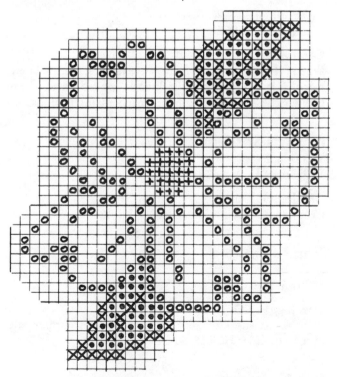

DOGWOOD

- 🔘 green
- ◎ pink
- ⊞ yellow
- ☒ dark green
- ☐ white

Daisy Chain
P.O. Box 140722
Dallas, TX 75214

Catalog, $2.00 (refundable).
Threads — silk filament, cotton for mini, Baiger metallics (5 types - filaments, braided, cords). **Notions:** needles, scissors (Gingher, Soligen, Scovill), Magnistitch, spring hoops. **Fabrics** (by sq. inch, or ¼ yard up) —Aidas, Hardanger. **Kits:** tote bag with insert, wood golf hood. (Also extensive decorative mini and other needlecraft kits, designs and supplies, books.)

Linda Dennis and the Finish Line, Inc.
P.O. Box 2712
Spartanburg, SC 29304

Send SASE for list.
"Ribband" **ribbon** for cross-stitch; barnyard stencils, others.

Designing Women United
601 E. 8th
El Dorado, AR 71730

Send SASE for information.
Cross-stitch — charted designs (geometrics, butterflies, cats, fish, rose, flowers, alphabet letters, others). Even-weave shirts — S, M, and L in 5 colors.

The DMC Corporation
107 Trumbull St.
Elizabeth, NJ 07206

See your dealer.
Full line of **threads:** embroidery, machine embroidery, metallics, Persian wool; other needlecraft threads, yarns. Manufacturer.

Joyce Drexler
921 E. Oak St.
Arcadia, FL 33821

Send SASE for prices.
Speed stitch **embroidery** kits, hoops, threads, other supplies.

"For Professional Looking Appliques, use machine embroidery thread, loosen the top tension on your sewing machine and use a stabilizer behind the background fabric. You can save time by using the same color bobbin thread for the entire applique. If your machine tension is adjusted properly, the bobbin thread will not show on the right side of the applique." — Courtesy of **Ginger Johnson** of Ginger Designs. She has been a designer and instructor for over twenty-five years.

Family Circle Kits
Box 450
Teaneck, NJ 07666

See copy of magazine, or send SASE for list.
Embroidery kits: cross-stitch, crewel, others; for home
and personal accessories.

Quilting design

Frederick J. Fawcett, Inc.
320 Derby St.
Salem, MA 01970
617-741-1306

Sample fabric swatches, prices, $1.00.
Linen embroidery yarn samples, $1.10.
Linen embroidery/fabrics — 100% linen evenweave, in
12 to 26 threads per inch, over 50" widths, 5 shades, by
yard. 100% linen twill — 54" width, by yard. Scottish
linen embroidery yarns, by skein in 3 weights, full line of
shades including Colonial colors. Linen lacing threads.
(Also other linen yarns, mesh canvas, and others.) Has
quantity prices and large order discounts.
(Also sells wholesale to businesses.)

Fibre Arts
6610 W. North Ave.
Wauwatosa, WI 53213

Catalog, $1.50.
Needlecraft: fabrics, kits; imported and antique accessories and specialties. Books.

The Finish Line, Inc.
P.O. Box 2712
Spartanburg, SC 29304

See your dealer or write for information.
Ribband™ **ribbons** — 60 styles, including polyester with
colored cotton trim for counted cross-stitch; others. Mus-
linband™ muslin edged with lace (for stencils, candlewicking, embroidery, etc.). **Accessories:** wood frames, bellpull
hardware (for Muslinband™ or Ribband™) tote bags (for
stenciling). Books — 14 how-tos including designs,
embroidery, stencil designs, others.

Foxxie Stitchery
Box 224
Ridgewood, NJ 07451

Catalog, $ .50.
Fabrics — Aida, Fiddler's cloth, Hardanger, others.
Embroidery and cross-stitch **kits:** Christmas accessories,
ornaments, hangings, tablecloths and sets; quilt covers,
calendars, pillows. **Supplies:** floss, other threads, waste
canvas, notions. Needlecraft frames. Imported scissors.
Designs, books. (And other needlecraft supplies.) Has
Mastercard, Visa; allows foreign orders.

Mary Fry
610 Springfield Ave.
Summit, NJ 07901

Catalog, $1.50.
Linen **fabrics, threads.** Evenweave fabrics: cotton, linen,
wool. **Kits:** Trapunto, blackwork, pulled thread, embroidery. Allows discounts for teachers/institutions.

Ginny's Stitchin's
106 Braddock
Williamsburg, VA 23185

Catalog, $1.00.
Cross-stitch fabrics, kits, designs, books.

Hand's On!
82 South St.
Milford, NH 03055

Catalog, $1.00.
Needlecraft supplies: imported and domestic materials.
(See also under HOME STUDY.)

S & C Huber
82 Plants Dam Rd.
East Lyme, CT 06333
203-739-0772

Catalog, $ .75.
Fabrics: linen, monks cloth, others. Over 50 **dyes.** (Also
has spinning/weaving supplies.)

The Huckery
P.O. Box 595, 158 Hempstead Ave.
Malverne, NY 11565

Catalog, $1.00.
Huck weaving kits/supplies: fabrics (cotton, variety of shades, 60" width), threads, patterns, books. Allows Canadian orders.

Kitsophrenia
P.O. Box 5042
Glendale, CA 91201
213-245-1919

Send SASE for details.
Handcut **shisha mirrors** (Pakistan), machine washable and dry cleanable; ⅝" sq. in silver, antique smoke, blue, green, amber. Round brass "shinies" ¾" metal discs; tin framed shisha mirrors (not washable).

Leonida's Embroidery St.
222 Osborne South #18
Winnipeg, Manitoba R3L123, Canada

Catalog, $ .50.
Needlecraft fabrics: Aida (linen, cotton), evenweave, wool twill, vanishing muslin, Hardanger, others. Embroidery hoops and frames. Books. (Other needlecraft supplies.)

LuRae's Creative Stitchery
P.O. Box 550
Bountiful, UT 84010

Free catalog.
Kits: quilts (trapunto, whimsical prints, others), pillows (fur, applique), embroidery motifs. **Designs/patterns:** alphabets, zodiacs, Christmas, monograms, others. Stamped goods (linens, dining linens). **Fabrics:** nylon, vinyl, others. **Threads** (for hand, machine): DMC, LaPaleta, Mettler, Talon metallic, others. Supplies/aids: embroidery hoops (for machine, hand), machine parts, transfer markers. Books (on machine embroidery).

The Needle Works
125 Westhampton
Aurora, IL 60505

Catalog, $1.00.
Counted cross-stitch fabrics, accessories, floss, charts.

Original Pattern Designs by Claudia
P.O. Box 37
Hope Mills, NC 28348

Catalog, $1.00.
Over 150 original pattern designs for sewing projects, embroidery and other needlework; including holiday, wood and slogan motifs, valentine, spring, animals, others.

Rainbow Crafts
404-5 Cranbury Rd.
E. Brunswick, NJ 08816

Catalog and graph, $1.00 (refundable).
Cross-stitch/candlewicking — fabrics, floss, books.

River Valley Needlecraft
R.R. #4
Stirling, Ontario KOK 3EO, Canada

Free catalog.
Supplies for embroidery, cross-stitch (and other needlecrafts). Markers, transfers, others. Books.

Suzicrafts
801 W. Harrison, Box 706 CP
Oak Park, IL 60303
312-848-4100

Catalog, $1.00.
Over 400 charted design books. Counted **cross-stitch** supplies, fabrics. Stencilling, quilting, candlewicking supplies. Holds sales periodically. In business since 1977.

Thumbelina Needlework Shop
1685 Copenhagen Dr., P.O. Box 1065
Solvang, CA 93463

Catalog, $2.00.
Embroidery **kits:** counted thread cross-stitch and others; contemporary and holiday motifs. **Fabrics:** congress, floba, monza, wool java, acrylic java, Hardanger, Aida, canvases, silk gauze. **Threads:** DMC, Danish flower and tapestries (full line). **Accessories:** brass rods, bamboo hangers, bell pull hardware. Books. (Other needlecraft supplies/kits.) Has Mastercard, Visa.

TJ's
2649 St. Clara Dr.
Macon, GA 31206

Catalog, $1.00 (refundable).
Counted cross-stitch designs for samplers, paperweights, jar lids, others. Supplies, accessories.

Patch Embroidery: "When doing sewing machine embroidery, draw the design to be sewn first on polyester background stabilizer (sometimes called 'trace-a-pattern'), then place in a machine embroidery hoop, double thickness, and apply the threads. When the design is finished, cut it out and apply to garment, first with glue stick, then with a zig-zag stitch around the edges. You have made your own applique patch! For best results use a blue stretch needle with your machine embroidery threads." — Courtesy of **Janet Stocker** of "Treadleart".

Toni's Transfers
2900 Heatherton Dr.
Florissant, MO 63033

Brochure, $ .50.
Embroidery iron-on **transfers, patterns/kits:** original "Country" motifs including "Strawberry Patch", "Flutters & Flowers", girl with umbrella, girl with curl, "Happiness is ... little boy" (with eyelet and gingham materials in kits); for pillows, tooth pillows, pictures and coordinated pictures, trims, others. Has quantity prices. In business since 1975.

Applique design

Touche' Applique
130 Kenneth St.
Greensburg, PA 15601

Brochure, $ .50.
Original **applique** kits/patterns, for machine (or hand) sewing: Kits with fabrics, trims; instructions and for machine writing and monograms. Appliques in English, French, Spanish.

Ukranian Gift Shop
2422 Central Ave., N.E.
Minneapolis, MN 55418

Catalog, $2.00.
Fabrics: Ukranian wool challis (by yard, or in shawls, kerchiefs). Hardanger, Aida, rayon/cottons, tapestry, wool/Dacron blends. DMC threads. (Eggeury supplies, Ukranian gift items.)

Walden
P.O. Box D
Elvia, NY 14059

Send for catalog.
Kits: candlewicking, quilting, others. **Supplies:** Muslin, Lily floss, 14 appliques, spring embroidery hoops. Extensive needlecraft booklets. (Other needlecraft supplies.) Has reduced prices, and preferred customer club for additional savings on payment of annual fee. Has Mastercard, Visa.

Vima, S.P.A.
Town & Country Village, 2727 Macroni Ave.
Sacramento, CA 95821
916-488-VIMA

Catalog, $2.00.
Embroidery **kits/pattern booklets:** Renaissance bell pull, textured floral motifs, needlelace sampler, embroidered venetian lace and contemporary needlelace motifs (florals, seashells, "jewels", medallions). Folk art baskets trims embroidery. **Supplies:** textured thread assortments, embroidery scissors (in heirloom sets; stork, folding, in sets with cases, antique, cross style, others — by Soligen). **Equipment:** magnifier lamps (Dzor, Lux-O, Big Eye). "Knitting" bags, totes. Needle sets. (And gift items — sewing oriented.) May have price specials.
(Also sells wholesale to businesses.)

Kaye Wood
4949 Eau Rd.
West Branch, MI 48661

Send SASE for list.
Books: *Monograms by Machine, Machine Embroidery and Applique Lessons,* others. (See also under HOME STUDY/EDUCATION).

B.   SMOCKING

Americraft, Inc.
P.O. Box 81342
Atlanta, GA 30366

Send SASE for details.
Smock Gathering machine — the "Read" 16 row model, others.

Barbie Beck English Smocking
1113 Caroline St.
Fredericksburg, VA 22401
703-371-3517

See your dealer or write for catalog.
Smocking **pleater,** patterns, design books, and leaflets.

The Berry Bucket
P.O. Box 4798
Martinez, GA 30907
404-860-4143

68 page catalog, $3.00.
Smocking supplies: pleating machines, variety of fabrics, laces, plates, others.

The Cleaver Hen
Rt. 1, Box 160
Rainier, OR 97048
503-556-5207

Send SASE for list.
Prepleated fabric for English smocked eggs, 2½" Christmas balls, samplers, inserts, etc. (Also has kits.)

Sandy Hunter, Inc.
P.O. Box 706
Flat Rock, NC 28731
704-693-8407

See your dealer or send SASE for information.
Smocking patterns (for adults, children, novelties), books.
Manufacturer.

Kara's Closet
779 E. Main St.
Branford, CT 06405

Catalog, $2.00.
English **Smocking kits/patterns**, plates. Books.

LBL Designs
P.O. Box 181082
Memphis, TN 38118

Send SASE for price list.
Over 22 **Smocking design plates** (including for a Christmas wreath).

Little Elegance, Ltd.
P.O. Box 14567
Richmond, VA 23221

Brochure, $1.00.
"Elegance" **fashion patterns:** children's pinafore apron, others; adults — Jane Page designs and charts, dot transfers in design form, smock **gathering machine.**

Little Miss Muffet, Inc.
P.O. Box 10912
Knoxville, TN 37919

See "The Smoc Box", or send $2.00 for "Smocking Gazette".
Complete line of **smocking:** Durand™ **pleater,** fabrics, kits and patterns. Educational kits for beginners. Books.

Madeline's Fabrics
1674 Montgomery Hwy.
Hoover, AL 35216

Send SASE for prices.
Smocking patterns including for children's dresses, others.

Sew Fine Fabrics
379 Atlanta St.
Marietta, GA 30060

See your dealer or write for information.
"Sewphisticated" **smocking books** — designs including for Ribband™ strips, others for adults, computer designs for home/office computer areas; bases — ovals, scoops, woven square, others.)
(Also sells wholesale to businesses.)

Small Fantasies
1448 Robinson Rd.
Grand Rapids, MI 49506

Catalog, $1.00.
Smocking patterns "inspired by yesterday's charm" (for children's and adults clothing including dresses, blouses, others.
(Also sells wholesale to businesses.)

> **Scouting Quilt Fabrics:** "Explore the drapery and better goods departments as well as the traditional quilting departments for fabric finds." — Courtesy of **Joyce Kelly** of Patches of Joy, Inc.

The Smoc Box
Box 10562
Knoxville, TN 37919
615-588-7373

Catalog, $2.00; Fabric swatches, $3.00.
Smocking kits patterns (prepleated fabric with materials, instructions) Children's garments, Christening dresses, women's garments, beginner primer, pillows, quilts, Christmas wreath, tree, 39 ball ornaments. **Design cards** (Little Miss Muffet, Ann Gentry, Linda Warren, Ellen McCarn, Ann Smith, Diane Bruce, Smock-A-Memory, Barbie Beck, Children's Corner). Durand 24 row **pleater**, Read 16 row pleater. DruDan Fabrics (batiste, broadcloth, gingham, gingham checks; Imperial rosebud prints, polished cotton, feathercord corduroy, wool challis blend). L.M.M. laces, soutache, embroidered edging. Susan Bates **floss. Aids:** Olfa cutter, mat, thread organizers and project kits, transfer pencil, blocker, ham, graph paper, styrofoam. Books.
(Sells wholesale to businesses through Little Miss Muffet — see index.)

Smoc-Kraft
103 Godwin Ave.
Midland Park, NJ 07432

Send SASE for details.
Smoc-Kraft English-style **smocking kits** (Pre-pleated, pre-cut, of poly/cotton) — baby's dress, boy's romper suit, yoke dress, pinafores, pinafore with panties, lady's apron, planter skirt (for flower pot); includes smocking instructions, designs, finishing suggestions.

The Smock Shop Shopper
1615 E. 4th St.
Charlottte, NC 28204

Send SASE for catalog.
English smocking supplies: patterns, gathering machines, design plates, fabrics, threads.

The Smockery
1034 Hartt Rd.
Erie, PA 16505

Catalog, $2.00.
Supplies, patterns, notions for **English smocking, French hand sewing,** soft sculpture, quilting.

The Smockery
312 North Main St.
Findlay, OH 45840

52 page catalog and price list, $3.00 (refundable).
Smocking **supplies** (full line); **pleater machines,** threads, designs, others.

The Smocking Bonnet
P.O. Box 555
Cookesville, MD 21723

Send SASE for complete listing.
English smocking: patterns, design plates, "Read" smock gathering machine (including 16 needle model), needles, thread racks; Imperial batiste and broadcloth **fabrics;** Swiss-Metrosene thread, DMC floss; "discount prices".

Smocking Daze
P.O. Box 706
Flat Rock, NC 28731
704-693-8407

See your dealer or write for information.
Smocking **patterns and books** by Sandy Hunter.

Smockits
Box 51
Seaford, DE 19973

Send large SASE for brochure.
Beginners smocking kit — pleated fabric, floss, needle, instructions.

Southern Smocking
5841 Dutch Creek Dr.
Raleigh, NC 27606

Catalog, $1.00.
English smocking supplies: designs, threads, needles, others.

Sugar 'N Spice Smocks
Box 30301
Raleigh, NC 27612

Send SASE for price list.
English smocking kits: pinafores, bonnets, pillows, others.

Tiny Treasures
1412 Whiting
Memphis, TN 38117

See your fabric store.
Smocking supplies: patterns, designer plates, Jane Soffos designs, original plate organizer, pearl buttons.
(Also sells wholesale to businesses.)

Velvet Mushroom
3727 Denver St.
Evans, CO 80620

Send SASE for information.
"Read" Smock gathering machines, replacement needles. "Immediate delivery".

C. QUILTING/PATCHWORK

Air-Lite Synthetics Mfg.
342 Irwin
Pontiac, MI 48053

See your dealer or write for information.
Quilt batts and rolls (Kodel fusion bond polyester) in cut batts — crib, twins, full, queen, king; 48", 96" rolls, doubled and folded.

American Heritage Co.
1000 Broadway
Kansas City, MO 64105

Catalog, $ .35.
Quilt kits (cotton/dacron) ready cut; 8 designs. Quilt tops, pillow kits.

Ann's Attic
Box 9736
Greensboro, NC 27408

Send large SASE for brochure.
Hand-tied **fringe starter kits** and supplies (100% cotton thread); muslin 108" wide.

Attic Treasures
Rt. 1
Trimble, MO 64492

Catalog, $3.00.
Old quilting patterns (and other needlecraft patterns).

Aunt Becky's
Box 6331
Spokane, WA 99207

Sample, $2.00 ppd.
Fringe protector (stainless steel, lightweight).
(Also sells wholesale to dealers.)

S. Baxi Co.
87-70 173 St.
Jamaica, NY 11432

Brochure, $ .25.
Patchwork kits: quilts, pillows. Fabric squares.

Bed Spreaders
#10 Vista Delmar
Camarn Island, WA 98292

Send SASE for prices.
Water bed quilt instruction booklet for "Quick-E" quilt, top kit (with precut pieces, instructions).

Bill's Quilt Frames
70093 Meadow View Rd.
Sister, OR 97759

Send SASE for complete details.
Tiltable *quilt frames* — handcrafted to exacting detail; tilts to any degree; in regular, queen or king widths.

Dorothy Bond
34706 Row River Rd.
Cottage Grove, OR 97424

Send SASE for details.
Book: *Crazy Quilt Stitches* — over 1000 authentic stitches taken from old crazy quilts 112 hand-illustrated pages.

Nicolette Booream, Inc.
P.O. Box 554
Philmont, NY 12565
518-672-4057

Catalog, $1.00.
Notions: English needles (applique, quilting, tapestry), threader, pattern tracer, seamer, transfer crayons and pencils, markers, beeswax, wood needle boxes (2 sizes), rulers, fabric paint, marker sets. Adjustable thimble, fabric glue stick (basting), plastic for templates. **Silk batting** (by leaf), for trapunto, clothing. **Patterns:** Mary Murphy's, others, for white work vests, quilted skirts; Quilting/ applique patterns for home accessories in variety of design. Quilting hoops and stands, needlework frame holder (floor model), Wood Shaker boxes (6 styles). **Fabrics** — 100% cotton prints and solids, cotton muslin (2 weights); Mountain Mist batting and pillow forms. Candlewicking design books. Holds sales periodically. Allows discounts to teachers/institutions and professionals. Manufacturer, in business since 1978. (And see QUILT PATTERN PER MONTH CLUB).
(Also sells wholesale to businesses).

Betty Boyink
818 Sheldon Rd.
Grand Haven, MI 49417

See your dealer or write for info.
Graph paper for quilters (12" sq. sheets in 24 page tablet).

Crossing Quilt Borders: "To find the right length for the borders of a quilt, measure the opposite sides and split the difference: Example, if one side is 71" and the other 72", border should be 71½". When stitched, one side will be eased and the other stretched, but the borders will be equal." — Courtesy of **Jeannie M. Spears** of Oliver Press, author of the book, *Mastering the Basics of Quiltmaking*, and a home study course.

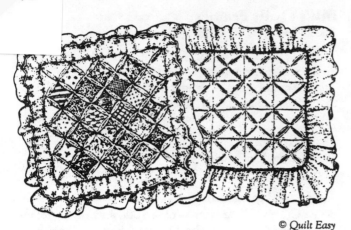

© Quilt Easy

Bunny Publications
Box 572
Williamsville, NY 14221

Brochure, $1.00.
"Kissy" Quilt designs including 12 cats, 13" Little Beach Boy, 9" sq. stained glass, 6" swan, chickens; "Stained glass" animals (cats, ducks, others).
(Also sells wholesale to businesses.)

Cabin Fever Calicos
5540 30th St., N.W.
Washington, DC 20015
202-686-0311

Catalog, $2.75.
"Palette of Color" 200 cotton solids swatches — quilt-weight, $2.75 ($3.00 in 1985). "Shimmery Solids" over 25 polished cotton swatches, $2.75 ($3.00 in 1985). Quilting **Fabrics** — "rainbows" 12 shades, quarter, half and full yards, — assortments in reds, roses, many other color hues. Designer patterns. **Notions/aids** — pounce wheel set, pressing and measuring items, seam rippers, rod seamer, pencils and pen markers, quilting needles, threader, protector, stitcher, metal thimbles. Quilting threads. Gingher scissors (4). Templates — miter marker, Lam-I-Graph™, template plastic. Olfa cutters, cutting mat. Color aids. Stenciling/quilting supplies (brushes, stencils), Fabtex textile paints. Quilters' projectors (enlarges quilt designs, other patterns) and reducing lenses, accessories. Drawing projector/stand. Quiltmaker's portable tracing boxes (5 sizes). Patterns. Books. Allows foreign orders. Has sales periodically; Mastercard, Visa.

Calico Hills Farm
6092 Liberty Rd., S.
Salem, OR 97306
503-581-6272

See your dealer or write for catalog.
Quilt patterns for 35½" wall quilt including "Goose in the Pond".

Calico Mouse
924 W. Sespe Ave.
Fillmore, CA 93015

Send SASE for prices.
Victorian applique/quilting patterns (and others) including **quilted Victorian cape.** Quilting kits and books. (Also sells wholesale to businesses.)

Calico 'N Things
P.O. Box 265
Marquette, MI 49855

Catalog and 250 swatches of fabrics, $3.25.
Jinny Beyer color-coordinated **fabrics. Quilting kits:** "Castle Wall" sophisticated 30" hanging (with Jinny Beyer fabric) in 3 colors, others.

Carney Creations
403 N. Gaylord
Ludington, MI 49431
Brochure, $1.00.
Designs for Hand Quilting (including for Hoop-framed wall hangings, others).

Carol's Crafts
Box 358, Ansonia Station
New York, NY 10023

Send SASE for prices.
Patchwork strips assortments (2" x 12") in reds, blues, pastels, Christmas colors.

Catseye Creation
Box 144
Hopewell, NJ 08525

Swatches and Catalog, $2.00.
Custom **Comforters** kits — Variety sizes, colors; limited Edition hand screened panels.

Chantilly Boutique
789 S.E. Baseline
Hillsboro, OR 97123
503-648-0325

Samples (2 x 2) and supply list, $3.00.
Full line of **Cotton fabrics** (100% cotton, designed by and for quilters) in coordinated colors/prints, "very special prices". Needlework supplies.

Chester Farms
Box 275
Rapine, VA 24472

Send SASE for information.
Wool batting (90" x 48" sheets), "Wool Fluffy Stuffing", carded or uncarded, in natural shades (2 lb. bags).

Chippewa Carding Mill
17 West Central St.
Chippewa Falls, WI 54729

Send SASE for information.
Wool batting.

The Church House
P.O. Box 789
Carlton, OR 97111

Send SASE for sample and information.
Transpatch™ **heat transfer patchwork patterns**
(transfers cutting/stitching lines to fabric with heated
iron) in packs with enough for double quilt; with
instructions.

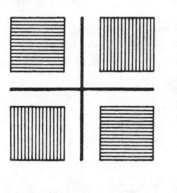

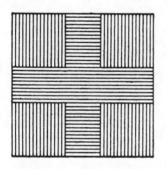

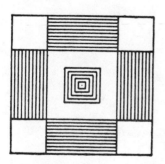

Cindy Taylor Clark
Rt. 202, Box 6
Alfred, ME 04002

Send SASE for information.
Quilt Blocks designs — "Colonial Life Series" (home
life, farm life).

Classic Quilts
P.O. Box 24
Cedar, MI 49621
616-941-1979

See your dealer or send SASE for details.
Pre-cut quilt kits (cotton) — top only kits for 84" x 92"
or 45" x 54", pillow kits.

Pat Cody
1561 Montclair Dr.
Ft. Worth, TX 76103

For machine quilting: Continuous line **quilting designs**
with differentiated sewing path, over 20 use ideas, $2.25.

Colonial Patterns, Inc.
340 W. 5th St.
Kansas City, MO 64105

See your dealer, or write for information.
"Aunt Martha's **quilting designs** collections and hot-
iron transfers (over 150 designs) for; State flags, state
birds, state flowers, new and old testaments motifs,
ABC's, others. **"Magic Margin"** guide (marks ¼" seam
allowances). Has toll free number for orders.

Come Quilt With Me
P.O. Box 1063
Brooklyn, NY 11202

Catalog, $1.50.
Extensive line of **quilting supplies;** Patterns, notions
(threads, needles, pins, others). Stencils (including folk-
art decorative tin quilt stencils, Schoolhouse, Rocking
Horse, Hearts). Others.

Comet Fibers, Inc.
845 Meeker Ave.
Brooklyn, NY 11222

Send SASE for list.
Batting (polyester; Crib to king sizes). Group discounts.

Quilt Tie-ing: "Use wool yarn rather than a blend
yarn to tie your quilts. The wool yarn holds the knot
better and doesn't fray." — Courtesy of **Eleanor A.
Burns** author of the book, *Quilt in a Day*, and other
books.

Contemporary Quilts
5305 Denwood Ave.
Memphis, TN 38122

Send SASE for details.
Quilting Frame Kit (Make-It-Yourself) — parts, including cast aluminum ratchet wheels and gears, for 108" x 24" floorstanding model; with instructions, drawings, specifications, supplies list.

The Country Cottage
Rt. 1, Box 179
College Grove, TN 37046

Send SASE for list.
Miniature quilt patterns; applique stitchery, "Colonial Williamsburg" design (part Williamsburg wallhanging collection — can be adapted to coverlets, shams, handbags, tree skirts, other uses).
(Also sells wholesale to retailers.)

Country Heirlooms
1125 East 3rd St.
Hope, AR 71801

Free brochure.
Quilting: Fabrics, and supplies (threads, aids, others), books, patterns.

Country Maid Gifts
Bowles Rd.
Stafford Springs, CT 06076

Brochures $2.00 (refundable).
Kits for **patchwork quilts** crib quilts (and dolls, latch hook, crewel).

Country Quilts
N70 W6344 Bridge Rd.
Cedarburg, WI 53012
414-375-4133

See your dealer or write for information.
Machine or hand **applique patterns** — country and folk art designs.

Covered Bridge Fabricworks
Box 884
Flagstaff, AZ 86002

Brochure, $ .50.
Quilting Kits: Screen print on fabric (with backing, materials instructions) for "primitive" hangings, pillows.

Craftsman's Harvest
1617 S. Fayetteville St.
Asheboro, NC 27203

See your dealer, or write for information.
Quilting/rug frame (4 sizes, 30" to 60" length work area, 18" width) with detachable rack, stand converts to trestle table with another top.

Cranmoor Collection
Box 1599
Toms River, NJ 08753

Send SASE for prices.
Patchwork squares (3½", 5½", 7½") package of 50 —solids and prints.

Quilting design

Cross Patch

Rt. 9
Garrison, NY 10524

Catalog, $1.00; 300 sample swatches, $3.00.
Calicos (prints/solids). **Quilting** kits, batting, patchwork. Applique and Quilt-as-you-go patterns. **Aids:** Plastic Stencils, templates, Hoops, frames, others. Books.

Mrs. Danner's Quilts

Box 650
Emporia, KS 66801

Send SASE for prices.
Quilting pattern books; **patterns** — in heirloom and other designs; for all sizes.

Dewey Designs

Box 2824
Lincoln, NE 68502

Brochure, $ .50.
Patterns for customizing flat sheets to fit waterbeds. **Quilt patterns.** Children's quilt appliques including koala, panda, snail, frog, other barnyard and pets; freight train cars and engine. (and patterns for personal accessories).

K. Dopp

15 Elsom Pkwy.
South Burlington, VT 05401

Send SASE for prices.
Patchwork packages (100 different prints of cotton, blends, by 4" squares).

Down on the Farm Originals, Inc.

P.O. Box 699
Shelby, NC 28150
800-438-0676 and 704-484-8750

See your dealer or send SASE for information.
"Critter Coverlette" patterns (32 designs, 42" x 54" size) — shapes of animals, truck, Santa, others. (Also needle craft kits.)

Dutch Girl Crafts

877 Greenbriar Lane,
Park Forest South, IL 60466

List, $ .50.
Heirloom quilt patterns (over 1,000 old and out-of-print designs). Other patterns.

Eastern Mountain Sports

1428 15th St.
Denver, CO 80241

Goose down filling.

R. V. Ethell

1700 Circle Lane
Zanesville, OH 43701

Send SASE for prices.
Quilt-as-you-go-patterns, in variety of flowers, motifs.

Extra Special Products

P.O. Box 777
Greenville, OH 45331

See your dealer or write for prices.
"Quickline" **Striping tool** — 12 measurements in one, 3" x 22½" long, works with rotary cutters, etc. Magnets —36 Quilter's designs.

Europa Old World Products

11811 Lincoln St.
Northglenn, CO 80233

Free brochure.
Down comforter kits (with baffle design for high loft) —pre-cut fabric; pre-measured down; instructions.

EZ Does It

7776 Golfcrest Dr.
San Diego, CA 92119

Patchwork On the Curve instructions (to transform patchwork or mini-patchwork patterns to use on curved borders — skirts, tablecloths, tree skirts, etc.), $2.50 ppd.

Fairfield Processing Corp.

P.O. Box 1157
Danbury, CT 06810

Send SASE for list.
Poly-fil™ polyester **fiberfill,** and batting. Ultra-loft™ heavyweight batting (for sleeping bags, comforters) — washable. Pillow forms. Manufacturer.

Famous Name Labels

P.O. Box 703
Westminster, CO 80030

Sample, $2.25.
Leather **finger guard** for quilting.

Blending Cotton with Blends: "When using 100% cotton fabrics for patchwork, to be applied to permanent press or blends, fuse lightweight fusible interfacing to the back side before you incorporate the patchwork into the garment. This will keep your cotton patchwork areas as fresh and crisp looking as the rest of the garment and will require no touch-up ironing after washing." — Courtesy of **Jane Hill,** designer/instructor, of Hillcraft.

Fiberspace

1232 E. Mason St.
Green Bay, WI 54301

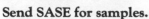

Send SASE for samples.
Quilting **fabrics and equipment** (also supplies, and equipment, for other fibercrafts).

The Frugal Fox

Box 372
Fontana, WI 53125

Send SASE for price list.
Fiberfill, quilt batts (custom cut), pillow forms. Manufacturer.

The Gibbs Manufacturing Co.

Canton, OH 44702

See your dealer or write for prices.
Gibbs quilting and needlecraft Hoops (hard wood, with spring tension). In business since 1884.

Gidden Patterns

P.O. Box EB
Beaumont, CA 92223

Send SASE for list.
Quilt **patterns:** "Rainbow Bear" patchwork design, (straight seam sewing), others.

Ginger Snap Station

P.O. Box 81086
Atlanta, GA 30366
404-455-6700

Catalog, $ .50.
Quilting: "Country" design kits/patterns; pillows (screened, trapunto, patchwork, others), over 20 quilt top and quilts, soft sculpture House/boxes, 14 soft frames kits. Christmas kits, soft sculpture/applique/quilt. (wreaths, hangings, stocking, hoop-picture, ornaments). Other Holiday items. Patterns, hand and machine appliques. Picture patches (screened muslin). **Fabrics —** 100% cotton (11 prints, solids); pre-quilted cotton; by yard. Quilt patches, Ginger shears, Olfa cutter. Threads, needles. (and doll/toy kits/patterns). Booklets, Books. (Sells wholesale — see "Yours Truly, Inc.").

The Gingerbread House

45 Prospect St.
Farmingdale, NY 11734
516-249-2368

Catalog, $1.00 (refundable).
Quilting **supplies:** threads, notions, aids, patterns, templates, books.

Glad Creations, Inc.

3400 Bloomington Ave., So.
Minneapolis, MN 55407

(1) Quilt fabric swatches, $2.00.
(2) Jinny Beyer Quiltprints Collection — 24 extra large swatches, $2.00 (OR — #1 and #2 swatches, both for $3.00).
(3) Supplies and notions catalog, $1.00 — or free with order for swatches.
Quilt block fabrics (100% cotton, 225 solids and prints) including Jinny Beyer prints, others. Quilting supplies/notions: Stencils, templates, full line of **threads, needles, hoops/frames, others.**

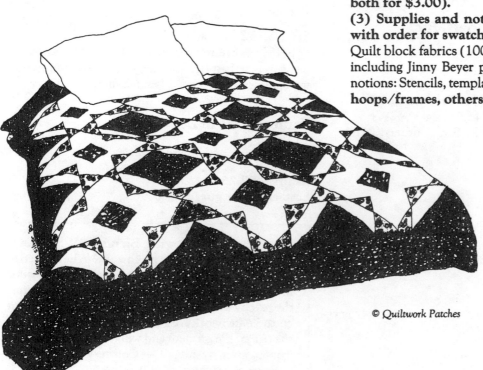

© *Quiltwork Patches*

The Glass Thimble
3434 North High St.
Columbus, OH 43214

Catalog and swatches, $1.00.
Quilting **Fabrics** — over 800 bolts and calicos; patterns, stencils, fabric-stenciling paints, brushes, others.

Good Company
P.O. Box 764
W. Caldwell, NJ 07006

Send SASE for brochure.
Quilting **templates** (clear plastic) in most basic shapes, special shapes; custom cut.

Goose Girl Creations
Rt. 2, Box 490
Buckner, MO 64016

See your local store or send SASE for information.
Quilting **patterns** for "stained glass windows", wall hangings and hoop pictures (including country designs).

Handwood Quilt Frames
Rt. 1, Box 1
Danville, NY 40422

Send SASE for information.
Handcrafted hardwood **quilting frames** — single and double winding bar styles for quilts up to 96" wide.

Hapco Products
46 Mapleview Dr.
Columbia, MO 65201
314-445-1019

See your dealer or write for information.
Quilting accessories: lap board (non-skid, portable, for assembling quilt blocks, etc.). Maple quilting frame, quilt display racks.

Heartfelt
Box 1829
Vineyard Haven, MA 02568

Brochure, Samples, $1.00.
100% natural **wool batting** (½", can be "peeled" into ¼") (single, double, queen and king bed).
Also sells wholesale to businesses.

Hearthside
Box 30305
Charlotte, VT 05445

Catalog and fabric swatches, $2.00 (refundable).
Quilting kits (pre-cut): wide variety of classic patterns.
Notions/aids: frames, hoops, needles, threads, thimbles, batting, patterns, fabrics, books.

© *Quiltwork Patches*

Hinterberg Design
6834 Enge Dr.
West Bend, WI 53095
414-263-5150

Free brochure.
Quilting frame kit (unfinished/finished wood, for easy you-assemble "in-seconds", dismantles for storage); 30" high, allows 96" x 28" work area. Has Mastercard, Visa.

Holubar
1975 30th St.
Boulder, CO 80303

Goose down filling.

Homecraft Services
340 W. 5th St.
Kansas City, MO 64105

Send SASE for list.
Quilt Patterns books: old-time, florals, state birds and flowers; award winners, others, with assembly instructions, yardage needs and piece count for all patterns.

Homestead Rustics
7014 N. Pearl
Oakfield, NY 14125

Send large SASE for prices.
Quilt books — ginghams, calicos, denims; prints, plains; polyesters. Quilt and pillow tops; quilting patterns.

Honey Bee Patterns
7647 Riverview Dr.
Jenison, MI 49428

Send SASE for color brochure.
Quilting patterns: "Goose doorstop", others; hoops, pillow kits/patterns, others.

Art in Applique: "Before beginning to applique a design to the background block — lightly trace entire design on background to aid in sewing all sections accurately in place, for balance and perfection." — Courtesy of **Cindy Taylor Clark** of Greenhouse Gallery — quilting artist and designer.

"Moonlight Mountains", © Bay Window Designs

Honey Pot Creations
Box 757
Eaton, CO 80615

Color brochure, $ .50.
Machine applique crib quilt patterns, including "Red Barn and Chickens" — with green worm.

The House of Joseph
Rt. 2, Box 162
Smithville, TX 78957

Send $2.00 for information (refundable).
Quilt **display racks** (5 styles, 5 finishes), Quilting and needlepoint **stands** (converts to small quilt racks). Wood wall rods with end brackets (for quilts). Also has crafted items.

Imbach Publications
246 Greengates
Corona, CA 91720

Send SASE for details.
Book: *Adventures in Patchwork*, by Gay Imbach (25 patterns for quilts/boutiques for dolls, wall or beds; piecing/assembly diagrams, 3" to 12" patchwork patterns, instructions, color illustrations).
"Dealer Inquiries welcome".

Katy
30 Colony Park Circle
Galveston, TX 77551

Send SASE for details.
Suncatcher **stained glass patterns** (use for applique, patchwork, etc.) over 70 motifs.

Kiddie-Komfies
Box 2095
Santa Ana, CA 92707

Send SASE for list.
Kiddie Komfies™ quilts **kits/patterns:** Animal shapes (for baby quilts, robes, wall hangings, rugs, etc.): Skunk, mouse, raccoon, teddy bear, panda, kitten, dog, squirrel, elephant, hippo; humpty-dumpty, clown, others. Has Mastercard, Visa.
(Also sells wholesale to businesses.)

La Plata Patterns
P.O. Box 820
Evans, CO 80620

Send SASE for price list.
Quilting books and patterns. May have price specials.

Leman Publications
Box 394
Wheat Ridge, CO 80033

Send SASE for details on books.
Quilting Books: beginner through advanced patterns and instructions; classic to contemporary designs. (And see QUILTS AND OTHER COMFORTS. Also publishes *Quiltmaker* and *Quilter's Newsletter Magazine*.)

Leone Publications
2721 Lyle Court
Santa Clara, CA 95051
415-948-8077

Send SASE for information.
Patchwork books by Diana Leone, including *Investments* (20 patchwork, applique and quilted vest patterns — including Log Cabin, Sashiko hand quilting and other designs; illustrated, with step by step instructions — fabric selection, to binding; for all sizes — adult, children). Other books include *The Sampler Book* and *Log Cabin Jacket*.

Limited Editions
195 Walnut St.
Montclair, NJ 07042

Send SASE for price list.
Baby quilt patterns — in actual shapes (kitten, honey bear, car, hippo, train).

Little Lamb Quilt Works
P.O. Box 2524
Dublin, CA 94566

Catalog, $ .50.
Quilting patterns/booklets for quilts (crib and doll sizes) including these designs: Teddy Bears, bumblebees/ butterflies, flower basket, spring lamb, alphabet, bear with baloons, sleepy cherub; others.

"Snooze Time" wall hanging quilt, © Bay Window Designs

Norma Locke
Rt. 1, Box 179
Gaston, OR 97119

Send SASE for list.
Sunbonnet Babies patterns (30 — old and new).

Mail-In Quilting Supplies
P.O. Box 603
Woodcliff Lake, NJ 07675

Catalog, $1.00.
Quilting **kits/patterns. Quilting stencils** (heavy template stock) in sets.

Marjean Creations
3201 Georgia
Kansas City, KS 66104

Send SASE for list.
Crib quilt **patterns** — "God Made Me" with 12 applique designs.

Judy Mathieson
5802 Jumilla Ave.
Woodland Hill, CA 91367

See your dealer or write for information.
Quilt block patterns for pillows, variety of motifs.

Mary McGregor
P.O. Box 154
Englewood, OH 45322

Send SASE for information.
Quilting kits/designs (with graphs): heirloom and other designs. DMC floss, hoops, others. (And needlepoint kits.)

Megan
2525 W. 6th
Topeka, KS 66606

Send SASE for list.
Over 100 full-sized **quilt patterns** — Kansas City Star, others.

Mehlco Crafts
Box 1205
Franingham, MA 01701

Send SASE for prices.
Patchwork squares (cotton blends): prints calicos, florals, solids; 8", 6", 4" sizes; by lb. or package.

Melcher
Rt. 1, Box 60
West Alton, MO 63386

Send SASE for prices.
Quilt blocks — 18", for embroidery, etc.; by dozen lot.

Memory's Rainbow
P.O. Box 764
Sogarland, TX 77478

Send SASE for details.
Instructions for "Elegant Kitty" **comforter** (of velvet, taffeta, and lace; for embroidery and monograms). (Also custom made.)

MO
P.O. Box 4454
Virginia Beach, VA 23454

Catalog, $1.00.
Brand name quilting supplies — stencils, patterns, notions (threads, needles, others), aids; — "Save 20%". Books, save "15%".

Carbonated Images: "I use **dressmakers** carbon paper to transfer quilting designs too intricate for making templates. Use the rounded hook end of a small metal crochet hook to trace over areas too detailed for a tracing wheel. It leaves a nice line and won't damage the quilt top if it tears through. **Note:** Always test dressmakers carbon paper on fabric before using to make sure it washes out!" — Courtesy of **Suzy Lawson** of Amity Publications, pattern designer.

Mountain Mist Catalog

117 Williams St.
Cincinnati, OH 45215

Catalog, $2.00.
Quilting **patterns** with plastic templates (for all bed sizes).
Designs: House Quilt, Double Irish Chain, Martha's
Vineyard, Old Fashioned, Rose, Old Mexico, Jacob's
Ladder, Mountain Star, Shoo Fly, Ohio Star, Mariners
Compass, Pennsylvania Dutch, Horn of Plenty, others.
Manufacturer.

Marge Murphy's Heirloom Quilting Designs

6624 April Bayou
Biloxi, MS 39532

See your dealer or write for information.
Quilting and trapunto designs: borders (11 designs,
1½" to 9" wide), shells and sails — 30 designs, many
others). Reversible shadow trapunto —clothing patterns
and quilt patterns.
(Also sells wholesale to businesses.)

Nimble Needle Boutique

4774 Horton Rd.
Jackson, MI 49201

Send $2.00 for swatches.
Fabric: calicos, small prints, matching solids, others.
Quilting **stencils.**

Nustyle Supplies

Box 61
Stover, MO 65078

Send $ .20 stamp for information.
Machine quilting **frames, quilting machines,** hand
frames. **Supplies:** threads, roll Dacron, batt Dacron. Business, established for forty years.

Oh, Kay! Cottage

P.O. Box 2834
Vancouver, WA 98668

See your dealer or send SASE for list.
Designs for quilting or applique: "Strawberry Times" for
pillows-cases, pillows; others.

Seminole Patchwork Sundress, © Hillcraft

Oklee Quilting Co.

Box 277
Oklee, MN 56742
218-796-5151

Send SASE for current prices.
Quilt batts (polyester), filling (polyester salvage) in 5 to
20 pound lots.

Kimi Ota

10300 61st Ave. So.
Seattle, WA 98178

Send SASE for details.
Book: *Sashiko Quilting,* by Kimi Ota (on Japanese stitch-
ery/quilting; traditional designs and stitching techniques).

P and S Fabrics

Box 257,
Ulna, SC 29378

Send SASE for prices.
Quilting packages: cotton blends, mill remnants — up
to 1 yard (in 3 lb. or 6 lb. lots).

Pangles Fabric and Craft Center
138 E. Main, Box 1098
Wise, WA 24293

Send SASE for price sheet.
"Panda — Puff" **quilting padding:** 96 x 108 quilt batting, quilt linings and pieces; **kits and frames.**

Paragon Needlecrafts
230 Fifth Ave.
New York, NY 10001

See your dealer.
Quilted wall hanging kits with French tapestry recreation, others. (And other needlecraft kits.)

Patches
Box 140
Dalton, MO 01226

Send SASE and $ .50 for list and samples.
Fabric squares: 50 piece assortments (4", 6" and 8") calicos, other cottons, velveteeen, corduroy, others.

Patchwork Patterns
P.O. Box 3461
Industry, CA 91744
213-692-4135

Send SASE for details.
Book: *Little Patchwork Things,* by Nancy Donahue (on miniatures — making, including 21 patchwork projects, 39 three inch quilt patterns) 34 color plates; 104 pages.

Pelikow
Box 225
Beverly, NJ 08010

Send SASE for prices.
Velvet remnants (¼ to ⅞ yds.) in assorted colors by pound or three pound lots.

Pickering's Patchwork Corners
8 Yamell Rd.
Tonasket, WA 98855

Send large SASE for brochure.
Quilting patterns for **machine/hand applique,** etc. (and fabric painting) — plants/flowers, wildlife, others.

The Pieceable Kingdom
340 E. Madison Ave.
Wheaton, IL 60187

See your dealer or send SASE for brochure.
Applique patterns, line of assorted motifs.

Pioneer Quilts
1115 Columbus
Rapid City, SD 57701

Send SASE for list.
Full line of quilting **patterns,** variety of designs. (Also sells wholesale to businesses.)

The Pisces Printer
Box 4625
Irvine, CA 92716

Send SASE for details and prices.
Quilts books: *Speed Quilts,* by Leslie W. Overstreet (60 fast quilt designs including Bear Paw, Four Patch, Nine Patch, Baby Blocks, Cathedral Window, Eight Pointed Star, others) with color plates, instructions, drawing. *Quilts from Graphic Prints,* by Leslie W. Overstreet (new technique of quiltmaking).

Plastic Patterns
P.O. Box 1606
Pearland, TX 77581

Catalog, $2.00.
Plastic quilting patterns — flexible, reusable pattern motifs, variety of designs.

Polly Anna Ltd.
5645 E. 9th St.
Tucson, AZ 85711

Send SASE for information.
Patterns/kits for quilt-sweater design. (Also ready-made.)

Powell Publications
P.O. Box 513
Edmonds, WA 98020

Send SASE for details.
Book: *The Finishing Touch,* by Shirley Thompson (over 120 full size designs for borders, lattice strips, blocks of all sizes.

Q. T. Designs
Box 421
Tipp City, OH 45371

Send SASE for list.
Patchwork templates — variety of shapes, of heavy plastic.

Every Bit Helps: "Lint from the filter in your dryer makes great stuffing material for small Christmas ornaments or trapunto projects ... and it's **free!**" — Courtesy of **Eleanor Barber,** designer, and publisher of *12 Months of Christmas* newsletter.

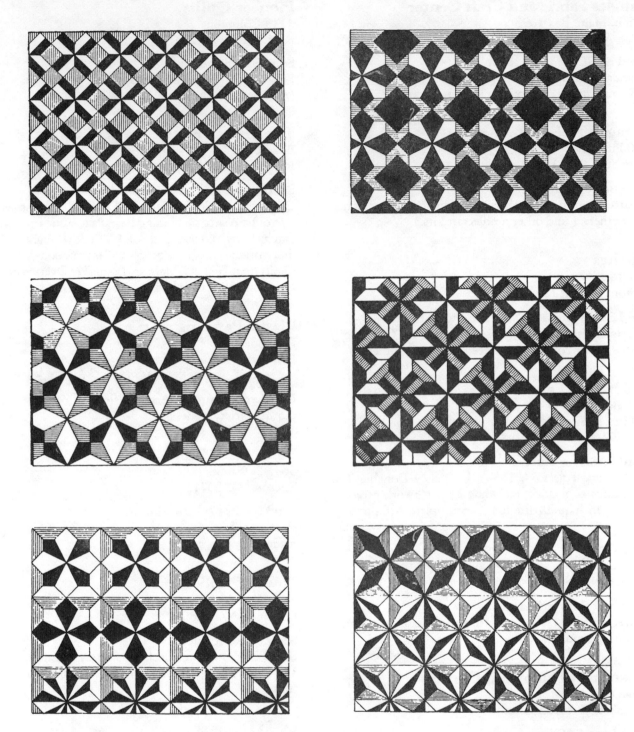

Inspiration for a simple quilt design

Quilt Basket

P.O. Box 3158
Quartz Hill, CA 93534

Catalog, $1.00 (refundable).
Quilting aids: — Ardco templates, quilting stencils, Olfa Rotary cutter, Gingher scissors, others. Fairfield batting. Quilting hoops, wood embroidery hoops. Notions (threads, needle, others). Patterns, books.

Quilt Easy

P.O. Box 321
St. Mountain, GA 30086
404-636-9405

Catalog, $ .50.
"Country Chic" **quilting kits/patterns** (for quilts and pillows): over 35 patterns including "Cathedral Window", 6 point star, Dresden, animal motifs, Dutch boy and girl, others. **Templates kit:** "Cathedral Window". (Also sells wholesale to legitimate businesses, quilting teachers, etc.).

Quilt Fair

201 N. Main
St. Charles, MO 63301

Free catalog.
Quilt **block sets:** nursery designs, others. Quilting supplies.

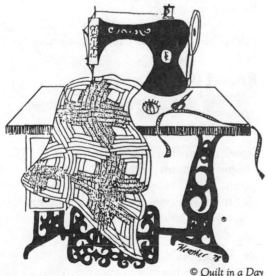

© *Quilt in a Day*

Quilt in a Day

3016 Quebrada Circle
Carlsbad, CA 92008

Send SASE for brochure.
Books: *Make A Quilt In A Day,* by Eleanor Burns (Log Cabin pattern) with quick-sew techniques for quiltmaking; through all processes, to finish. Others: *The Sampler, Bunnies and Blossoms,* and *Country Christmas Sewing,* feature full size patterns and directions for sewing projects. (And has patterns and fabric kits for accessories.) (Also sells wholesale to businesses.)

Quilt Line

1639 12th Ave.
Rockford, IL 61108

Send SASE for prices.
Seam marker (all metal, 10" x 3" unit — marks quilt seams — quilt piece against back step of unit, press down on flexible strip, then ¼" seam line is drawn).

Quilt Patterns Per Month Club

P.O. Box 554
Philmont, NY 12565

Catalog, $1.00.
Members subscribing to this pattern club receive patterns, discount of 10% on quilting supplies, new product announcements, monthly sales and a newsletter. (See **Nicolette Booream, Inc.** for product information.)

Quilt Shop

Booneville, MS 38829

Send SASE for prices.
Quilt **scraps** (cotton blends) checks, plaids; in 12 lb. and 17 lb. lots.

The Quilt Shop

4525 50th St.
Lubbock, TX 79414

80 page catalog, $1.00.
Quilting **supplies:** full line of kits/patterns, fabrics, books.

Quilter's Corner

92 Main St.
Tappan, NY 10983

Send $1.75 for sample.
Quilters Quarter™ — quarter inch measures (for patchwork); accepts Canadian orders.
"Wholesale Inquiries invited".

Quilters' Comfort

4 Cottage Place
Utica, NY 13502

Send SASE for details.
Quilt **frames/stands** (adjustable height — 4 models); and quilt frame plans, for you-make.
"Dealer inquiries invited."

> "**Quilting** is meant to be enjoyed, rather than endured. Always make a sample block before embarking on an entire quilt, only to find that you hate doing it. Most of all, relax and enjoy the craft." — Courtesy of **Aloyse Yorko** of Yorkcraft, editor of *Quilt* magazine and author of books and patterns.

Quiltessence

Box 27143
Phoenix, AZ 85061

Send SASE for list.
Sandpainter quilting **designs** (inspired by ancient medicine chants) (also patterns for purses).

Quilts and Other Comforts

Box 394
Wheatridge, CO 80033

Catalog, $1.25.
Quilting **patterns/kits:** full line of designs for quilts: heirlooms, designer, classics, contemporary; storybook; all sizes — adult, children, baby. Patterns are full size, with directions. Kits use all cotton fabrics. Star kits for quilts. Quick and easy, and other pillow kits. Designs, templates, pattern collections, colonial collections. Cotton **fabrics** — unbleached muslin, fabric packets (of greens, coppers — prints in ¼ yd. pieces), rainbow sampler; cottons by yard, 24 solid shades. Quilt-as-you-go frames (adjustable hoops), frame stands. Graph papers. Plastigraph™ graph/ template sheets (developed by the firm for quilting stencils). May have coupon specials.

Quilts by Jeannie May

917 Lakeview Ave.
St. Paul, MN 55117

Catalog, $1.00.
Quilting patterns: including for English piecing or celtic technique, others; pattern sets (suns designs, others); dot-patterns, applique motifs, Christmas, dragons, monsters, others. Accessories patterns. Quilting slogans (transfers): "My Mom's A Quilter ...", and others. Paper templates. Has quantity prices. In business since 1971.

Quilts, Etc.

1500 South Hwy. 301
Dade City, FL 33525

Catalog and over 150 swatches, $1.00.
Fabrics (100% cotton) chintzes, solids, prints by V.I.P., Concord, others. Quilting supplies — full line, "reasonable". Also has custom-made Amish quilts.

Quiltwork Patches

430 N.W. 6th St., Box 724
Corvallis, OR 97330

Catalog, $1.00 (or $2.00 with fabric samples).
Quilting kits (with pre-cut fabric pieces; coordinated prints/solids): quilts and quilt tops (complete kits with muslin quilt back and batting; crib size with flannel backing). Pillow kits. Designs include "Sawtooth", "Hester's Garden"™ and others. **Supplies:** notions (pins, needles, threader/magnifier, gripper), aids: ripper, magnetic seam guide, thimbles (leather, metal), threads.

Develop a quilt design from a woven motif.

The Quiltworks

218 Third Ave.
Minneapolis, MN 55401

Write for catalog.
Quilting and trapunto **stencils** in 100 designs, or blank nylon sheets. (Also has toll free number for orders.)

Round Brush Designs

9 Hemlock Rd.
Brunswick, ME 04011
207-729-9395

Brochure and order information, $ .75.
Original "Country **Stencils**" — two part, pre-cut transparent nylar; variety of designs in 3-5 patterns per pack (for quilts, pillows, floor cloths, placemats, others). (Also sells wholesale to retailers.)

St. Peter Woolen Mill

101 W. Broadway
St. Peter, MN 56082

Catalog, $1.00 or send SASE with inquiry.
Wool batting (2 lb. and up). Other needlecraft supplies.

Sew It Seams

P.O. Box 370
Gulf Breeze, FL 32561
904-932-5319

See your dealer or write for information.
Quilting **kits** — picnics spread, vests, jackets, shirts.

Mrs. Shiell's Quilt Shop
241 E. 6th Ave.
Tallahassee, FL 32303

Send SASE for prices and details.
Patchwork pattern **templates** for 12" blocks — cut around printed plastic shapes; collection of six, sets makes 48 blocks.

Joann Simmons
Rt. 2, Box 14
Ash, NC 28420

Send SASE for price list.
Quilting scraps: satin, nylon, polyester, others; by pound.

Sonlight Creations
P.O. Box 46
Olathe, KS 66061

Send SASE for information.
Pre-printed quilt **kit** — for baby bed (35" x 43") in rabbits and rainbow design.

Squares
P.O. Box 6164
Charleston, SC 29405

Send SASE for list.
Quilting **fabric squares** (4½") — pastels, darks; calicos, plaids, solid woven polycotton; by 1 lb. (approximately 300); or 5 lb. cutting table scraps.

Stained Panes Studio
1474 Post Rd., Box 15
Fairfield, CT 06430

Stained glass **catalog** of design full-sized drawings (use for patchwork, applique, etc.) $3.25 ppd.

Staple Fibre Fill and Batting Co.
141 Lanza Ave.
Garfield, NJ 07026

See your dealer or write for information.
Polyester **fibre fill,** bonded batting (4 sizes), pillow forms; variety of sizes, weights, and shapes.

Starlight Studio
P.O. Box 12001
Portland, OR 97212

Pattern catalog, $1.00.
Quilt **patterns** for machine applique, etc.

The Stearns and Foster Co.
P.O. Box 15380, Lockland
Cincinnati, OH 45215

Mountain Mist Country Store Catalog, $1.00.
Over 130 quilt **patterns/designs.** Batting (poly/cotton), quilt backing, "Fiberloft" filling, pillow forms. Manufacturer.

The Stencil House
RFD #9, Box 287
Concord, NH 03301

Brochure, $1.00.
Stencils (mylar), including "Shaker Tree of Life" design in 2 sizes — stencils cut and uncut; with instructions.

Stitches with Love
128 Laconwood
Springfield, IL 62703

See your dealer or write for brochure.
Machine applique **patterns** — teen girls and boys items, dimensional pictures.

Storybook Quilts
4738 Manzanita
Carmichael, CA 95608

Quilt patterns catalog, $ .50.
Applique catalog, $1.00.
Applique kits/patterns for: placemats, tablecloths and runners. Quilt patterns/kits: children's animals, "Cactus Pete" designs, others; pattern and applique kits, others.

Swiss-Metrosene, Inc.
7780 Quincy
Willowbrook, IL 60521
312-325-2767

See your dealer or write for information.
Quilting thread — Swiss made, 100% Egyptian long fiber cotton, 10 colors, by spool. Athena dress form (adjustable at bust, waist, hips); solid foam with nylon cover, on stand. "Madiera" metallic threads (by 100 yd. spools) in 6 colors and variegated colors (washable and dry cleanable).

> **Many Professionals Agree that Leather Type Thimbles are Best for Quilting.**

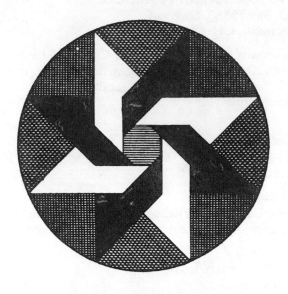

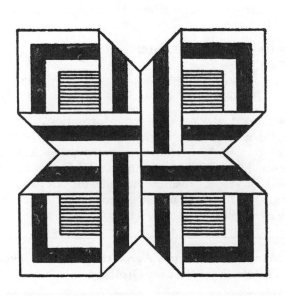

Textile Sample Co.

Box 290
New City, NY 10956

Send SASE for prices.
Patchwork squares — pre-cut first quality cotton and cotton blends (prints, solids, ginghams, florals, plaids, stripes).

That Patchwork Place, Inc.

P.O. Box 118
Bothell, WA 98011
206-483-3313

See your dealer or send $1.25 for catalog ($1.50 in '85).
Books: *The Basics of Quilted Clothing,* by Nancy Martin (guide to clothing construction, with over 30 basic designs and variations, directions, full size templates). Books on patchwork, strip quilting, others. "Country collection" patterns (clothing).

Tiffaniques

275 Walnut Lane
Oak Brook, IL 60521

Send SASE for price list.
Patchwork squares (solids, prints — 3¼" or 5½", 7½" sizes) by package of 50, with instructions.

Toddler Bible Pattern

402 Hawthorne
Kalispell, MT 59901
406-257-4185

See your dealer or write for prices.
"Toddler Bible" quilt block embroidery patterns — 20, for quilt, cloth book, pillows, hangings; illustrations for crib quilt and cloth — quilt book.
(Also sells wholesale to distributors, retailers and teachers/institutions.)

The Treadle Works

118 Westridge Dr.
Portola Valley, CA 94025

Free brochure.
Quilting kits: Amish designs — wall hangings, pillows (cotton-poly fabric, pre-cut, batting, backing).
(Also sells wholesale.)

Elizabeth Voris

P.O. Box 4474
San Pedro, CA 90275

Send SASE for prices.
Seashell **patterns** for applique quilt (actual block size, 12").

© *Robin's Nest Designs*

Wetmore Mercantile
930 West Glenn
Tucson, AZ 85705

Send SASE for prices.
Quilts **kits** — "colonial patches" in double, queen; 14"
pillows. Patches, separately.

Women's Circle Patterns
Box 124, Old Chelsea Station
New York, NY 10113

Needlecraft catalog, $1.50.
Quilting **patterns** — modern patch type, 50 states design,
"pussycats-on-a-fitness-kick", and other patterns. (See
also under clothing).

Wood-Tics, Inc.
2027 29th Ave., N.W.
New Brighton, MN 55112
612-633-8688

See your dealer or send $2.00 for catalog.
Quick Trace™ quilting stencils.

Woodbine Cottage
1984 Ballina Rd.
Cazenovia, NY 13035

Send SASE for prices.
Wool **batting** from Corriedale sheep.

"**Machine Quilters:** The secret of pucker-free
machine quilting lies in your treatment of the **backing,** not in your basting stitches. Make sure the
backing is stretched fairly tautly all the time you're
basting." — Courtesy of **Robbie Fanning** of
"Open Chain", author of *The Complete Book of
Machine Quilting* and other books.

Wrights Home Sewing Co.
South St.
West Warren, MA 01092

See your dealer or write for information.
Cotton bias tapes — 32 solid colors, 18 calicos and pin
dot prints; extra wide, double fold (for quilting, etc.).
Satin blanket binding (12 colors).

Yorkcraft
Box 98
West Redding, CT 06896
203-438-7555

Send SASE for brochure.
Quilting books/patterns: (by Aloyse F. Yorko): quilting accessories, samplers, instructions, patterns — variety
of motifs. Has quantity prices and large order discounts.

Yours Truly, Inc.
P.O. Box 80218
Atlanta, GA 30366

**See "GINGER SNAP STATION" (retail outlet) for
products.**

7
Clothing

Listings in this section present sources of kits, patterns, fabrics and books for garments; and also includes accessories and trims in the catagories of BRIDAL FASHIONS and INFANTS/CHILDREN'S WEAR; maternity and "new mother" clothing is included with the later category.

A. FASHIONS

(Sources for today's clothing; see also OUTDOORS, or the index, for specific items.)

Altra Sewing Kits
5541 Central Ave.
Boulder, CO 80201

Free catalog.
Activewear kits (matching separates) — sport shorts, pants, Denver jacket, others; with all materials, instructions. Has toll free number for orders (or "questions") —800-621-8103. Has Mastercard, Visa.

Bo Sew Accents
P.O. Box 426
Woodland Hills, CA 91365

Catalog, $1.00.
Over 1200 **sewing patterns** (full size) of: Kappie, Forget-Me-Not, Karnival Kreations, Sew Easy, Sandbox Gang, McCall's, Patch Press, Apple Dumplins', Instant Interiors, Craft Course, Ginger, Jean Hardy, Daisymae, Calico Hills Farm, Mountain Mist, Simplicity, others. Patterns include for all adult and chilren's clothing (and others for home and person).

Bristles and Needles
2724 N.E. 62nd Ave.
Portland, OR 97213

Send SASE for brochure.
Painted fabric designs and **patterns/kits** for quilted panel vests, border bouquet jacket or long vest, purse pattern (with painted flap and designs); all with instructions. (Also sells wholesale to dealers.)

Burda Patterns, Inc.
Box 2517
Smyrna, GA 30081

See your dealer or call toll free (1-800-241-6887) for name of nearest store.
Clothing patterns (all sizes on one pattern) of "Elegant European fashion" including for women's fashions, with "system for achieving perfect fit" — skirts, blouses, dresses, others.

Butterick Fashion Marketing Corp.
161 Sixth Ave.
New York, NY 10013

See your dealer or write for information.
Full line of fashion patterns including Fast & Easy™, Designer clothing, See & Sew budget patterns, "Sew, Pack And Go", and others. (And home accessories, holiday items, dolls and toys.)

Facing Applique Pieces: "Interface fabric with an iron-on interfacing FIRST. Then, lay applique pattern pieces on top and cut out. This gives you an exact 'fit' and you don't have to trim away any excess interfacing. Also, it MAINLY prevents 'puckering' when appliqueing by machine. I found this extremely helpful for any type of applique project. Some say to use a grocery bag underneath to prevent puckering — **but** this method works very well, and **better!**" — Courtesy of **Nanci Cowles,** pattern designer, of The Calico Candlestick.

Bonnie Weiss Centi
P.O. Box 142
Jamestown, NY 14701

Booklet: *Re-Lining Coats and Jackets* — (and hints on organizing patterns), $2.50.

Creative Expressions
149 Hazeltine Ave.
Jamestown, NY 14701

Send SASE for list.
Sewing **how-to booklets** on relining coats/jackets, bias tape application, others.
(Also sells wholesale to businesses.)

Creative Sewing Co.
1448 Tradewinds Ave.
Sacremento, CA 95822

Send SASE for details.
Book: *Ultrasuede™ Fabric Sewing Guide*, by Krestine Corbin — presents techniques for standard pattern use with the fabric, insuring the "crisp cut look" with illustrations including for fashions (capes and others).

Lourdes Culkin
17 Jasmine Rd.
Levittown, PA 19056

Send SASE for details.
Book: *Sweater Sewing*, by Lourdes Culkin; on cutting and constructing sweaters from sweater bodies (panels and sweater knit yardage).

Designer Jeans Inc.
45 E. Gentile St. #2
Layton, UT 84040

Free catalog.
Jeans supplies: Denim fabric, pockets, kits, accessories, zippers, rivets, snaps, threads; notions. Jeans labels. Books: *Designer Jeans Made Easy*, by Peggy Layton.
(Also sells wholesale to businesses.)

Fashionetics, Inc.
P.O. Box 146
Armonk, NY 10504

Send SASE for details.
Book: *Discover Fit, Fashion And You*, by Leona Rocha

A. Fischer
421 S.W. 5th, #713
Portland, OR 97204
503-246-4761 or 224-2183

Send SASE for prices.
Shoulder pads (for jacket, coat, dress).

Frostline Kits
Frostline Circle
Denver, CO 80241

Free Sew Classics catalog (specify).
Over 30 ready-to-sew **clothing kits** (with pre-cut fabrics all notions, instructions) blazer, blouse, skirts, slacks fashion coats, jackets; accessories.

Gem Publications
P.O. Box 2499
Melbourne, FL 32901

Send SASE for brochure.
Book: *The Custom Touch*, by Mary J. Wadlington (patternmaking for "replica of" the body; over 200 pattern designs. Has quantity discounts, and for teachers/institutions and professionals.

Goose Tracks
9127 Rutland Ct.
Stockton, CA 95209
209-951-5000

Color brochure, $ .75.
Applique patterns — (full sized, all sizes, included in one). Applique patterns; women's and children's jackets, vests.

Happy Hands Needlecraft Shoppe
4949 Byers Ave.
Ft. Worth, TX 76107

Send SASE for list.
Clothes patterns by Durelle: "Parisiamie Wrap" dress (or robe, coat), caftan, apron, smock, French style dress.

Hillcraft
P.O. Box 2573
Boca Raton, FL 33427

Free brochure.
Spiral patchwork patterns for: sundress, "Log Cabin" skirt, "Wild Goose Chase" jacket (open neckline, full length or three-quarter sleeved, reversible); all patterns full-size pieces, multi-sized for 6-20). Spiral patchwork Christmas items patterns. Manufacturer, in business since 1981.
Sells wholesale to businesses, teachers/institutions, professionals.

Homeland
P.O. Box 835
Nampa, ID 83651

Send SASE for details.
Illustrated manual on creating designer jeans — features techniques, pocket designs and patterns; step-by-step instructions.

In Stitches
512 Almond
Nampa, ID 83651

Send SASE for details.
Book: *Everything About Jeans*, by Herta Hales (step-by-step instructions on jeans-making); 125 illustrations, 15 pocket patterns (child's, adult's, 66 pocket designs). (Also sells wholesale to dealers.)

Jesse's Spring
11713 Chapel Rd.
Clifton, VA 22024

Brochure and price list, send large SASE.
Patchwork patterns (full sized, all sizes included) — jacket, tunic, vests, skirt/vest.

C. J. Kidd
4215 186th Pl., S.E.
Issaquah, WA 98027

Send SASE for price list.
Books (illustrates designer techniques and construction tips for professional ready-to-wear look in sewing projects); *Warm-ups* (using velours, terries, sweatshirts). *Designer Tops* (for over 30 different tops). *Swimwear and Cover-ups* (fit, line, and design). *Sew For The Little Girl In Your Life* (for 4-12 year old using "Three Color Approach" with variations on tops, skirts, knickers).

Kieffer's Lingerie Fabrics and Supplies
1625 Hennepin Ave.
Minneapolis, MN 55403

"Kwik-Sew" patterns catalog, $2.75.
Sewing patterns: women's jogging outfits, suits, bathing suits, dresses, blouses, others; children's four-sizes-in-one patterns, others. (And has complete line of lingerie/swimwear fabrics and trims.)

Kwik Sew Pattern Co.
300 Sixth Ave.
Minneapolis, MN 55401

5035 Timberlea Blvd., Unit #7
Mississauga, Ontario L4W 2S3, Canada

377 Montague Rd., West End
Brisbane Queensland 4101, Australia

See your dealer or send $1.00 for catalog.
"Kwik-Sew" fashion patterns (for all family members): women's suits, bathing suits, hooded pullover, sundress and jacket, jogging suit (and hooded style); children's 4-sizes-in-one patterns.
Manufacturer.

Luchard, Inc./Lucette
P.O. Box 13261
Albuquerque, NM 87192

Send SASE for complete details.
Lucette pattern system pants pattern/manual (for variety of styles, and modifications for shorts, coulottes, jumpsuits).

McCall Patterns
230 Park Ave.
New York, NY 10169

See your dealer or write for information.
Full line of fashion clothing patterns: Brook Shields Signature Collection, Designer clothes, "Easy dresses" and "14 Plus™" sizes. (Also has personal and bridal accessories, smocking and candlewicking patterns, monograms/motifs; home accessories, and dolls.)

Jennifier Morgan Designs
P.O. Box 1073
Sisters, OR 97759

Catalog, $3.00.
Lamb suede clothing kits (original classic fashion designs by Jennifier Morgan) of pre-cut lamb suede, with materials for you-sew; 18 colors; t-shirts, t-shirt dress, culottes, tapered knickers, gathered waist pants, designer jeans, fly front jacked (unlined). Service: custom garmenting, in leather. Also readymade garments as above. Jennifier Morgan clothing is offered through 18 outlets in the western states. In business since 1980.
(Also sells wholesale to retailers, professionals, and teachers/institutions.)

Needle Knows
P.O. Box 44268
Phoenix, AZ 85064

Send SASE for details.
Book: *Sew On Ultra Suede*; with patterns, illustrations, instructions, designs for cutout work, and more.

A Sleeve Seams Professional: "Only people who sew at home use a ⅝" seam allowance when setting-in sleeves. Use a ⅜" seam allowance as the professionals do. Run a line of basting ¼" from the raw edges on cap of sleeve and armhole of front and back. (Remark notches and shoulder dots so you don't loose them in the next step.) Trim extra seam allowance on the basting lines. It will be much easier to set-in the sleeve smoothly, without puckers."
—Courtesy of **Rosalie Lemontree** of "The Fashion/Sewing Newsletter", professional with a degree background and association with the educational department of McCall Pattern Co.

Patches of Joy
8050 S.W. Wareham Circle
Portland, OR 97223
503-246-6389

Send $2.00 for catalog and price list.
Patchwork patterns (full-sized): bib overalls, vests, vest and skirt set (Seminole), jackets (string patchwork, ribbon joined, others); peasant skirt, blouse and shawl. Allows 10% discount to teachers/institutions. (Also sells wholesale to businesses.) Manufacturer, in business since 1976.

Pearls Co.
Box 3088
New Haven, CT 06515

Send SASE for catalog.
Fashion lace sewing kits: blouses, skirts, dresses. Based on system of straight seams; no pattern using polyester laces.

The Piecemakers
RFD 3, Box 21
Plymouth, NH 03264

Brochure, $1.00.
Quilted kits/patterns: vest in "Flying Geese" patchwork (multi-size pattern and instructions with heart quilting pattern for straps; for machine and hand piecing); others. (Also sells wholesale to dealers.)

Polaris Publications
4273 Polaris Parkway
Janesville, WI 53545

Send SASE for details.
Book: *Fit For Fashion* — a guide to pattern alteration and fitting with step-by-step directions; also covers preliminaries — choosing fabrics, wardrobe and alterations/ measuring instructions.

Pollack's Furrier's Supply Corp.
160 W. 29th St.
New York, NY 10001

Write for catalog, or send SASE with inquiry.
Furriers supplies: lining materials — rayon fleece, silk, linnet, pellon, flannel, others. Hot iron cloth, hair cloth. French fleece. **Aids/tools:** furriers knives, blades, needles, tweezers, Wiss scissors/shears. Seam rollers, tagger, stretcher, seam napper, Kyles shapers, pullers, markers, belt pliers. Adhesives, fur dyes, beltings; fur and sewing machines. In business since 1943.

Yvonne Porcella
3619 Shoemake Ave.
Modesto, CA 95351

Send SASE for details.
Books: *Pieced Clothing*, and *Pieced Clothing Variations* (patterns for simple clothing construction).

Mary Roehr Custom Tailoring
645 N.E. Royal Court
Portland, OR 97232

Send SASE for list.
Book: *Speed Tailoring* ("made-easy"). How-to booklets *Narrowing Lapels* and *Narrowing Neckties*.

Sew Easy Lingerie
107 New York Ave.
Jersey City, NJ 07307

Send SASE for details.
Lingerie patterns: complete line, of multi-sized per pattern.

Sew Know-How
P.O. Box 12102
Fresno, CA 93776

Free brochure.
Sewing patterns/books by Artefabas: *How to Make 19 Shirts From One Pattern* (blouses), *Quick Sewing Tips*; others. **Patterns:** 6-way blouse, wrap skirt. Allows discount to teachers/institutions.

Sew Natural
211 East Palace
Santa Fe, NM 87051
505-982-8389

Send SASE for information.
"Hollyhock Dress" pattern — long, wide sleeved; and contrasting prints and solids for piecework sleeves, bodice, etc.; others.

Sew Pak Enterprises
102 Fox Run Circle
Clarks Summit, PA 18411
and:
7090 Onieda St.
Beaver Dam, WI 53916

Send SASE for information.
Sew Pak™ learn-and-do packs: tailoring, interfacing, fusible shoulder pads, sleeve heads; 2 weights. "Button holes can be Beautiful" pack with sliding buttonhole foot (high or low shank). "Seamless slips".

Sew Pretty
9440 Meadow Lane
Des Plaines, IL 60016

Free brochure.
Lingerie kits: camisoles, gowns, slips.

Sew-Wise Designs
P.O. Box 8653
White Bear, MN 55110

Catalog, $ .50.
Sewing kits: lingerie, appliques (and other needlecraft).

Sharon-By-The-Sea
5276 Hollister Ave. #153
Santa Barbara, CA 93111

Catalog, $2.00.
"Sharon's Stitchery Styles" clothing kits/patterns (men's, women's, children's): shirts, skirts, vests, blouses, others with inserts for variety of decorating techniques.

Short Cummings
16605 N.E. 30th
Bellevue, WA 98008

Send SASE for prices.
Boxer Shorts patterns (full sized) for men's, boy's sizes. Allows Canadian orders.

Simplicity Pattern Co.
200 Madison Ave.
New York, NY 10016

See your dealer, or send $ .35 for leaflet: "Action Packed Sewing" (specify).
Full line of fashion patterns for all family members, including "Easy to Sew", Beginner's Choice™, extra-sure moneysavers; and for "Young Jr. Teens" and larger sizes.

Dorothy Stringer
2633 Woodley Place
Falls Church, VA 22046

Book: *Custom Tailoring,* by Dorothy Stringer. Methods for tailoring "to sew the $1000 suit".

Summer and Winter
400 Hawthorne
Williamsport, PA 17701
Catalog, $2.00 (refundable with $10 order).
Bridal information free upon request. **Clothing patterns** of these designer's: Folkwear, Past Patterns, Bridal Elegance, Sunrise, Piece Time, Hillcraft, Fashion Blueprints, Judy Mathieson, Docie Doe, Goose Tracks, Patches of Joy, others.

T Shirts
P.O. Box 1270
Stanwood, WA 98292

How-to booklet: sew basic tank tops, t-shirts, sweaters, $3.00.

Ultra Fit
237 Van Courtland Park Ave.
Yonkers, NY 10705
914-963-9837

Send SASE for details.
Fitting system outfit (of washable stretch fabric, padded braid defining major lines of the figure): pin pattern or fabric to outfit to adjust size; in ladies leotard or tights, child's/teenage jumpsuit; all sizes. Has Mastercard, Visa.

Vogue Pattern Service
P.O. Box 549
Altoona, PA 16603

See your dealer.
Full line of fashion patterns: "Very easy", American Designer collection (Bill Blass, John Anthony, Perry Ellis, Anne Klein, Calvin Klein, Oscar De La Renta). And patterns for belts, hats, handbags; Easter and Christmas accessories and dolls.

Women's Circle Patterns
Box 124, Old Chelsea Station
New York, NY 10113

Fashion catalog, $1.50.
Sewing patterns for ladies clothing: dresses, easy-sew coulotte dress, other dresses, loungers, smock outfits, others; some multi-sized.

Workbasket Patterns
Box 151, Old Chelsea Station
New York, NY 10113

Catalog, $1.50.
Patterns for fashions: Women's dresses, skirts, blouses, sundresses, others; potholders.

Period Sleeve Seams: "Always leave a 1" adjusting seam under the arm for fitting when making a vintage garment up to the years 1910. It was customary. Also the sleeve seam had ¾" of ease in Victorian and Edwardian times. The armhole was small and very high compared to today's standards. It was high to allow for freedom of movement because it had so little ease." — Courtesy of **Saundra Ros Altman** of Past patterns.

B. INFANTS/CHILDREN'S WEAR AND ACCESSORIES

Sources for infants and children's clothing, accessories and baby care items are included in this category, as are maternity and "new mother" garments. (And see FASHIONS category).

Animal Crackers
P.O. Box 7455
Tacoma, WA 98407

Free brochure.
Patterns (full size) for: Tie Chair — securer (holds child in straight back chair to 25" tall — folds to fit in diaper bag) in 4 versions. Cover-up apron, back pack; toys (parrot, fish, crocodile).

Babe Too
Route 2, Box 3
Inman, KS 67546

Send long SASE for flyer.
Patterns for breastfeeding mothers: Dresses, blouses, nightgowns (with hidden bustline openings).

Baby Basics
P.O. Box 925
Estacada, OR 97023

Send SASE for details.
Projects directions: Baby layette, diapers, shirts, shoes, carriers, toys, etc. (with new and reused materials).

Caines Company
Box 84
Greer, SC 29652

Brochure, $ .50.
Baby items patterns: Quilt, fitted sheet, bumper, mobile, diaper stacker, seat cover, bibs, nursing pads, wall hanging.

Calico & Straw, Inc.
P.O. Box 469
Carver, MA 02330

See your dealer or write for free brochure.
Patterns: Backpacks, school cases and briefcase; with appliques in cat and dog designs. Reversible aprons and bibs (child's, preteen's, adult's). Nursery hanging organizers, diaper stacker, dolls.
(And sells wholesale to businesses, teachers/institutions.)

Charing Cross Kits
Main St., P.O. Box 79855
Meredity, NH 03253
603-279-8449

Catalog, $1.00 ($2.00 in '85).
"Clothkits" English imported sewing kits (screened designs on cotton and cotton blend fabrics — children's, adult's, teen's clothing; with notions, instructions): Children's pantaloons, overalls, dungarees, T-shirts, tops, hats, jumpers, dresses, shorts (most sizes). Women's T-shirt dresses, others; track suits, short sets, tops, pants, skirts, pinafore, jackets, night wear, lingerie, kimono. Men's jogging sets, T-shirts. Bedding kits (duvet covers, pillow cases). **Baby** carry bags and organizers. Children's hat/badge kit, satchel kit, coordinated accessories. Doll kits. Holds sales. Allows discount to teachers/institutions, professionals. Has Mastercard, Visa. In business since 1977.

Cheeks
Box 3222
Sonora, CA 95370
209-533-0961

Send SASE for prices.
Baby carrier kits (newborn to toddler) front or back carry, with double pouch, pocket — notions, hardware, pattern. Refill kits (at discount) for sew and sell. ("You'll get faster and faster at sewing the carriers," says Nancy Pierson, Cheeks spokesperson, "Three hours is probably average after your first two.") Manufacturer, in business since 1980.
(Also sells wholesale to businesses.)

Cherub Enterprises
P.O. Box 1247
Chester, PA 96020

Catalog, $1.00.
Baby Items patterns: "Noah's nursery set" mobile, quilt, diaper stacker, wall hanging, organizer; others.

Creative Express, Inc.
P.O. Box 4666
Rolling Bay, WA 98061

Cooperative catalog/newsletter, $1.00.
Children's patterns: Backpacks (2 sizes) aprons, baby carrier, diaper bag, portable high chair pants (attaches to regular chair), soft bag. Dresses (sun, party), overalls, playsuits, contour diapers. **Accessory packs** (zippers, buttons, Velcro webbing D-rings — as needed for above patterns). **Aids:** Olfa cutters, transfer pens. **Notions** threads (on cones) webbing, cording, buckles, clamps, buttons, interfacing. **Fabrics:** Pack cloth, waterproof nylon. (And see PATTERN CLUB, below.)

Creative Express Pattern Club
P.O. Box 4666
Rolling Bay, WA 98061

Catalog/newsletter, $1.00.
This sewing-for-children club has a yearly membership fee that gives these benefits: Free patterns for children's items, discounts on bulk notions, exclusive pattern and how-to data offers, newspaper, bimonthly moneysaver coupons. (See also above listing.)

Designs by Shirly
427 Franklin Ave.
Moberly, MO 65270

Brochure, $ .35.
Baby Accessories patterns (full size): Diaper stacker, crib toys and quilt (animal motifs), tote bag; and other accessories and needlecraft supplies. Has quantity prices.

Ginger Designs
Box 3241
Newport Beach, CA 92663

See your dealer or send SASE for information.
Children's wear patterns (boys and girls) — with guide sheets, each includes 5 sizes (2 through 6) with applique or patchwork as an option; in these items: reversible jumper, blouse, coats, jackets, dresses, shirt and pants, dress/ blouse/skirt, blazer dress and jacket, front button dress and slip. Full sized doll (mannequin) patterns. "All the latest 'designer tricks' are included in the patterns," says President, Ginger Johnson, of her designs.
(Also sells wholesale to distributors and retailers.)

The Great Stitch Factory
5255 S.E. Hacienda
Hillsboro, OR 97123

Send SASE for prices.
Baby "TV" booties (3 sizes).

Grow Clothes
1759 Mummasburg Rd.
Gettysburg, PA 17325

Brochure, $ .25.
Patterns and kits: Children's clothing — allows expansion to "get 3 times the wear from each outfit you sew" —girl's pullover dress, boy's jumpsuit (long or short); others.

Hand-Me-Dones
844 Oleander Dr.
Loveland, CO 80537

Ballet shoes patterns (send shoe size), $2.00 and SASE.

Life-size dolls wear children's outfits, © *Ginger Designs*

Homespun Creations
P.O. Box 6125
San Jose, CA 95150

See your dealer or send SASE for list.
Patterns: Aprons, pajama bags, diaper and book bags, quilts (and sock and cloth dolls).

J-Birds
3910 King Arthur Ct.
Winston-Salem, NC 27104

Send larg SASE for swatches/photos.
Girl's sundress kit: Pre-cut, to size 4, gingham — 4 colors.

Katidonn Enterprises
Box 771446
Steamboat Springs, CO 80477

Send SASE for list.
Child's easy-sew backpack pattern (Also in ready-made). Others

> **Buttonhole Tips:** "If working with **stripes,** put all buttonholes on one stripe. It's real classy to use buttons that match the stripe on which buttons are to be sewn." — Courtesy of **Artefabas;** lawyer, teacher, and author of *Super Quick Sewing Tips.*

Kimcraft
Rt. 2, Box 22
Ripon, WI 54971

Send SASE for price list.
Sunbonnet pattern (sizes to fit 3 months through childhood), others.

Lynn-Gayle Distributing
2083 Crabapple
Shreveport, LA 71118

Send SASE for details.
Baby comforter kits/patterns: Lamb motif; (with instructions), others.

M.O.M. Patterns
1331 Terry Ave. #204
Seattle, WA 98101

Send SASE for brochure.
Maternity patterns: Dresses, blouses, skirts, pants, shorts, others.

Make-N-Takes By Marilyn
P.O. Box 910
Estacada, OR 97023
503-630-6706

"E-Z" baby basket patterns/kits with patterns with frame; totes babies up to 6-7 months; 12" wide, 29" long with safe handles, "stronger than wicker", special frame for basket holds up to 65 pounds; features removeable, washable fabric cover.
(Also sells wholesale to businesses.)

Sharin Moznetti
4438 156th Pl., S.E.
Bellevue, WA 98006

Send SASE for information.
Baby clothes patterns including premature sizes.

Patch Couturier Patterns, Inc.
9925 S.W. 59th Ave.
Portland, OR 97219

See your dealer or write for prices.
Patterns: Girl's patchwork skirt (sizes 5-6-7 — without pattern adjustment), others.

Patchwork Pony
89-37 86th St.
Woodhaven, NY 11421

Catalog, $1.25.
Patterns: Bear quilt, crib sheet, hobby horse, donkey, pony. Music boxes.

Pitter Patterns
9539 45th N.E.
Seattle, WA 98115

Catalog, $1.00.
"Designer" infant/toddler patterns for clothing and accessories (dresses, sleepers, shirts, others).

Raindrops & Roses
P.O. Box 14615
Portland, OR 97214

Send SASE for price list.
Patterns, including for a versatile maternity nursing dress (sizes 8-16).
(Also sells wholesale to businesses.)

The Sandbox Gang
P.O. Box 2704
Huntington Beach, CA 92647

See your dealer or write for catalog.
Children's accessories patterns (with appliques): Nursery organizers, laundry bags, comforters.

Savage's Beasts
854 N.E. 58th St.
Seattle, WA 98105

Send SASE for prices.
"Quick Creature Costumes" patterns for create-a-monster (heads, gloves, spats) for people 4 ft. or taller; "for adventurous souls with little or no sewing experience."

Scrap Happy
296 E. 5th
Eugene, OR 97401
503-343-7091

Send SASE for list.
Children's clothing patterns: "Simple and quick to sew," country fashions; multiple sizes in one pattern; over 8 dresses (sizes 2-12) purses, others. Has Mastercard, Visa.
(Also sells wholesale to stores.)

Sew What
45 Maple Ave.
Pelham, NY 10803

Brochure, $ .50.
Animal slippers kits/patterns (full size, fur-fabric): Bear, dog, cat, elephant designs.

Special Patterns
P.O. Box 217
Lopez, WA 98261

Send SASE for details.
"Premie" patterns set (especially designed for 3-6 lbs. baby): Cap, gown, T-shirts, sleepers.

Stuff It's Patterns
P.O. Box 1803
Roswell, GA 30076

Send SASE for price list.
Designer nursery patterns: Crib bumper pad, quilt, diaper bag, seat pads and covers, others.

Sunrise Industries
395 S. Geneva Rd., Box 1316
Orem, UT 84057
801-224-4207

Free brochure.
Infants/children's clothing patterns (in sets — each pattern with at least 12 garments, multisized in 4 different age groups, from preemie infants through size 12): Western wear, sleep wear, school clothes, dresses, semi-formal wear, swim wear, sports wear, others.
Manufacturer, since 1977.
(Also sells wholesale to businesses.)

Diana Thorpe
1515 W. 5th Ave.
Kennewick, WA 98336

Send SASE for list.
Baby clothes patterns — premature sizes.

Cheryl Tillman
218 Algonquin
Pekin, IL 61554

Send SASE for list.
Patterns: Baby carrier, baby chamois moccasins (size ½ to 2).

Travel-Pals
P.O. Box 16924
Portland, OR 97216

Send SASE for prices.
Children's carseat covers patterns: With pockets for toys, books, bottles, etc.; custom patterns for Strollee, Century, Century Infant Loveseat.

Wee Ones
Rt. 1, Box 36
Okanogan, WA 98840

Send SASE for brochure.
Baby accessories patterns/kits, plastic "whipper snaps" for baby sleepers, others.

Your Favorite Aunt
P.O. Box 331
Kenilworth, IL 60043

Catalog, $1.00.
Patchwork kits/patterns: Children's vests (denim, calico, others) with appliques, in 4 sizes; others.

"Use This Slick Trick for all roll-up sleeves on blouses, shirts, dresses and jackets, IF the fabric is about the same on both sides. (1) Decide how far up the sleeve will be rolled, above or below the elbow. Place a pin at that point. (2) Stitch sleeve seam from under arm to the pin. Make a knot there. (3) Clip both seam allowances to the knot. Turn sleeve right side out. (4) Pin the unstitched seam with wrong sides together and edges meeting. Start at know and finish stitching the seam. (5) Press open both parts of the seam. (6) Machine-hem the bottom edge with narrow hem on outside of the sleeve."
— Courtesy of **Jane Shaner,** publisher of *The Silver Thimble.*

C. HISTORIC & ETHNIC CLOTHING

Listings in this category include sources for American Indian and other American historic costumes, and for costumes from many countries, worldwide — from early times to the present.

Bluenose Wools

114 Henderson St.
Chapel Hill, NC 27514

Send SASE for brochure. Catalog and price list, $3.00.
Clothing patterns: Folkwear, Past Patterns, Ethnic Patterns. **Buttons:** Wood, bone, Mother-of-pearl, porcelain, pewter, metal, others (and spinning/weaving supplies). Has quantity prices. In business since 1978.

© Fashion Blueprints

© Chris Rex, Folk Fabrics & Garments

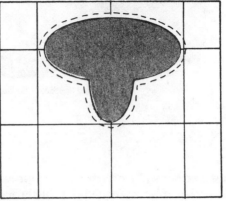

Crazy Crow Trading Post

Box 314
Denison, TX 75020
214-463-1366

Catalog, $2.00.
American Indian and historic clothing kits: Capote
(blanket) coats, buckskin pants, dresses (plains style —
wool, calico) rifle frock (coat), half-legging, woman's
buckskin leggings. Buckskin bag, tobacco bag, others.
Footwear kits: Hard-sole, soft-sole moccasins, buckskin
high top moccasins. Indian costume parts kits (bustles,
warbonnets, others). Historic garment patterns. Trims
(see Section 4). **Supplies:** Fabrics (calicos, wools, broadcloth, others), leathers, leather thongs. Threads (and other
craft supplies and Indian items). Books: Needlecrafts, others, tipimaking, clothing beadwork, history, others. In
business since 1970. Has quantity prices, discounts to
teachers/institutions and professionals.
(Also sells wholesale to businesses.)

Eagle Feather Trading Post

706 W. Riverdale Rd.
Ogden, UT 84403

Catalog, $2.00.
American Indian supplies: Leather kits, parts, skins;
other leathers. Green River Forge (historic) clothing patterns. Iron-on transfers, ball point paints. **Trims:** Beads,
ornaments, bells, conchos, feathers, shells, sewing
notions, fringes.

Edges Design Co.

20250 Wilder Ct.
Salinas, CA 93907
408-663-0633

Send SASE for brochure.
Books: *Design & Sew It Yourself*, by Diane Ericson Frode
and Lois Ericson (workbook for creative clothing with
design exercises, data on practical application — ethnic
and historic, to contemporary — garments techniques,
and materials suggestions for decoration and structural
effects). And *Print It Yourself* (fabric painting and printing
techniques) and *Ethnic Clothing*. Has quantity prices;
allows discount to teachers/institutions.

Ethnic Accessories

P.O. Box 250
Forestville, CA 95436

Catalog, $1.50.
Folkwear patterns (full line) men's women's and children's ethnic garments; and historic clothing of 19th century (Victorian, Western and prairie styles, others). Garments of turn of the century through 1940's. **Supplies:**
Shisha glass, goat lacing, Kanagawa thread (Japanese
metallic — 2 weights). **Fabrics:** "Lappas" African
damask, Guatemalan Morga — by yard. Books: Costume,
techniques, design, patterns (ethnic, exotic, smocking,
others). Non-needlecraft related items.

Ethnic Wear

R.D. 1, P.O. Box 109
McVeytown, PA 17051

Catalog and swatches, $1.00.
Frontier fashions and ethnic clothing **patterns, cotton
fabrics.**

Waxy Sewing Aid: "To sew **rickrack** without
frustration, place a strip of **wax paper** on top of the
rickrack. Sew through paper and rickrack. Tear off
wax paper." — Courtesy of **Artefabas;** lawyer,
teacher, and author of *Super Quick Sewing Tips.*

Japanese kimono, © Folkwear

Fashion Blueprints

P.O. Box 21141, Dept. N
Minneapolis, MN 55421

Catalog, $1.00.

Ethnic clothing patterns (24 designs; with improved blueprint format, each pattern multisized — small through extra large — for women, men and children): Chinese jacket and vest, Lorean coat and jacket, Thai wrap dress and top, Japanese robes and "Tsumugi Hippari" shirt. Vietnamese "oudai" tunics and pants, Mandarin jacket and vest. East Indies jacket and pants, Kashmir tunic and top, Judean bridal dress, Bethelehem jacket, Nomad dress, coat (adult, child). Mexican wedding shirt, dress and top (women's, children's). Volga shirtdresses and tunic, Dahomeyan-African dress and top. Early American: Pa. Dutch shirt (men), prairie skirt/petticoat, short gown and apron, Sioux ribbon shirt. (Tibetan shirt and vest features Japanese Sashiko stitch-techniques. All patterns are adaptable to a variety of style changes, and decorative trims and details.) May have price specials.

(Also sells wholesale to businesses.)

Folk Fabrics & Garments

3230 St. Matthews Dr.
Sacramento, CA 95821
916-481-8775

Send SASE for details.

Book: *Comfort Clothes* by Chris Rex (on West African garments, including patterns for caftans, bare midriff and other tops, full pants, tunics, Dashiki and other skirts, men's robes, tunic, shirts, others. A chapter on fabric embellishments (dyeing, batik, block printing, embroidery) variety of neck opening templates are included.
Chris Rex heads the Art Dept. of American River College in Northern California. She spent time in West African bush country and researched clothing and fabrics of the area.

Folkwear

Box 3798
San Rafael, CA 94902
415-457-0252

See your mail-order outlet, or write for information. Sewing patterns for antique clothing: Victorian vintage vests, English smocks, prairie dress, Victorian shirt, Edwardian underthings, calico day dress, skirts, Gibson girl blouse, river boatman's shirt, others. **Ethnic patterns:** Japanese (kimono, field clothing), Chinese (jacket, skirt). Dresses from Gaza, Syria, Afghan nomads. Shirts from Egypt, France — smock, Romania, Nepal, Russia, Yugoslavia, Navajo Indian. Tibetan panel coat, Turkish coat. Sarouelles pants. Others. Patterns adjust for all sizes; some adapt to both men and women; complete size range in each pattern, printed on heavy stock; some with creative handwork designs options. Manufacturer, in business since 1976.

Green River Forge, Ltd.

P.O. Box 715
Roosevelt, UT 84066
801-353-4586

Informative catalog — with historical notes and clothing data, $3.00 ($4.00 in '85).

Over 30 clothing patterns (historically accurate, 18th and 19th century): Women's gowns (hooped, high waisted, Southwestern ruffled skirt), coats, 4 Indian dresses. Men's patterns: Waistcoats, coats, shirts, breeches, Revolutionary war uniform, Spanish coat and pants, capote, others. Boy's shirt and pants. Books on clothing (including *The Art Of Makin' Skins* — how to make clothing, moccasins, tents), others. In business since 1971.

(Also sells wholesale to businesses.)

Grey Owl

113-15 Springfield Blvd.
Queens Village, NY 11429

Catalog, $1.00.
American Indian clothing/costume kits: Sioux War
bonnets, shirts, headdresses, dance bustle costumes,
dresses, accessories, leathers. And full line of other Indian
craft supplies and trims.

Hawaii's Pattern People
(See ''Pattern People'')

The Old World Sewing Pattern Co.

Rt. 2, Box 103
Cold Spring, MN 56320

Free brochure.
Clothing Patterns, accurate 19th century, screened on
brown paper, for today's sizes 8-12 — empire and roman-
tic gowns, bustled, crinolined gowns, men's frock coat,
informal suit. Has quantity prices. Brides who buy a pattern can get free information on headpiece.

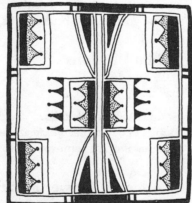

Past Patterns

2017 Eastern, S.E.
Grand Rapids, MI 49507

Turn of the Century Catalog, $5.00.
Historic fashion patterns: Authentic, late 1800's to
present, on heavy brown paper — Women's gowns, petticoats, blouses, suits, clock, nightwear; men's suit, duster;
full range of garments from 1911-1950's, for women,
children. Mastercard, Visa.
(Also sells wholesale to businesses.)

Pauloa Patterns
(See Pattern People)

Pattern People

P.O. Box 11254
Honolulu, HI 96828

Catalog, $1.00.
Hawaiian fashion patterns: over 36 women's long
dresses, short dresses, wrap clothes, pants, bikinis; men's
shirts.
(Also sells wholesale to businesses.)

Plume Trading Sales Co.

P.O. Box 585
Monroe, NY 10950

Catalog, $1.00.
American Indian clothing kits/patterns: Warshirts, 5
vests, 3 leggings/breechclout sets, dress, headdresses; costume trims, accessories, leathers. Has some quantity
prices.

Traditional Fine Ethnic Products

P.O. Box 2683
El Cajon, CA 92021

Brochures, send SASE.
Norwegian costume kits: Bergen Bunad and Graffer
Bunad outfits; shirt, skirt; woven braids, pewter
buttons/clasps.

Arapaho bag and Sioux shirt

"Square Dance Costumes have a great deal of
fullness in the skirts — using gores, circles, or trimed
darts at the waist. Due to the fullness, uneven hem-
lines are a constant problem. **After** cutting garment
and **before** assembling, stitch straight lines from
hem edge toward waist (in best matching thread
available) over **most** biased areas. It will then be
unnecessary to hang for days to accomodate the sag,
for it will be eliminated. — Courtesy of **Mary Jane
McClelland,** of Fit For You.

D. BRIDAL FASHIONS AND WEDDING ACCESSORIES

Aik's Satin and Lace
1705 77 Ave. East
Tacoma, WA 98424
206-922-6114

For paper doll, pattern pieces and catalog, $2.00 (refundable).
Pattern kit to design specifications: mix and match bodices, sleeves, skirts for own gown; mail completed paperdoll for pre-cut kit — complete with fabrics, laces, trims and notions. (Also has readymade from kit.)

Bridal Elegance
1176 Northport Dr.
Columbus, OH 43320

Send SASE for list.
Bridal fashion patterns: Interchangeable styles — skirt variations, for gathered or flat train; other mix and match formal gown parts, bridesmaids dresses patterns.

Bridal Illusions
P.O. Box 345
Bay City, MI 48707

Send SASE for details.
Book: *Guide to "Professional Secrets" for Veils* designing and making, for semi-formal to formal wear.

Cinderella Flower and Feather
57 W. 38th St.
New York, NY 10018

Send SASE for list.
Wedding: floral parts, glues; flower sprays, clusters, wreaths, feathers.

CR's Crafts
Box 8
Leland, IA 50453

Catalog, $1.00.
Wedding accessories kits: Bouquets, "rabbit" fur muff, ring pillows, garter; readymade accessories. (And doll patterns, kits, supplies.)
(Also sells wholesale to businesses.)

Craft and Floral Supply Co.
P.O. Box 68
Temple City, CA 91780

Catalog, $1.00.
Wedding accessories: silk flowers (flowermaking supplies), ribbons, net.

Craft Source
9121 E. Las Tunas Dr., P.O. box 68
Temple City, CA 91780

Wedding catalog, $2.00.
Flowermaking supplies, bouquets, decoratives. Dyes.

Econocraft
940 Industrial Blvd.
New Albany, IN 47150

Send SASE for price list.
Flowermaking supplies: Pretty Petals, Country Flowers, others; wedding accessories. (Other needlecraft supplies.)

KC Originals
571 No. Madison
Ogden, UT 84404

Send SASE for prices.
Nylon bridal veil netting — 150 colors.

Keepsake Designs
571 N. Madison
Ogden, UT 84404

Send SASE for details.
How-to book: *Bridal Keepsakes*, by Charlene Miller (make ring pillows, purse, sachets, garters); others. Has quantity prices, large order discounts.
(Also sells wholesale to businesses.)

Keepsakes, Ltd.
P.O. Box 484
Glen Ellyn, IL 60137

Send SASE for details.
Keepsake bridal handkerchief kit — converts to christening bonnet later; with gift card for bride or baby.

Mill End Store
8300 S.E. McLoughlin Blvd.
Portland, OR 97202

Send SASE for current offerings.
Bridal fabrics (full lines): taffeta, satin, chiffon, Georgette, tissue faille, organza, velvet, others. Laces — all types; lace collars and medallions. (And has other fabrics.)

Simplicity Pattern Co.
901 Wayne St.
Niles, MI 49121

See your local fabric store.
Book: *Bridal Sewing and Crafts*, (instructions for gowns selection and fitting, shopping tips; bridal accessories) bridal party items — bouquets, smocked purse, ring pillow. Other wedding, shower and gifts ideas.

E. SPECIALTY FASHIONS

C. M. Almy & Son, Inc.
37 Purchase St.
Rye, NY 10580

Catalog, brochures, $2.00.
Ecclesiastical clothing kits: Vestments, clerical items, choir robes; "choir" **fabrics** (polyester blends, textures, satin), damasks, brocades, linings (some metallics), tapestries, etc. Fringes, cording, tassels, bandings, appliques.

Fit For You
781 So. Golden Prados Dr.
Diamond Bar, CA 91765

Catalog, $ .50 (refundable).
Square dance costumes patterns: Variety of styles — skirts, dresses, slips. Notions.

Gwen Forrester
58 Pine Hill Rd., R.D. #1
Framingham, MA 01701

For skating/dancing costumes: trim, beads and appliques catalog, $2.00.
Lycra spandex swatches, $2.00.
Fabric swatches, $1.00 each.
Milliken visa, matching boys/girls fabrics, stretch satin, Glitterskin, Milliskin.

Jean Hardy Patterns
2151 La Cuesta Dr.
Santa Ana, CA 92705

Catalog, $1.00.
Western/action clothing patterns: Tennis dress, blouses, skirts, misses sport set, pep squad skirts, dresses, shirts, lingerie, body suits, square dance skirts, dresses, sports sets. Men's items. Riding outfits.

Skating Patterns by Trudi
Box 362
East Longmeadow, MA 01028

Free catalog.
Skating/dancing costumes patterns (child's 3 to adult 18) — skirts (gored, wrap, others), leotards, briefs, boys/mens bolero, suits pants, others. Custom-sized men's patterns.

Silk Flowers are Made from Silk Organza, or Rayon Organza (About Half as Expensive as Silk) — Both Have Been Termed "China Silk".

F. READYMADE CLOTHING

This category gives sources for plain, reasonable clothing for "you-decorate" (by embroidery, applique, etc.; or by stencil, paint, dye).

Clothcrafters Co.

P.O. Box 176
Elkhart Lake, WI 53020

Free catalog.
Plain fabric readymades: cotton flannel sheeting, netting, cheesecloth, sleeping bag liners, polishing cloths, cloth bags. Reasonable prices.

Cotton Pickin'

P.O. Box 462
Forestville, CA 95436
707-887-1651

Send SASE for brochure.
T-shirts (100% white cotton) all sizes (men's, women's, children, infants); "wholesale".

Gohn Bros.

Box 111
Middlebury, IN 46546
219-825-2400

Free catalog.
Amish and plain clothing: canvas gloves, suspenders, denim caps, infant clothing. Lingerie, underwear, cotton socks; men's jackets and vests, nylon jackets, denim pants, t-shirts, sweatshirts, other men's and boy's shirts. Manufacturer, since 1900.

Orion Company

4105 Bent Oak Ct.
Douglasville, GA 30135

Send SASE for prices.
Hospital scrub shirts — medium, large, or extra large size; 100% cotton, white.

Sara Glove Co.

16 Cherry Ave.
Waterbury, CT 06704

Catalog, $1.00.
Lee jeans, factory outlet work clothes, shoes. Bargains on new shirts, Lee jackets, gloves, coveralls, others.

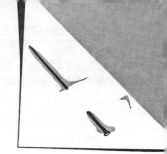

8
Personal Accessories

Supplies sources for this section cover Fashion Accessories for adults (see CHILDREN'S CLOTHING AND ACCESSORIES, and BRIDAL FASHIONS AND ACCESSORIES for other, personal accessory items, or consult the index for specific supplies).

Accento Craft
100 Anclote Rd.
Tarpon Springs, FL 33589

Send SASE for brochure.
Handbag handles. "Thread ease" threader. Other needlecraft items.
(Also sells wholesale to businesses.)

Caldwell Lace Leather Co.
Caldwell St.
Auburn, KY 42206

See your dealer or send SASE for details.
Leather kits: handbags, billfolds, others. Leather lacing, leather pieces, trims (by lb. bag) variety of colors. Book. In business since 1863.

Calico Express, Ltd.
P.O. Box 494W
Marion, IA 52302
319-393-4520

Catalog, $1.00.
Original **patterns/kits** for: Denim tote bag, crayon apron, baby bibs, cover-apron, racquet cover, girl's purse, others. (And home accessories.)

Carol & Pat Original
P.O. Box 1252
Springfield, VA 22151

Catalog, $1.00.
Handbag kits: complete kit for machine sewing (with Ultrasuede™) in 5 colors; or partial kit, without fabric; clutch types, shell clutch, bamboo — handles pouch, disco bag, gathered clutch, "snap-hex facile" frames, portfolio; cases (cigarette, eyeglass, key) complete and partial kits. Some quantity kits (hardware for 3 handbags, 1 pattern/instructions). **Purse hardware:** frames, chains; handles, lucite bottom. Rivet setter. In business since 1979.
(Also sells wholesale to businesses with separate "dressmaker wholesale price list" without patterns. Retailers/businesses should send tax and business license number for free information.)

Chantpleure
445 E. Hickory St.
Hinsdale, IL 60521

Send SASE for prices.
Needle/scissors case kit — Victorian "folded Hearts" case with ribbon-tie closure.
(Also sells wholesale to dealers.)

Charda Classics
117 S.W. Scott St.
Ankeny, IA 50021

Send SASE for prices.
Wood Bermuda handbag handles and linings.

Designer Patchwork: "To create a designer look when making patchwork clothing select fashionable colors. Jackets and vests are the most interesting when five or more fabrics are used in a combination of colors and size of prints. Florals, paisleys, geometric designs, mini dots and calicos are effective for a fashion look." — Courtesy of **Joyce Kelly** of Patches of Joy, Inc.

Cold Creek Kits
8917 Sandusky-Clyde Rd.
Castalia, OH 44824

Free Brochure.
Soft luggage (sewing) kits, Variety of sizes.

The Crafters
Box 6068
Wilmington, DE 19804

Send SASE for brochure.
Bermuda handbag kits/patterns. (classic style — variety of fabrics, 10½" sq.); Wood handles (finished/unfinished, in 6 shapes, hinged or unhinged).

Crane Hill Farm
8062 Black River Rd.
Watertown, NY 13601

Catalog and fabric samples, $ .75.
Designer wallets kits/patterns (of "Two-sized" calico fabric), checkbook clutch, credit card folder, shaped glasses case.

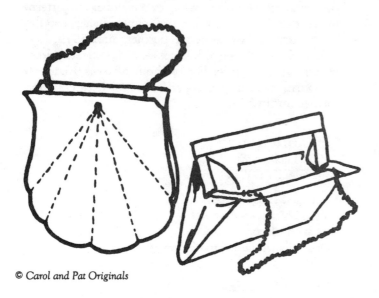

© Carol and Pat Originals

Dazians, Inc.
40 E. 29th St.
New York, NY 10016
(Also in Beverly Hills, Boston, Chicago, Dallas, Miami)
212-686-5300

Free catalog.
Novelty buckram hat frames: pillbox, beanie, Western, sailor woman's, saucer brim, conical poke, "Garden Party", "Gay Nineties", tricorne, drum major's, fez, sombrero, coolie, headband, cloche, short topper, Dutch girl, jockey, cadet, others. (Also complete line of theatrical fabrics and trims, readymades.)
Allows discount to professionals; Some quantity prices.

Dewey Designs
Box 2824
Lincoln, NE 68502

Brochure, $ .50.
Accessories patterns: Wallets, duffle bags, Visor-organizer, and others.

Essex Wood Products
Box 27
Deep River, CT 06417

Free brochure.
Bermuda bag liner/wood handle kits, with patterns for button-on covers (and complete line of wooden ware). Has Mastercard, Visa.
(Also sells wholesale to businesses.)

Flying Fingers
P.O. Box 9197
Richmond Heights, MO 63117
314-647-1335

Catalog, $ .75.
Kits (quilting-applique, patchwork): purse and tote bags, packable-hat with pockets (adult, child), patchwork long skirt, golf skirt, others. (And home accessories kits.) Manufacturer.

Pat Golbeiski
1504 S.E. Main
Portland, OR 97214

Pattern for Obi belt (for any size waist), $2.50 ppd.

Louis A. Green & Co., Inc.
Forbes Industrial Park, Box 221
Chelsea, MA 02150

Free literature.
Full line of Webbing — 100% cotton, vat-dyed webbing and binding (for tote bags, belts, other canvas items). (Also has cords.)

Iowa Pigskin Sales Co.
R.R. 2
West Branch, IA 52358

Sample swatches, $2.00.
Pigskin handbag kits. Book *Creating With Pigskin* (and pigskin by square foot).

J. R. Enterprises
Box 4371
Thousand Oaks, CA 91359

Sewing pattern for travel bags: 3 sizes (for jewelry, cosmetics, etc.); others, $1.50. Other patterns.

© *Kountry Kitchen Kapers*

Jacmore Needlecraft, Inc.
2337 McDonald Ave.
Brooklyn, NY 11223

See your dealer or write for information.
Bag handles, belt buckles, bellpull **hardware,** metal novelties, metallic threads (other items).

Kits
Box 182
Madison Lake, MN 56063

Send SASE for list.
Hand muff kits: Acrylic "fur" (children's size), velveteen patchwork (woman's) wool lined, in 4 colors. (And knitting kits.)

Kocak's Briar Patch
977 Oak Lane
Orange Park, FL 32073

Brochure, $2.00.
Pattern/kits for aprons — Holiday and shower motifs.

Kosmo Products
P.O. Box 501
Mt. Prospect, IL 60056

Send large SASE for price list.
Kits: Shoe organizer bag, pillows and quilts (patchwork), pajama bag/pillow, Children's shoe bag holders, diaper stacker/laundry bag, "hen" pincushion/notions holder. (Other needlecraft items.)

Kountry Kitchen Kapers
5530 S.W. 90th Ave.
Portland, OR 97225
503-292-1481

Send SASE for information.
Patterns including for easy-make **smock-apron** (for 3 sizes) — 1 yard of 60" fabric with leftovers for hotpads. (Wholesale inquiries invited.)

Lynnline
Box 813
Steila Coom, WA 98388

Catalog, $1.00 (refundable).
Sewing Patterns: soft wallets, reversible purse, European quilt and patch handbag, others.

Madhatter Press
3101 12th Ave., So. #5
Minneapolis, MN 55407
612-722-8951

Free brochure.
Book: *From The Neck Up: An Illustrated Guide to Hatmaking,* by Denise Dreher. A text of fourteen lessons (on design, pattern-making, construction for felt, straw and fabric covered hats; turban draping; block making; and renovation). Step-by-step hatmaking techniques are presented with over 400 clear illustrations. Sixty ¼" scale patterns for historical and contemporary hats (for men and women) are included as is a chapter of materials/equipment suppliers. The volume stresses professional methods and improvisations for beginner and advanced work.
Denise Dreher is a professional milliner and lecturer with numerous T.V. and movie credits to her costuming ability including for *The Empire Strikes Back.* (See also under "Resources")
Has quantity discounts.
(Also sells wholesale to businesses.)

New Life for Furs: "By shortening the front panels of a mink or any other FUR stole, you can give the garment a NEW look ... as a cape or shrug. No cutting necessary. Simply attach 3 MALE snap parts to the LINING of each of the two front panel ENDS (spaced one at each side, and one in middle). Then sew 3 FEMALE snap parts to the LINING in lower bust area to match the positions on the panel ends (one set in the RIGHT bust area ... one set in the LEFT bust area). Once completed, all you do is snap panels into position on the bust area lining ... and PRESTO ... you have a cape or shrug 'look'. Simply unsnap, and you are back to a regular stole, as originally." — Courtesy of **Arthur M. Rein,** noted furrier.

BUTTERFLY

- ◉ black
- Ⅴ red
- ⊘ coral
- ⊡ yellow

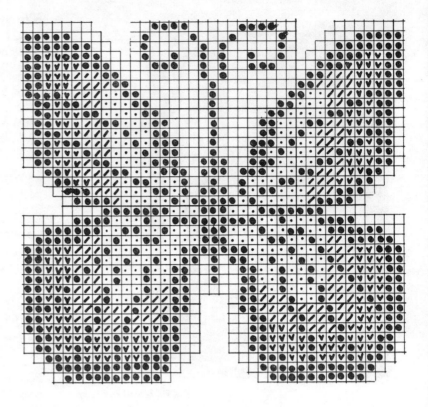

POPPY

- ⊡ red
- ◉ black
- ⊘ green

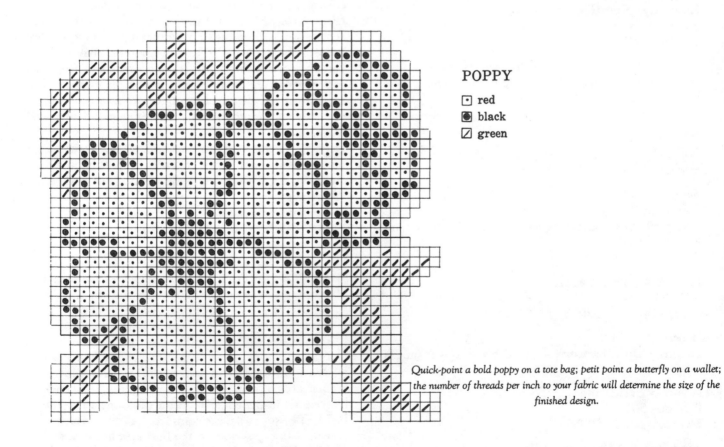

Quick-point a bold poppy on a tote bag; petit point a butterfly on a wallet; the number of threads per inch to your fabric will determine the size of the finished design.

Miller's Craft Corner

Box 7232
Columbus, GA 31908

Catalog, $1.00.
Handbag parts: "Marbella" handles — 9 shapes, wood handles — 23 shapes/sizes, wood beads. (And macrame and flowermaking supplies.) Has Mastercard, Visa.

Multi-Woods International

P.O. Box 3517
Wilmington, NC 28403

Handbag kits — finished wood handles, pattern for liner and cover; 4 styles.
(Also sells wholesale to businesses.)

My Sister and I

P.O. Box 536
Montville, NJ 07045

Brochure, $ .25.
Personal accessories patterns: Cases (checkbook, eyeglasses) bookcover, others.

N & N Designs

5275 Mt. Vernon Pkwy.
Atlanta, GA 30327

Send SASE for prices.
Button-on purse cover designs (5 different, 3 sizes each with applique instructions.)
(Also sells wholesale to businesses.)

Needle In The Haystack

P.O. Box 834
McMinnville, OR 97128

Send SASE for price list.
Accessories kits: Aprons (pre-cut fabric): Crayon pinafore (sizes 2-4), barbecue apron/hot pad. (And home accessories kits).

Pattern Perfect

380 No. 8th St.
El Centro, CA 92243

Send SASE for list.
Patterns including for beach tote/towel wrap, others.

Pocketpoint, Inc.

438 Humphrey St.
Swampscott, MA 01907

Free catalog.
Carrybag kits (with needlepoint/cross stitch pocket/panels) Also has completed bags for you — needlecraft only.

Quakertown Sheepskins

Rt. 309
Quakertown, PA 18951

Send SASE for prices.
Sheepskin inner soles for shoes, boots. Variety of sizes.

Quiltessence

Box 27143
Phoenix, AZ 85061

Send SASE for list.
Patterns: Indian "Windwalker" purses (traditions of Hopi, Navajo, Zuni Indians in 3 designs). Victorian heart **music box kit** (quilted).

Barney Roberti Daughters & Sons

Youngsville, PA 16371

Free literature.
Handbag handles — maple hardwood, 10 styles.

Stitches 'N Stuff Depot

P.O. Box 549
Zoar, OH 44697

Send SASE for prices.
Purse kits (candlewicking initials/sewing): 10" x 8" with velcro closure, 3 colors, with materials, instructions. Candlewicking **alphabet patterns** (with floral accent).

Timberline Sewing Kits

Box 126-F2
Pittsfield, NH 03263
603-435-8888

Free brochure.
Luggage/totes kits: Bike bag, 2 packs, totes, cargo and garment bags, drawstring sacks (5 sizes). **Others:** Cordura™ billfold, wallet, accessory pouch, belt, reflective belt. Comforters kits (4 bed sizes). And outerwear clothing. May run sales. Allows discount to teachers/institutions. Manufacturer, since 1976.

Color You Young: "Navy blue and red are one of the most youthful color combinations. It can take 10 years off the appearance and costs much less than a face lift! A common color mistake to avoid with navy blue and red is wearing a navy blue outfit with red shoes, belt, beads. Shoes should always be the same color or darker than the hemline. In this particular case, red shoes draw the eye right to the foot and away from the face." — Courtesy of **Ruth Zimmerli** of Color Compliments. She is a professional color analyzer/consultant.

Useful Uniques
557 N. Mill
Plymouth, MI 48170

Send SASE for price list.
Soft sculpture kits: hand mirror, reversible handbag, photo album, others.

V.I.P. Crafts & Fabrics
1412 Broadway
New York, NY 10018
212-730-4600

See your dealer or write for information.
Kits: Checkbook covers, book covers, pillows, sachets, child's purse, others. (And fabrics — cottons and blends).

Wallets 'N Things
17281 Edwards
Southfield, MI 48076

Send SASE for list.
Patterns and kits for fabric **checkbook wallets.**

Washington Millinery Supplies, Inc.
8501 Atlas Dr.
Gaithersburg, MD 20760
301-963-4444

Catalog, $5.00.
Millinery supplies: Hat materials (heavy faille, chrinoline; wire frames, ribbon wire, others), plain horsehair hat forms, derbies, others. **Veiling:** nylon, sheers, organzas, others. **Laces** — full line including Chantilly, Schiffle, Venice; cluny, nylon, stretch, novelties, satin, others. **Boutique trims:** Beads, pearls, combs, feathers, ribbons (full line) rhinestone, buttons, flowers (Magic silk, satin, velvet). Tiaras and headpieces. **Steamers. Adhesives:** Bridal glue, Sobo, others. **Service:** Custom dyeing. (Also sells wholesale to businesses.)

9
Decorative Home Accessories

Company listings in this section offer kits, patterns and supplies for HOLIDAY decoratives; or ROOMS — kitchen, living or bedrooms or bath; or for LAMPMAKING and SPECIALTY SEWING. (And see the index or other section throughout the book, for specific items.)

Americana Applique
Rt. 1, Box 876
Union, MO 63084
314-583-8754

Color brochure, $1.00 (refundable).
Patterns — Eighteen Original full-size "country" designs (for hand or machine applique) with color photo; for hoop pictures, quilt and other uses, including: Hearts and Birds, Angel-welcome, Quilt Birds, "Whaler's Luck", Fruit Basket, rooster, sitting hen, others. Manufacturer, in business since May, 1982.
(Also sells wholesale to businesses, professionals, teachers/institutions.

Amity Publications
78688 Sears Rd.
College Grove, OR 97424
503-942-7501

Send SASE for catalog.
Amish/country patterns/kits for quilts, hangings (country scenes); quilting blocks/pattern sheets (3 design sets). Dolls. Book: *Amish Inspirations* by Suzy Lawson (full-size patterns for 46 Amish quilts; 38 quilting motifs; with instructions, 12 border variations; how-to's; 136 pages, soft cover.
Manufacturer, in business since 1981.
(Also sells wholesale to distributors, retailers, professionals, teachers/institutions.)

Appliques by Country Crafts
Rt. 1
Breckenridge, MO 64625
816-738-4496

See your dealer or write for brochure.
Applique/patterns: 18" designs including for 14" hoop/hanging.

Arts 'N Designs
1400 W. Flournoy St.
Chicago, IL 60607

Catalog, $ .50.
Soft sculpture patterns for astrological signs (and other crafts).

At Last
P.O. Box 549
Holmdel, NJ 07733

Send SASE for list.
"Quackers" calico duck patterns/kits — soft sculpture, for hearth, doorstop, etc. Allows Canadian orders.

"**Gathering With a Cord** is not a trick!! Sewing long length straight stitches into the fabric and then pulling on them can cause damage to fine fabrics. The seam allowance can actually be frayed away like fringe. Instead take a long piece of soft cord the entire length of the fabric to be gathered, and lay it at the ⅜" point of your seam allowance. Using a regular zig-zag on the widest width and longest length, stitch over the cord. Do not catch the cording with the needle. After sewing the area to be gathered, simply pull on the cord to create the desired fullness. Handle the gathered section of the garment as you would normally, sewing it to the other units with ⅝" seam allowances. Then remove the cord, but leave the zig-zag stitches to help overcast the edge." — Courtesy of **Irene M. James** of I. M. James Enterprises, from her book, *Sewing Specialties*.

"Hill Top Farm", © *Bay Window Designs*

"Country Checkerboard", © *Bay Window Designs*

Bay Window Designs
201 First, Box 402
Forreston, IL 61030
815-938-3117

See your dealer or send SASE for information.
Applique patterns (original "Country" designs, full-size, with color photo) for hoop pictures, hangings: scenics, cat snoozing, pilgrims, "Back Porch", "Washstand", others. Country soft checkerboard (for applique or stencil). Finished models available. In business since 1981. Plans adding to line of country patterns adaptable for both applique and stencil techniques.
(Also sells wholesale to distributors, retailers, professionals, teachers/institutions.)

Bazaar Boutique Craft Patterns
8902 Granada Hills
Austin, TX 78737

Brochure, $1.00.
Over 40 soft-sewn patterns including for tissue-box House (boutique size), "bunny ball", others. Accepts MasterCard, Visa.

Judy Bean Crafts
P.O. Box 281
Kirbyville, TX 75956

Brochures, $1.00.
Kits/patterns: Holiday items — angel, reindeer, ornaments; kitchen accessories — potholders, mats; "stained glass" design quilts, pillows. Others.

Lanna Blumberg
Rt. 1, Box 82
Newberg, OR 97132

Send SASE for list.
"Duck Decoy" patterns: Green Winged Teal, Hooded Merganser, Canadian Goose; other waterfowl.
(Also sells wholesale to businesses.)

Bo Dew Accents
P.O. Box 426
Woodland Hills, CA 91365

Catalog, $1.00.
Sewing patterns/pattern books (over 1200, full-size) from most major manufacturers; for home accessories including soft sculpture decoratives, pillows, quilts, (all sizes, types, styles), laundry bags, nursery organizers, comforters, carrying cases, potholders and other kitchen covers, cozies, and decoratives. Lampshades, Folkwear victorian boudoir linens, draperies and slipcovers, tablecloths, others; in country/Americana, contemporary, and classic designs. Christmas and Holiday decorative item patterns — good selection. Dolls and toys patterns. Notions: weights, measuring tools, "Elasti-guide" elastic aid, pins, marking and transfer pencils, magnifier, threader. Scissors — Gingher shears, folding, left handed. Gold and silver markers (felt tipped, marks fabrics, ribbon and other items.) (And full line of fashion clothing patterns.)

Jeanette Boettcher
18483 Ravenwood
Saratoga, CA 95070

Send SASE for prices.
Velvet strawberry sachets kit (or for Christmas ornaments, etc.).

Bonette's
3035 N. Arlington
Simi Valley, CA 93063
Catalog, $1.00.

Kitchen decor patterns (for hand/machine, quilting): potholders, bunwarmer, basket covers, wall decor, others (in chicken, rooster, kitty, teddy, mouse, pig and butterfly designs.)

Cab's Trunk
639 S. Quincy
Hinsdale, IL 60521

Send SASE for Brochure.
Soft-Sculpture patterns/kits — Baskets (6", 8", 10" round with handles). Pillows (including personalized graduation colors and year, others.)

"Quilt Birds", © Ann Heitkamp, Americana

The Calico Candlestick
88 Rosewood Dr.
Avon Lake, OH 44012

Catalog, $1.00 and long SASE.
Original Patterns for **"Country" accessories:** "Heather the Hen" centerpiece, Sunbonnet girl detergent cover, calico basket, potholders (fry pan, chicken in Basket, calico cottage, sunbonnet kids) "Candy Shoppe" house-sculptured box, with patterns for "taffy" and lollipops, 2-slice toaster cover, Christmas tree ornaments set patterns. (Designer Nanci Cowles had a patchwork Easter basket in *Crafts* magazine, April '83.)

Calico Construction Co.
Box 64717
Baton Rouge, LA 70896

Brochure, $1.00.
"Country Calico" kitchen patterns (patchwork and applique) — 6 refrigerator magnets, 6 potholders, 6 towels, 3 table runners, broom cover, phone book cover.

Calico Express, Ltd.
P.O. Box 494W
Marion, IA 52302
319-393-4520
Catalog, $1.00.
Original patterns/kits for: tissue holders, potholders (patchwork), photo album covers, toaster and blender covers, matching placemats and napkin rings, kitchen ensemble set, sewing machine cover, doll and baby quilts, pillow tops, baskets, gift bags, holiday items, patchwork wreaths. (also personal items.)

Calico Factory
P.O. Box 4794
Vancouver, WA 98662

See your dealer or write for information.
Patterns for toaster covers, organizers, book covers, "Basket-tier" hanging baskets, others.

Calico Reality
P.O. Box 328
Perry, OH 44081

Brochure, $1.00 and large SASE.
Patterns: "Snapper" calico fish serving caddy, tissue "cottages", applique pillows for TV guide and remote control (12" x 16") including "Afternoon Soap Opera", "Sports-A-Holic", "Pets Prime Time", "Captivated Kits", "Late Night Toes"; others.

Calico Wall Works
314 South Willard
Ottumwa, IA 52501

Catalog, $1.75 ($1.00 refunds).
Over 35 original designs by Irene Goudy including for **hoop-framed pictures,** others.
(Also sells wholesale to businesses.)

Fabric Shaper Illusions: Fabric "slimmers" — any dark, opaque colors and/or small prints, of dull finish and thin fabric. **Fabric "body boosters"** — any bright or light colors and/or large prints, shiny finished and bulky fabrics. — Courtesy of **Margaret A. Boyd.**

Cappels of Dayton

2767 Holman St.
Dayton, OH 45439
513-293-6884

Catalog, $2.00.
Decorator patterns/pattern booklets: fowl (calico hen doorstop, other hens, mallard country goose, Canadian goose, duck with eyeglasses), stencil hoop-pictures, doorstop; soft sculpture baskets, baby motifs hangings, hoop-pictures ("country" applique designs), Christmas (standing tree, Santa, gingerbread dolls, ornaments, tree skirt, patchwork stocking, others. Halloween pumpkin, 56" tall stuffed skeleton, door decorations, others. **Pillow kits:** Stenciled, 9 candlewicking pillows (and pattern books). Wood framing **hoops** (4" — 18" sizes). Cloth dolls, teddy bear, others. In business since 1972.

Carol Art

P.O. Box 479
Woodburn, OR 97071

Brochure, $1.00.
Easy to sew patterns/designs for appliqued/quilted **Hoop-framed pictures** "Limited Edition" series, ("the Prospector", "Country Kitchen", others).

Carousel Crafts Co.

P.O. Box 42549
Houston, TX 77042
713-784-3551

See your local store, or write for information.
Puffet™ quick stitchery kits — Christmas ornaments/package trims (over 60 designs), stockings, embroidered ornaments, Soft sculpture kits for halloween designs, Thanksgiving, patchwork wreath, pillows, soft jewelry boxes, hanging organizers (pocketed), shoe bags, chicken pincushion, calico hen calendar; others, (and dolls/toys.) Allows discounts to teachers/institutions — on orders over $150.00.
Manufacturer, in business since 1968.
(Also sells wholesale to businesss.)

Carrousel Patterns

P.O. Box 1370
Vancouver, WA 98666

Send SASE for prices.
Soft sculpture Wall hangings patterns (full-sized); bonnet girl and dog on leash, others.
(Also sells wholesale to businesses.)

Cas's Country Crafts

312 E. Pipeline Rd.
Hurst, TX 76053
817-282-5201

Send SASE for prices.
Soft sculpture patterns/kits: "Designer Swan" and "Designer Geese" decorative (20", with trapunto quilted design for wings, kit in white satin with ribbon). "Designer Swan Caddy" kit/pattern — serves as container.
(Also sells wholesale to businesses.)

Cathy Needlecraft

One Tuxnis Rd.
Tarriffville, CT 06081

See your dealer or send SASE for list.
Stencil/quilted pillow kits (fabric silk-screened).

Cher's Kit and Kaboodle

P.O. Box 3537, #110
Austin, TX 78764

Send SASE for catalog.
Soft sculpture kits — for boxes, decorative items (seasonal, holiday) coiled baskets, designer frames, dolls, clown bookends, goose, "lamby", frigies, Nap mat (clown design), felt gift tags.

Colonial Crafts of Charlotte

P.O. Box 221343
Charlotte, NC 28222

Catalog, $1.00.
Accessories kits for Calico wreath, applique pillows, others.

Country Collage, Inc.

P.O. Box 797
Flemington, NJ 08822

Catalog, $1.00.
Accessories Patterns/kits: Tea cozies (hen, flower, whale), No-sew holiday wreath (pre-cut and sewn fabric parts, form, box, notion), Others. Has Mastercard, Visa.

Country Mouse Patterns

P.O. Box 306
Mt. Freedom, NJ 07970

Catalog, $1.00.
Holiday accessories patterns: Santa and Mrs., Victorian wreath, snowman face, garland, candy cane, others.

© *Instant Interiors*

Country Post

P.O. Box 1821
Kettering, OH 45429

Brochure, $1.00.
Country and folk art applique kits and patterns including for hoop framed pictures.

P. Cox Design Studio

P.O. Box 9825
Ft. Worth, TX 76101
817-731-3648

Free brochure.
Patterns (full-size) for "Cat Cozy" cat bed/house, "Doggie Den" bed (in designs of a variety of breeds), quilts ("Caladium" World Without End adaptation, "Christmas Fan" design and Lovebird comforter — "Bride's Keepsake"; quilted angel tree-topper or puppet; others. (Also sells wholesale to businesses.)

The Craft Barn

600 Fairview, S.E.
Salem, OR 97302

Catalog, $2.00 ($1.00 refund).
Patterns/kits — fabric wallhanging, **kitchen** creations and decorator items, toys.

Crafts and Patterns

P.O. Box 1127
Woodland, CA 95695

Catalog, $1.00 and large SASE.
Over 45 full-sized **patterns**: "calico bathroom" items —hand toilet sign, outhouse towel bar, flat roof outhouse for toilet tissue, peak roof outhouse for facial tissue, outhouse wall hanging; others. (Also Holiday items.)

Crafts and Patterns

P.O. Box 1127
Woodland, CA 95695

Catalog, $1.00 and large SASE.
Over 45 patterns including for holiday decorating (Christmas, Halloween, Thanksgiving) — door and wall hangings, placemats, potholders and others (also bathroom decor items).

Cranberry Creek

P.O. Box 12434
Overland Park, KS 66212
913-381-5931

See your dealer or write for brochure.
Window Quilt Pattern™ of traditional method, with matching window warmer and pillow patterns. (And has a stuffed teddy bear kit.)

© *Amity Publications*

Creations From Imagination Unlimited

P.O. Box 7015
Federal Way, WA 98003

Brochure, $ .50.
Patterns including for "unicorn" wallhanging (adapts to baby's quilt) for machine applique, others.

The Creative Connection

P.O. Box 184
Stratham, NH 03885
603-772-3203

Samples, specifications and prices, $1.00 ($1.25 in 1985).
Window Fleece™ 4-layer **insulating fabric** (with inner mil film and Hollofil™ layers, channel quilted, 90" or 45"; translucent (white); by yard. Window fleece, natural 5 layer poly/cotton blend with 2 inner fiber fil and mil film layers (front layer a non-woven fabric). Insul-Trac™ **hardware kits** for shades (track, snap tape, seal edge, glide stops, caps, rod), in variety of widths (24" to 96") and lengths 24" to 120"). Has quantity prices, large order discounts (20% for $100.00+); allows discount to teachers/institutions. In business since 1982.

Handy Hand-Rest: "For your console sewing machine, sew a quilted mat to fit the space where your right hand rests (or left, if you are left-handed). It protects the wood surface and can also serve as temporary pincushion." — Courtesy of Margaret A. Boyd.

Creative Cricket

Stratham, NH 03885

Catalog, $1.00.
Lampshade supplies: for cut and pierced types. Shades — calico, silk, linen. Frames, rings, fabrics, trims, designs. (Also sells wholesale to businesses.)

Creative Critters

4240 Woodland Dr.
Post Falls, ID 83854

Duck decoy kits (9" x 13" finished size): burlap fabric printed, with dark brown ducks and markings, muslin for lining, wood base; instructions.

Creative Makings by Martie

P.O. Box 4445
Glendale, CA 91202

Catalog, $2.50.
Pattern designs (full size): Quilted and Egg-shaped placemats (5 variations) Soft sculpture baskets, hearts, purses, toys, patchwork eggs. Tea cozies, nesting dolls, Christmas accessories (ornaments, trinket bags), patchwork baskets. Fabric adhesives. Others.

Creative Patterns

Box 163
Brea, CA 92621

Catalog, $1.00 (refundable).
Patterns/kits: Home decorating accessories, quilts, Christmas ornaments, dolls, others.

D & M

P.O. Box 382
Pleasant Grove, UT 84062

Send SASE for list.
Patterns: quilted wine holder (for bottle and corkscrew), others.

D & S Mercantile

Box 93
Wantagh, NY 11793

Send SASE for information.
Soft box kit (for jewelry, diaper pins, etc.) 6" x 6" x 4", (with pre-cut fabric, trims; 4 calico colors), others.

D-Carol

P.O. Box 16489
Greensboro, NC 27406

Sample patterns and brochure, $2.00.
Patterns (for calico or felt appliques) — Christmas ornaments, cards, accessories (Dickens characters, old fashioned boy and girl, others); (other needlework kits).

Dorothy Dear Old Fashioned Fabric Designs

P.O. Box 903
Forest Grove, OR 97116

Brochure, $1.00.
Home accessories kits including for Angel pillow (silk-screened/Victorian angel from the artwork of Dorothy Bittleston Smith) for sew and stuff. Others.

Design Source

P.O. Box 168
Marsing, ID 83639
208-896-4811

Send SASE for brochure.
Kits/patterns for felt soft sculpture home accessories: wall dolls (cowboy, cowgirl, ballerina, footbll players over 30" sizes). Rainbow door decor, gumball pajama bag. Holiday items: Mrs. Santa candy holder, Rudolph/Noel banner, Angel advent calendar, "HoHoHo" and "Joy" wall hangings. Books: felt how-tos. Kits/Patterns packed in ziplock bags with color illustration. "Fast and easy," says Nance Kueneman, "using quick-stitch felt technique." Manufacturer, in business since June, 1981. (Also sells wholesale to businesses).

Designs by Shirley

427 Franklin Ave.
Moberly, MO 65270

Brochure, $ .35.
Patterns (full size): Christmas decoratives, placemats, quilts (and baby accessories).

Designs by Tekla

4045 Hwy. 194
Duluth, MN 55811

Instructions, $2.50.
Sew ruffles and lace **lampshade cover** (fits over old shade, removes for laundering).

Designs Etc.

Box 414
Schertz, TX 78154

Send SASE for prices.
Patterns for large flower **pillows** (like real flowers) rose, magnolia, daisy, sunflower, gardenia, pansy, daffodil.

DML Originals

P.O. Box 1033
Cheshire, CT 06410

Idea catalog, $1.00.
"Country" patterns/kits: Puff-patchwork tote, pillow, basket (calico pre-cut square), others.

© *Design Source*

The Fabric Patch
12 Hickory Lane
Algonquin, IL 60102

Free catalog.
Patterns and kits (original designs) for quilt, pillow, totebag.

Flying Fingers
P.O. Box 9197
Richmond Heights, MO 63117

Catalog, $ .75.
Quilting kits (applique, patchwork): rocking chair cushions, pillows, tooth fairy pillow, angel and animal designed quilts, wallhangings; angel braided wreath, (and clothing, personal items).

Frying Pan Patterns
P.O. Box 134
Herndon, VA 22070

See your dealer or write for information.
Needlework designs (country and others) — leaflets; books (Christmas, silhouettes, Unicorns, Kitchen-aids, holiday keepsakes, others).
(Also sells wholesale to businesses.)

The Gandernest
2801 N. 58th St.
Omaha, NE 68104

Send SASE for list.
Quilting patterns including for fan-shaped baskets ("Butterfly Basket") with soft-sculptured butterfly, "Rose Basket"; suitable for May baskets, wall or door decorations.

Gleason Creations
4459 Crestwood Circle
Concord, CA 94521

Brochure, $ .50.
Refrigerator magnet patterns/kits — sets for fabric, fruit, vegetables, with applique and embroidery.

Gracie-Linn Originals
1812 E. Carleton
Adrian, MI 49221

Send SASE for list.
Candlewicking flyswatter kit (fabric, batting and trims, materials, pattern), others.

Grandma's House
R.R. 4, Box 35
Springfield, IL 62707

Send SASE for prices.
Cathedral window pillow kit (for 12" size) with muslin, calico; instructions.

Grandmother's
Box 507
Langhorne, PA 19047

Send SASE for price list.
Patterns: **placemats** (4 basics, for 13 variations) and unusual shapes; **potholders** (5 motifs with 10 variations), Baby bibs.

Green Gables
3606 W. Washington Blvd.
Los Angeles, CA 90018

See your retailer or send SASE for details.
Focal Point™ **Designer patterns** for custom lamps, matching comforters, pillows, table dressings, etc. **Lamp frames** — over 100 styles, electrical parts kits (keyed with lamp patterns).
Manufacturer.

Greenbrier Publishing Co.
Box 546
Dayton, OH 45449

See your dealer or write for brochure.
Patterns for stuffed toys, applique pictures, wall hangings, Christmas skirt, others.

Salvage Selvages: "Whenever possible, those 'fabric decorating' should use the full fabric width and take advantage of the ravel-free selvage edges." — Courtesy of **Gail E. Brown** of Instant Interiors.

© *Yours Truly, Inc.*

Greenhouse Gallery
R.R. 1, Box 6
Alfred, ME 04002
207-324-7903

Brochures, $1.00.
"Colonial Life" Series applique patterns (for hoop-frame hangings) including Home Life (girl with flowers), Farm Life (boy with farm items), Applique patterns — whale, barnyard animals. Stained glass motifs; butterfly, 3 calico cats, folk couple sampler, country schoolhouse patterns. Miniature appliques or **Christmas** ornament patterns (4), tree-top angels patterns. Others.
(Also sells wholesale to businesses.) In business since 1979.

Hare Designs
P.O. Box 414
Naperville, IL 60566
312-420-7321

See your dealer or write for Brochure.
Calico and Spice Ball kits (assorted calicos and 6 spices).

Constance Hazzard
Box 17455
Salt Lake City, UT 84117

Send SASE for list.
Patterns for kitchen accessories: Reversible appliance covers ("mischievous cat" design) — blender, mixer, toaster (3 sizes), can opener.

Hill-Looney, Inc.
Box 1533
Wewoka, OK 74884

See your dealer or write for information.
Edna Looney felt kits for holiday tablecloths, banners, stockings, others.

Home Sewn Company
P.O. Box 206
Novi, MI 48050

Catalog, $1.00 (refundable).
Hoop-framed picture patterns sailing boat, tulips and butterfly, "Crystallum" in vase, "welcome" hanging. Cat doorstop/pillow. In business since 1982.
(Also sells wholesale to businesses.)

Homespun
Box 314
Fairfax Station, VA 22039

Full size patterns: calico doorstops/pillows — Mother Goose in bonnet and scarf; others.

How Clever
206 Indiana
Elmhurst, IL 60126

Catalog, $1.00.
Soft sculpture patterns (full size): tissue box covers, tea cosies, closet hampers (2 sizes), sachets; planter covers —to match decor or special occasions.

Hugg's Handicrafts
120 Main St.
Tuckerton, NJ 08087

Send SASE for brochure.
Calico centerpiece kits: flower arrangements, holiday; others.

In Stitches
Box 1747
Boca Raton, FL 33429

Brochure, $1.00.
Strawberry jam soft fabric jar — instructions and kit.

Instant Interiors
P.O. Box 1793
Eugene, OR 97440

See your dealer or send SASE for catalog sheet.
Booklets: easy-make accessories how-to, including bed covers, furniture covers, fabricing everything, fabric space makers, table toppings, lampshades. Has quantity prices.

Kalico Kastle
45 N. Lone Peak Dr.
Alpine, UT 84003

Brochure, $1.50.
Holiday soft sculpture patterns/kits: Angels, candy cane and basket, wreath, birds, tree skirt. Has Mastercard, Visa. Allows overseas orders for patterns.
(Also sells wholesale to business.)

Kalico Keepsakes
Rt. 2, Box 199
Ottumwa, IA 52501

Catalog, $1.00.
Over 30 applique designs for round and oval **hoop-framed pictures:** patterns and kits (kits include full size pattern, fabric batting, backing, instructions; color choices).

© Mats Etc., Inc.

Karen's Kreations
Box 2024
Heath, OH 43055

Brochure, $ .75.
Soft sculpture "fat cat" (and mouse) doorstop pattern, others.

Kathy's Korner
P.O. Box 222
Kenilworth, IL 60043

Catalog, $1.00.
Soft Sculpture pattern/kits: baskets, wreaths, Easter and Spring items. "Country Garden Seeds" pillows kits/patterns. "Village Square" Quilt/Hanging, others.

Kiddy Guides
P.O. Box 22649
Beachwood, OH 44122
216-991-4771

Send SASE for information.
Kiddy Guide™ patterns including for child's window treatment ensemble pattern (adjusts to any size window curtain/ruffle/ties and shade), with applique guides. Mastercard, Visa.

The Knitting Etc. Corners
Box 494
Canfield, OH 44406

Catalog, $ .50.
Pillow kits: screen printed fabric; assortment of designs, for piecing, quilting, assembling; in choice of colors. (And needlecraft kits.)

Let's Quilt 'N Sew-On
Box 29584
San Antonio, TX 78229

Catalog, $1.00.
Quilting kits/patterns: wall hangings, place mats, pillows, quilts (baby, adults), comforters; tote bags, others. (Also sells wholesale to dealers.)

Linda's Crafts and Gifts
12050 State Rt. 56
Mechanicsburg, OH 43044

Send SASE for list.
"Rooster" country-look tissue box cover (square) kit and pattern.

Lion's Pride Patterns
P.O. Box 194
Maple Plain, MN 55359

Send SASE for details.
Soft sculptured baskets (3 styles), others.

Little Brown House Patterns
P.O. Box 671
Hillsboro, OR 97123

Send SASE for brochure.
Original **"Country" soft sculpture** patterns: hen, ducks, Victorian doves, patchwork pillows, calico cat (and toys). Models — available readymade.
(Also sells wholesale to retailers.)

She Felt You Should Know: "Felt wall hangings can be placed on the wall with straight pins if desired to avoid additional nail holes in wall when hanging decorative items. Also, the blunt end of a bamboo skewer is excellent for stuffing fiberfill into intricate curves of felt designs to ensure filling out all areas of item (stems, leaves, ears, etc.)." — Courtesy of **Nance Kueneman** and **Sue Church** of Design Source — designers, authors of Plaid Enterprises, Inc. booklets.

*Create a family heirloom by duplicating your coat of arms
in your favorite needlework, courtesy Jan Hostage*

Mats, Etc., Inc.
409 N. Hickory, P.O. Box 192
Appleton City, MO 64724

See your local store, or write for color catalog, $1.00.
Prefinished fabric "country" look home accessories, for
hand-decorative sewing (cross stitch, embroidery, candlewicking, stencils, etc.) — for **kitchen, bath, holidays;**
handbags, others. **Trims** — muslin ruffles, cluny lace,
eyelet laces, ruffles in variety of prints, pleated ruffles,
Aida cloth trims and patches with ruffles or bound edges.
Riddler's cloth patches, bound edged or ruffled. Manufacturers, since 1978.
(Also sells wholesale to businesses.)

Mom's Place
1413 Sunset
Richland, WA 99352

Send SASE for brochure.
Soft sculpture decorations patterns: Goose, duck, turkey, chicken, unicorn, others; with instructions. "Quantity discounts."

Moneypenny Enterprises
P.O. Box 7
Morro Bay, CA 93442

Send SASE for list.
Full-size patterns for **sewing machine covers** — "Lady
Melina" doll, with storage pocket, swan (cover or soft-
sculpture), others.

Needle in the Haystack
P.O. Box 834
McMinnville, OR 97128

Send SASE for price list.
Kits: Quilts, hangings, Christmas decoratives (and aprons,
others).

Needleworks
P.O. Box 7052
Pine Bluff, AR 71611

See your dealer or write for information.
Prefinished accessories for needlecrafting/trims, including: Aprons, place mats, baby bibs, oven mitts,
others.

Nook & Cranny
P.O. Box 5178
Tyler, TX 75712

Send SASE for list.
**Patterns including for curved/contoured backrest
pillow** (with ruffle or roll); others.

Orange Delights
1108 Darby
Orange, CA 92665

See your dealer or send $1.00 for catalog.
Patterns/kits: The Hen O' the House and Family™, and
"The Cock O' the Walk" 3-D roosters and chickens
pattern, with wood leg and base kits. Pattern for soft
sculpture chamber pot and bowl (with quilting). Finished
pine ironing board (fold-up, on easy wall mount, wood
with brass hardware) includes pattern for ironing board
cover — or get checkerboard cover, separately.

Osage County Quilt Factory
3632 S.W. 38th
Topeka, KS 66610

See your dealer or send SASE for details.
Quilting/applique patterns for hoop-framed pictures
including: Tulip Basket, Hearts & Doves, May Basket, leaf
designs, "Country" motifs, tulip designs, album quilt,
Christmas designs, others.

Patchs of Joy
8050 S.W. Wareham Cir.
Portland, OR 97223

Send $1.00 for catalog and price list.
Patchwork/applique patterns (full size) for soft sculptures, wall hangings: Victorian and colonial houses/scen-
ics, fabric kites, 45" parrot, giant flowers, cat-tail's and
grass, 29" butterfly, sun shapes, rainbow, moon, stars,
clouds, giant desert cactus, unicorn or pegasus. Sewing
machine cover pattern, and for pillows, racquet cover,
others. Candlewicking kits. Design books. "Knights-
bridge": English inspired coordinated accessories (appli-
que/patchwork) appliance covers, cosy, placemats, seat
cushions, apron, hanging. **Aids:** Olfa cutters, mat; loop
turner, loop setter, thread cutter. (And patchwork
clothing kits/patterns.) Allows discount to teachers/
institutions. Manufacturer, in business since 1976.
(Also sells wholesale to businesses.)

Patchwork 'N Things
P.O. Box 3725
Granada Hills, CA 91344

See your dealer or write for brochure.
Kits/patterns: Pillows, totes, quilts, Christmas items, toys.

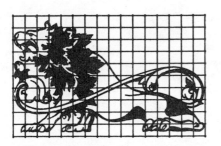

The Pattern Factory
823 Main, Suite 1B
Sumner, WA 98390

See your dealer or write for catalog, $1.50 ($2.00 in '85).
Quilting patterns, "Country" designs (full size) including for: Basket Cats, soft sculpture wall "rocking animals", holiday items, stained glass tulips, country critters — pillows and hoops, totes, "House Welcome" and "Skinny Pockets" banners, other banners, hoop-pictures, quilts, others. **Fabric patches** — silk-screened patterns on poly/cotton fabric, over 50 "country designs" — animals, holiday, children's, "sunbonnet" kids, others; and in small sizes for ornaments. **Unfinished wood racks** for magazines, etc., for fabric covers — with instructions (can utilize screened patches or patchwork, etc.). Silk screen sampler design book. Allows foreign orders. Has educator discount for teachers and guilds.
(Also sells wholesale to distributors and retailers — free catalog.)

Patterns
Box 923
Buffalo, NY 14240

Send SASE for list.
Patterns — kitchen accessories — fruit or vegetable motifs. Also toys patterns.

Patterns by Barbara
P.O. Box 502
Chama, NM 87520

Send SASE for list.
Accessories patterns for "Calico Hen" Kleenex box cover, napkin holder; calico wreath thread/scissors holder; others.

Pernicketies
P.O. Box 291
Black Diamond, WA 98010

Send SASE for list.
Bowl cozies patterns (for 2 styles/sizes); others.

Piecemaker Pattern Co.
2405 Butternut Circle
Salt Lake City, UT 84117

Send SASE for list.
Accessories patterns including for sofa sewing caddy (in calico and quilted fabrics) with pockets, pin cushion, and strawberry for needles.

PJ (Very) Limited
934 Meadow Crest Rd.
La Grange Park, IL 60525

Send SASE for details.
Fabric box kits including "Flop Box" (flat when opened) for secured scissors, threads, etc.; with tips/instruction book.

Plain & Fancy
P.O. Box 145
Lorain, OH 44052

Catalog and swatches, $2.00.
Amish quilting patterns including for hoop-framed pictures or pillows in four seasons motifs. **Amish colored fabric** (14 ½-yd. pieces) for Amish motif pattern. "Calico carry all" three-pocketed tote bag kit — strip piecing, finished to 6" x 13" x 16".
(Also sells wholesale to businesses.)

Platypus
Box 396, Planatarium Station
New York, NY 10024
212-874-0753

Catalog, $1.00.
Pillow kits: Four white work "Learning Projects" kits with quilting method of trapunto, other techniques, with handbook, materials, full size patterns, illustrated procedures, through to making an envelope pillow cover, and stretch and framing stitchery. And full line of cloth dolls/animals patterns. In business since 1970.

A Stuffing Alternative: "Can't get your patterns back in the envelope? Hang them over a hanger instead! I use the same "basic" patterns repeatedly. My favorite patterns are on a hanger waiting for me. A real time saver!" — Courtesy of **Marilyn Bardsley,** Certified Sew/Fit Counselor, Sewing Magic.

The Puddleduck
4403 Karls Gate Dr.
Marietta, GA 30067
404-977-2230

Brochure, $1.00 ($1.25 in '85)
Patterns/kits for soft sculpture/applique/quilting
(including with alphabet, for personalizing): "Sunny Day Cloud", and train hangings; crib quilt/hanging of "Miss Puddleduck" with balloon, "The Tugboat", crayons, ice cream cones, Christmas quilted table runner and placemats (patchwork), Advent Christmas tree hanging. Others.
(Also sells patterns wholesale to distributors and retailers.)

Rachel's Patterns
P.O. Box 495
Hermitage, TN 37076

Instructions for country ruffled pillows, $2.00.

Rainbo Patterns
Box 500
Minocqua, WI 54548

Send SASE for list.
Holiday folk banners patterns (full size, 2' x 3' — washable, storable): Christmas wreath, Easter bunny, Halloween, Thanksgiving turkey, others.

Rainbow Designs
2374 North 850 West
Provo, UT 84604

Send SASE for details.
Bed linen patterns: Fitted waterbed sheets and pillowcases; king, queen and standard, 4 styles.

Raspberry Hill Patchworks
2277 Edgewood Dr.
Grafton, WI 53024
414-377-9116

See your dealer or write for information.
Patterns — "Water Fowl Collection": Canada goose, common loon; mini-goose, mallard, mute swan.

Renie's Touch
P.O. Box 4944
Spokane, WA 99202

Send large SASE and $1.00 for brochure.
Bathroom accessories patterns: Ribbons/lace string quilt toilet seat cover, Kleenex box cover, spare tissue holder; others.

RI Kreations
P.O. Box 181
Baldwinsville, NY 13027

Send SASE for prices.
"Puffy Personals" kits — 9" letters to spell name, etc. for stitch and stuff (with Velcro fasteners and hanging rings) in multicolors or baby pastels.

Rooster Products
1765 Chestnut St.
San Francisco, CA 94123

Send SASE for details.
Soft sculpture children's wall decorations kits: Animals including dressed bear, rabbit, others.
(Also sells wholesale to businesses.)

Rumpfie Creations
R.D. 1, Box 477
Goshen, NY 10924

Catalog, $1.00.
Patterns/kits: Mobiles and wallhangings, including satin "Clown Hanging from Balloons", others.

Salmagundi Farms
P.O. Box 789
Coupeville, WA 98239
206-678-5888

Write for catalog.
Lampshade frames and kits: Over 55 styles, new classic, Tiffany styles, others. Wiring kits, patterns.

The Scrap Sack
Rt. 5, Box 90
Warsaw, IN 46580

Brochure, $1.00.
Soft sculpture kits/patterns: "I'm Puffin" cat doorstop, "Pig-in-A-Poke" tote bag; others.

Sew Sweet Creations, Belwood Center
4515 Alamo
Simi Valley, CA 93063

Catalog and fabric samples, $1.50.
Soft sculpture basket kit: (9" diameter; print fabrics in 6 colors). "Calico Miss" magnet/sew kit. Others.

The Sewing Centipede
P.O. Box 218
Midway City, CA 92655

Brochure, $ .50.
Pattern/kits: "Mouse" design kitchen broom cover. Sculptured macaw, toucan. Quilts.

Fozie Bear™, © Vogue Patterns

"Holiday Charmers on Parade", © Butterick Patterns

Shades of Olde
P.O. Box 4075
Boulder, CO 80306

Free brochure.
Lampshade kits (sewn) for variety of fabrics, 10 shapes. Holds sales, allows wholesale to teachers/institutions. (Also sells wholesale to businesses.)

Shape Up
16372 W. Lee Lane
Prairie View, IL 60069

Catalog, $1.00.
Fabric frames patterns: shaped in animals, and whimsical characters.

Simplicity Pattern Co.
200 Madison Ave.
New York, NY 10016

See your dealer or write for information.
Patterns: pillows, desk/dresser items, machine cover, draperies, nursery items, Marjorie Puckett designs (boxes, trays, baskets, others). Christmas accessories.

The Special Touch
7034 Pembridge
San Diego, CA 92139

Instructions, $2.00.
Toilet seat and tank lid cover set.

Sugarplums
113 Kensington
Lafayette, LA 70508

Send SASE for price list.
Patterns/kits: hoop-frame "Fat Cat" picture, others.

Sweet Dreams Designs
P.O. Box 14777
Chicago, IL 60614

Brochure, $1.00.
Original soft sculpture patterns including for "Rainbow Sunshine Balloon" — 10" with sun, hearts, and rainbow design; others.

That Patchwork Place, Inc.
P.O. Box 118
Bothell, WA 98011

See your dealer or send $1.25 for catalog ($1.50 in '85).
"Country collection" patterns: soft sculpture, banner, calico decorator, ironing board cover, pillows, bedding, others, books.
(Also sells wholesale to distributors, retailers.)

Sewing Aid, You-Make: "Wooden dowels covered with a tube made from quilted fabric make wonderful **pressing hams** for small projects such as doll clothes, and stuffed animals; as well as for tight places on larger items. Make a set from ¾", 1", and 1½" dowels. Cut fabric to fit around the dowel + ½" (to allow for ¼" seams). Sew, turn right side out, and insert dowel. Close ends." — Courtesy of **Andrea W. Warner** of Andee's Arti-Facts.

Bettie Tolley
P.O. Box 869
Acton, MA 01720

Send SASE for brochure.
Kits: bun warmer, others; in "calico country" style.

Tomorrow's Treasures
P.O. Box 1982
Placentia, CA 92670

Catalog, $1.00.
Soft sculpture holiday decoratives patterns: calico deer ornaments, dressed Teddy bears, 3" felt bears, others; cat family, 12" calico rocking horse, others. (Also sells wholesale to businesses.)

Vogue — Butterick Pattern Service
P.O. Box 549
Altoona, PA 16603

See your dealer or send SASE for information.
Patterns for home accessories: kitchen and picnic linens, Easter items, kitchen accessories, Christmas decoratives and ornaments, others. (Also dolls, full line of fashion garments and personal accessories.)

Warm Window
P.O. Box 27136
Seattle, WA 98125

See your dealer or write for prices.
"Warm Window" insulated **shade material** for make-it-yourself (or custom made).

Windle
P.O. Box 3091
Margate City, NJ 08402

Send SASE for brochure.
Full size pattern: mallard duck (8" size), instructions; others.

Window Wear
P.O. Box 70243
Eugene, OR 97401

Instructions book on making roman shades, $2.50.

You and Me Patterns, Inc.
Rt. 1, Box 179
Owatonna, MN 55060

Send SASE for list.
Patterns for liners for wood slat bushel baskets.

Young Ideas
#7 Travelers Way
St. Charles, MO 63301

Send SASE for details.
Patterns/kits for covered dish carrier; (for dinners, pies, etc.).

10
Furniture & Upholstery

(And see the index for specific items elsewhere in the book.)

Barap Specialties
835 Bellows Ave.
Frankfort, MI 49635

Catalog, $1.00.
Upholstery: Equipment, tools (cutters, clamps, others), repair kit, grommet kit, calipers. **Furniture patterns,** seat weaving materials.

Brown Sales Corp.
Box 4384
Madison, WI 53711

Send SASE with inquiry.
Polystyrene pellets (by bag) for bean bag chairs.

By Vea Prints
729 Heinz Ave. #2,
Berkeley, CA 94710

See your dealer or send SASE with inquiry.
Hand-printed fabric: "Magic Meadow" design, 29" square, for futon (Japanese folding bed), floor pillows, or hangings.

C. T. Textiles
340 E. 57th St.
New York, NY 10022

Send $1.00 and SASE with inquiry and color choice.
Upholstery leathers — smooth grain and suede skins —by square foot.

Calico Corners
210 105th Ave., N.E.
Bellvue, WA 98004

Send SASE for price details.
Book: *The Calico Corners' Guide to Upholstered Walls,* (how to panel-upholster with fabric).

Fan's Furnishings
P.O. Box 58503
Louisville, KY 40258

Send SASE for details.
Instructions for furnituremaking using foam shapes (for lounge chair, sofa, bed; for home, van, camper, boat, cabin).

Freeman and Co.
416 Julian Ave.
Thomasville, NC 27360

See your dealer or send SASE for information.
Furniture for needle arts (mahogany 18th century reproductions of Chippendale, Hepplewhite periods) wood furniture fabric upholstered for needlework.

The Futon Co.
412 W. Franklin
Chapel Hill, NC 27514

Send SASE for prices.
Cotton futons, folds into couch; for you-cover (or ready-made covers).

Futon Mattress Co.
37 Wooster St.
New York, NY 10013

Brochure, $2.00.
Futons, bed frames (and furniture, screens and readymades).

Jack's Upholstery & Caning Supplies
Oswego, IL 60543

Catalog, $1.25 (refundable).
Upholstery: Button molds, machine. Nails, needles, .springs, tacks, threads, staple gun, air compresser, hammers, pliers, gimp, welt, blues, twines, webbing. Fasteners. Fabrics (mock cambric, cotton, dacron, denim, canvas. Foams. Caning supplies. Tools, books. Has quantity prices.

Jim Dandy Sales

Box 30377
Cincinnati, OH 45230

Free catalog.
Upholstery supplies: webbing, twines (button, mattress, spring; cotton, jute, paper), cane webbing, cane. Fabrics: burlap, canvas, muslin, denim, heavy cottons — by yards, roll. Pool table material; velvets, brocades, vinyls and patterned vinyls, others. Tools/aids: stretchers, hammers, wire and barbed webbing, tacks, mallets, heavy needles; spring repair kit. Casters, furniture legs, stools. Zippers, nails. Books. Has some quantity prices, Mastercard, Visa.

Leisure Seats

P.O. Box 917
Marietta, GA 30065

Send SASE for details.
Pattern for **folding sling rocker** (of canvas, denim, or macrame).

Ltd. Additions

P.O. Box 1340
Rohnert Park, CA 94928

Send SASE for price list.
Sofa sleeper patterns — "seamstress quality" (for sofa, folds-out-to-bed style) in twin, double/full, queen. "Can be made in less than five hours with basic sewing know how."

Marson Patterns

P.O. Box 31
Union Lake, MI 48085

Send SASE for list.
Patterns: bean bag chairs — 180" circumference model, clown chair (108").

Peach Blossom Futon

3273 Ibis
San Diego, CA 92103

Send SASE for list.
Cotton filled futons (traditional Japanese sleeping mattresses) in adult sizes, children's sizes (for you-cover). (Also has readymade futon covers, comforters).

Poppy Fabric

2072 Addison St.
Berkeley, CA 94704

Send SASE for price data.
"Shiki Buton" pattern (Japanese bed) — three designs/ sizes with diagrams, directions; for mat, case, pillow/seat, comforter.

Quilted Safari

3029 Deodar St.
Costa Mesa, CA 92626

Send SASE for list.
"Safari bag" **sleeping bags patterns** (for sewing machine quilting): shark, hippo, lion, walrus, elephant.

Sew Much Fun

560 Carlson Dr.
Lebanon, OR 97355

Send SASE for complete list.
Patterns including for soft-stuffed "sleep 'n go" baby bed with matching "Teddy Bear" appliqued quilt and pillow; others.

Sew 'N Stuff

2855 E. Appalachian Ct.
Westlake Village, CA 91362

Brochure, $ .75.
Sewing patterns and kits including Drowsy Droid™ "sleepover bag", others.

Shaker Workshops

Box 1028
Concord, MA 01742

Catalog and samples, $ .50.
Canvas (100% cotton) chair webbing tape in 12 traditional Shaker colors (with weaving instructions).

Tandy Leather Co.

Box 2934
Ft. Worth, TX 76113

Free catalog.
Upholstery weight leathers (and other leathers) sewing hand tools, punches, accessories, dyes, others.

Tioga Mill Outlet

200 S. Hartman St.
York, PA 17403

Fabric swatches, $1.00 — specific color scheme, yardage requirements.
Upholstery fabric — variety of colors, patterns.

Upholstery Aids

Box 313
Old Bethpage, NY 11804

Catalog/manual, $2.00.
Reupholstery supplies, tools.

11
Dolls, Toys & Miniatures

Companies in this section offer (A) kits and patterns of "little folks" and their clothing, of other toys; and (B) for dollhouse (scaled miniatures) items. (And see FABRICS, TRIMS, and the index for specific items.)

A. DOLLS/TOYS

Adam & Eve's Fig Leaf
18906 Beach Blvd.
Huntington Beach, CA 92648

Send SASE for prices. Furry animal patterns.
Cat, racoon, panda, mouse, giraffe, dogs, frog, rhino, hippo, turtle, elephant, snail, skunk, squirrel, pig.
Accessories kits: Eyes, nose, fur.

All Dolled Up
P.O. Box 81
Kings Park, NY 11754

Send SASE for list.
Doll clothing patterns (3 sizes) easy-sew, others.

Amity Publications
78688 Sears Rd.
College Grove, OR 97424
503-942-7501

Send SASE for catalog.
Patterns for Amish dolls: 21" doll with hat, dress, apron and pants: with quilt; 21" Amish boy with felt hat and clothing; with puppy. (Also has Amish design patterns for quilts, hangings.)
(And sells wholesale to businesses, professionals, teachers/institutions.)

Andee's Arti-Facts
1641 North Mary Dr.
Santa Marica, CA 93454

Send $1.00 and SASE for brochure and preview list.
Doll patterns with part dough or oven-clay bodies (heads, etc.) rest stuffed: 14" Clutter Fairy, 6" Littlest Angel on Cloud, 15" clown, 14" boy with black eye, 20" girl (yarn hair), 14" mermaid, 15" girl and boy jointed dolls, inset eyes dolls (20" girl, 42" "Babysitter", 15" girl Genie, 18" Purple People Eater creature). "Cottage carrying case and 6' rag doll (girl or boy). Quilted hangings "quotes" patterns. Pillow patterns. May have sales. In business since July 1981.
Owner Andrea Warner is working on new "Grumbles" fantasy creatures patterns. (Also publishes a newsletter.) (Also sells wholesale to businesses.)

Animal Crackers
P.O. Box 7455
Tacoma, WA 98407

Free brochure.
Stuffed animal patterns (full size): Parrot, fish, crocodile, others. (Also has child's tie chair securer pattern.)

Art Etc. Studio
Rt. 1, Box 266B
Wimberly, TX 78676

Send $ .25 and long SASE for brochure.
Doll patterns: Boy and girl infants, boy and girl toddlers (19") on hot-iron transfers. **Supplies:** Dolskin™ doll body fabric (100% cotton, hand dyed muslin of "skin color"), long stuffing needles (3½" and 5").
(Also sells wholesale to dealers).

Needling Fiberfill: "Use a long, strong yarn darner needle to help rearrange fiberfill to get the look you want for your doll." — Courtesy of **Sandra Price**, designer, of San Lou.

"YOU CAN'T COME IN."

Atlanta Puffections

P.O. Box 13524
Atlanta, GA 30324

Catalog, $1.00 (refundable).
Puffs™ soft patterns/kits (patterns full size) from assorted fabrics; 8" boy, girl, twins; 9" bride, groom, attendants (faces made from polyester doubleknit). Astronaut Puffs™ 7" boy and girl (with silver metallic costumes). Others.

Aunt Sharon's Creations

P.O. Box 8581
Fountain Valley, CA 92708

Brochure, $ .50.
"Shelf People" doll patterns: soldier, elf, angel, reindeer, cowboy; full-sized.

Baja Ma Originals

1344 Mountevideo St.
Placeutia, CA 92670

Send SASE for list.
"Fantasyland" soft sculpture pattern/kits: 16" unicorn, winged Pegasus (with feather boa), pony, dragon; mermaid, Indian girl, Cleopatra, others.

Barrett International

726 State Ave.
Holly Hill, FL 32017

Send SASE for list.
"Huggy" snap-together doll kits — 10" bunnies or bears (calico and solid print fabrics); others.

Mary Bastian

RFD #1,
Claremont, NH 03743

Send SASE for list.
Doll patterns including for alien doll — "huggable size", others.

Berene

P.O. Box 10697
Golden, CO 80401

Brochure, send SASE.
Noisemakers for dolls/toys (etc.): squeekers, Mama criers, animal voices, musical movements, eyes, noses, others. Patterns for toys.

Big Mouth Puppets

P.O. Box 1593
Beaverton, OR 97075

Send SASE for list.
Big mouth puppet kits/patterns (with pre-cut craft fur): 36" frog, monster, others; in 20 colors. (Also has readymade puppets.) Has quantity prices (inquire).

BJC Artistic Enterprises

279 E. Grant St., P.O. Box 608
Lebanon, OR 97355

Catalog, $1.25.
Original rag doll patterns (over 50) including for jointed dolls, large sized, double-doll, others. Book: *Romance With A Rag Doll* by Barbara Carroll; (How-to, includes 3 full-sized patterns).

Black Forest Originals

Box 2358
Palm Desert, CA 92261

Send SASE for details.
"Kitchen Witch" soft sculptures doll kit (with fur wig, wire, supplies).

Dovie Blankenship

4708 W. 26th Ave.
Gary, IN 46406

Send SASE for details.
Sock doll patterns: 17" doll — boy, girl (from cotton work socks).

Bluegrass Babies
596 Cherokee Rd.
Raceland, KY 41169

Catalog, $1.00.
Cloth doll patterns (full size) — reproductions of famous characters, movie stars, antique dolls, singers, actors, others (including Snoopy, Donnie and Marie, Elvis, Batman, Superman).

Bodie's
808 3rd Ave.
Sheldon, IA 51201

Brochure, $ .50 and SASE.
Cloth doll patterns — original designs for 20" size soft-sculptures (fingers, toes, eyes) joint moveable arms and legs.

Eileen Bonifaci
2339 Roslyn Ave.
Duluth, MN 55803

Information and sample adjustable doll clothes pattern, $2.00 and SASE.
Doll skirt pleater (9" x 12") for ¼", ½" or larger pleats.

D. A. Brinkman
154 Gordon Dr.
Spartanburg, SC 29301

See your dealer or write for prices.
Soft animal patterns (5" — 15") pigs, ducks, cats, cows.

Buckwheats
P.O. Box 336
Riderwood, MD 21139
301-823-3058

Brochure, $1.00.
Original soft sculpture patterns/kits: "Fine Feather Friends" 15" swan, 10" mallard duck; 14" mouse family, mini-creatures (mouse, cat, rabbit), 24" rabbit, doorstop cat. Christmas: cane, 17" elf, 26" Santa, 16" free-standing angel, and skating reindeer. Moosehead with antler spread of 32", 20" carrot. Allows 10% discount to teachers/institutions.
(Also sells wholesale to businesses.)

Butterick Fashion Marketing Corp.
161 Sixth Ave.
New York, NY 10013

See your dealer or write for information.
Doll/animal patterns: Noah's ark and animals hanging; dolls (clown, baby, others), teaching toys, clothes. "Teddy Chair" sit-upon; chess/checker and backgammon board. Growth tree. Others.

Button Enterprises
143 Madison
Ogden, UT 84404
801-394-9153

Send SASE for list; or sample set, $2.00.
Doll clothing patterns (for 11½" teens): sets for girls (blouse, skirt, dress, slip, nightgown, robe), boy (suit-pants and coat, shirt, pajamas, bathrobe). In business since 1976.

By Diane
1126 Ivon Rd.
Endicott, NY 13760
607-754-0391

Catalog (update flyers), $1.25; fur sample charts, $2.00.
"Fuzzy Friends" toy patterns/kits: sea creatures, hippo, elephant, rhino, lion, giraffe, kangaroo, panda, raccoon. Beaver, otter, mink, badger, skunk, frog, dog, cat, cow, duckling, parrot, deer, poodle, camel. **Teddy bears kits/patterns:** jointed (12", 20", 28" tubby, 24" jointed cub); 29" walking bear. **Arm puppets patterns/kits:** Teddy, rabbit, fox. **Hand puppet kits/patterns:** Teddy, koala, pup, mink, raccoon, panda. Holds promotions periodically.
(Also sells wholesale to businesses.)

Caldwell's
3853 Goodnight Ave.
Pueblo, CO 81005

Catalog, $1.00 (refundable).
Doll parts: hands, feet, masks, eyes, others. **Animal:** eyes, noses, masks. (and other embroidery and needle-work supplies.)

Calico and Straw
P.O. Box 469
Carver, MA 02330

See your store or write for free brochure.
Reversible doll patterns (full size) for 20" cloth doll and wardrobe (for happy, sad, and sleepy faces; with yarn hairdoos). Doll accessories patterns (for 20" doll) — bib, diaper, tote bag, quilt; heart appliques.
(Also sells wholesale to businesses and teachers/institutions — write for details.)

Dolls in the Flesh: "Colored broadcloth and knits are basic necessities for cloth dolls — in 'flesh colors'. This means the palest peach, created from a mix of pink, yellow and white; and a range of tans and browns, rather than pastel pinks that make cloth dolls look garish and phoney." — Courtesy of **Colette Wolff** of Platypus.

Calico Junction
P.O. Box 232
Chino, CA 91710

Brochure, $ .50 and SASE.
Patterns (full sized) for 23" "huggable" bear, jointed, with bib; others. Allows foreign orders.

Camille's Designs
517 S. Milwaukee St.
Theresa, WI 53091

Send large SASE for brochure.
Stuffed doll patterns and kits — 14" clown, 18" baby doll; cradle; body fabrics (by yard).

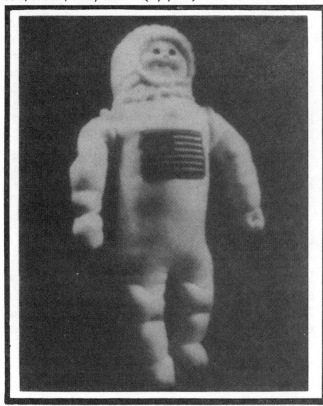

© A. Cannon Originals

A. Cannon Originals
P.O. Box 8195
Columbus, GA 31908
404-563-1625

Send SASE for list.
Original soft-sculpture doll patterns: simple sculpture Space Alien (6" to 36" size), 20" astronaut, 18" elf. Others include: 26" Captain, 26" Captain's mate, 26" girl, "Miss Priss" dolls, 22" baby first year, 15" premature baby (wears newborn clothes), 12" bunny, 24" "Killer Shark". In business since 1982.
(Also sells wholesale to distributors and retailers.)

© A. Cannon Originals

Cape Cod, Ltd.
Box 391
Teaticket, MA 02536

Full color catalog, $2.50.
Baby doll (soft porcelain-like plastic, with glass-like eyes), 12½" with **full christening outfit pattern.** (Has other doll parts, accessories, how-to books.)

Caravan Crafts
P.O. Box 6641
Omaha, NE 68106

Send SASE for list.
Stuffed toy kits/patterns nice for 6" bean bag clown, others.

Carlisle Creations
9059 Sugar Tree Trail
Huntsville, AL 35802

Send SASE for price list.
Toy patterns including "Country Mouse" (3¾") dressed, others.

Carlson
Rt. 1, Box 75
Deary, ID 83823

Send SASE and $ .50 for brochure.
Doll and toy patterns including "Sweetie Pie" 18" doll posed as crawling baby; others.

Carolee Creations
787 Industrial Dr.
Elmhurst, IL 60126

Catalog, $1.00.
Sew Sweet Dolls™ patterns/kits: 43" Emily, Alexander; 16½" to 18½" girls, 18" bride, others. Fleece **body fabric** (60", by yard).
Has toll free number for orders, Mastercard, Visa.

Carousel Crafts Co.
P.O. Box 42549
Houston, TX 77042

See your retailer or write for information.
Doll kits: baby, kitchen angel, man and woman dolls, others; clothes. Teddy bear with travel tote. Crib mobile, grow chart, others.

Carriage House Antiques
2 Lincoln Way West
New Oxford, PA 17350

Brochure, $1.00 and long SASE (refundable).
Doll clothes supplies: buttons, 18 laces, snaps, hair yarns. **Fabrics:** body broadcloth, ginghams, moire taffetas, satins, imported fine fabrics. May have sales. Allows foreign orders.

Cathy's Creations
190 Overpeck Ave.
Ridgefield Park, NJ 07660

Catalog, $1.00.
Stuffed critter jump-ropes kits and patterns. Other cloth dolls, toys; "wholesale prices".

Charing Cross Kits
Main St., P.O. Box 79855
Meridith, NH 03253
603-279-8449

Catalog, $1.00 ('83 — '84); $2.00 ('85).
"Clothkits" rag doll kits — 17" boy and girl dolls with "folk-country" look (hair and features printed on 100% cotton fabric), kit with polyester filling, in pink or brown skin; with clothes. Separate wardrobe kits, bedding kits (pillow, blanket, sheet); clothing fits most slim 16" dolls. (And full line of women's and children's clothing kits in "folk-country" style.)

Charles Marie's
5721 Andrews Hwy.
Odessa, TX 79762

Send SASE for brochure.
Cloth doll patterns: 15" elf, 24" boy and girl, 30" cloth; Santa dolls; others.

Cher's Crafts and Things
P.O. Box 34752
Omaha, NE 68134

Send SASE for prices.
"Strawberry" clothes patterns — for 5½" Berry Folks (nine-piece wardrobe), instructions.

Cincinnati Craft
P.O. Box 207
Circleville, OH 43113

Catalog, $1.00.
Doll parts: faces, heads, accessories. (Other arts/crafts supplies.) Has Mastercard, Visa.

Cindy's Pantry
22982 La Cadena Dr.
Laguna Hills, CA 92653

Free 32 page catalog.
Patterns for doll and clothes (and quilts).

Colleen's Cottage
P.O. Box 1089
Mt. Shasta, CA 96067

Catalog, $1.25 and large SASE.
Ethnic cloth doll patterns (for 11" to 20" basic cloth doll, with face instructions according to nationality specified), and ethnic costumes — all nationalities; each costume pattern with face/hair style for the outfit. Allows foreign orders. May have special prices. (Also publishes *The Cloth Doll* magazine.)

Colonial House of Dolls
300 S. York St.
Mechanicsburg, PA 17055

Catalog, $2.00.
"Dolly Dustless" protective doll covers (clear, flexible, dome shaped vinyl for 8" to 24" dolls). **Doll stands** for 3½" to 42" dolls. Other supplies. Has quantity prices. Mastercard, Visa.

Conchocrafts
2989 CT
Sanangelo, TX 76902

Send 3 stamps for catalogs.
Doll patterns: nineteenth century doll bodies (with instructions). Books. (Other needlecraft supplies.)

Sewing on Doll Features: "Make sure you let eyes dry thoroughly before attaching hair. After doll is completed, spray with Scotch-gard™." — Courtesy of **Sandra Price,** of San Lou.

Conni Su Originals

P.O. Box 365
Montrose, CA 91020

See your dealer or write for information.
Soft sculpture animal patterns for 22" goose, 10" duck.

Connie's Designs

P.O. Box 3557
St. Paul, MN 55165

Send SASE for prices.
Soft toy animals kits (life-like, use "Stac-Rame" technique): owls, squirrels, raccoon. Has Visa, Mastercard.

Cosi Cottage and Co.

326 N. National Ave.
Fond du Lac, WI 54935

Send SASE for list.
Maugelsous "Sew 'N Love Living Dolls" kits. **Supplies:** fabrics, pillon, batting and stuffing, Velcro, notions.

Country Handicrafts

P.O. Box 572
Milwaukee, WI 53201

Send SASE for list.
Doll patterns (full size) including 11" Norweigian ice skating doll (by Loretta Daum Byrne), others.

Country Maid Gifts

Bowles Rd.
Stafford Springs, CT 06076

Brochure, $2.00.
Patterns for stuffed dolls and animals (and quilts; also for crewel).

CR's Crafts

Box 8
Leland, IA 50453

Catalog, $1.00.
Plush "fur" kits/patterns: animals (Teddy bears, monkey, others), wrap-around puppets, dolls (with plastic heads/hands). **Supplies:** Fur fiberfill, fabrics, flesh cotton body fabric, ribbons. Animal parts, music boxes. Doll parts. Has quantity prices.

Cradle Creations

P.O. Box 441
Stone Mt., GA 30086

Send SASE for prices.
Soft sculpture baby dolls patterns — 10" boys, girls with 7 hairstyles, garment patterns.

The Craft Crib

P.O. Box 44
Morris, IL 60450

Send SASE for brochure.
Soft toy puppy kit, puppy and accessories kit; patterns.

The Craft Source

P.O. Box 836
Mokena, IL 60448

Catalog, $1.00.
Doll parts: heads, faces, others.

The Craft Tree

Hall Rd.
Barrington, NH 03825

Catalog, $1.50 (refundable).
Doll kits: Mr. and Mrs. Santa, Mr. and Mrs. Black America. Doll parts: heads, faces, heads/arms sets, bodies, torsos. Animal eyes: rabbit, cat, frog, bear, dog. Stuffed **animal kits:** koalas, lamb, sheep, monkey. **Supplies:** craft fur, squeakers, hats.

Cranberry Creek

P.O. Box 12434
Overland Park, KS 66212
913-381-5931

See your dealer or write for brochure.
"The Brampton Bear", classic **teddy bear kit** (fur, with leather paws) and patterns.

Creative Playmates

1430 Billings
Houston, TX 77055

Write for details.
Toy "entertainment center" playmates (appliqued) kits and patterns — "Country Town", "Frontier Days", train, others.

Cricket Factory

Box 213
Apple Valley, CA 92307

Catalog, $ .50.
Doll patterns: 13" baby (easy sew), others.

Critters

246 Orchard Ave.
Somerdale, NJ 08083

Catalog, $2.00.
Patterns/kits: stuffed animals, sports equipment, kites, rainbows, others.

Curious Characters
2609 So. Blauvelt
Sioux Falls, SD 57105

Send SASE for prices.
Soft sculpture baby doll/puppet patterns (full size): 10" Emily, also serves as "body pillow".

Daisymae Dolls
P.O. Box 1135
Orem, UT 84057

Send SASE for prices.
Soft doll patterns (16" to 20" sizes): girl and boy "country" dolls, baby dolls; (also baby clothing patterns).

Dare
8122 Meadow Lane
Munster, IN 46321

Send SASE for information.
Patterns including for **antique bunny doll** with overalls, others.

The Decorated Chair
P.O. Box 18
Pickerington, OH 43147

Brochures, $1.00.
Soft sculpture patterns: country folk art dolls and Pickerington Village house — doubles as purse, others.

Dena's Dolls
1774 Antero Dr.
Longmont, CO 80501

Catalog, $1.00.
Cloth doll patterns (full sized) for 16" and 22" girls, with dresses, clown, doll in football uniform (with helmet); others. Has quantity prices.

Designs by Kimberly Dee
P.O. Box 2837
Mission Viejo, CA 92690

Catalog, $1.00.
Cloth doll patterns (full size) for "Jillybean", and other boys and girls, 13" to 16" sizes, with clothing patterns.

Diann's Originals
P.O. Box 694
Park Ridge, IL 60068

Brochure, $1.00.
Original cloth doll kits (with handpainted faces) 20" girl, clothing patterns.

Dillon's Dolls
P.O. Box 2478
Newport News, VA 23602

Brochure, $1.00.
Cloth doll patterns: Grandma and grandpa, baby and brother, Mrs. Santa, others; 15" doorstop mouse. Pattern books for Christmas, country, Christmas ornaments.

Apt Applique — Machine Style: "Top quality thread is an important ingredient in frustration free machine appliquing. It helps eliminate thread breakage, skipped stitches, and a dull, uneven appearance. It is a necessity for a satin smooth finish!" — Courtesy of **Ann Keitkamp** of Americana Applique, professional seamstress/designer.

Dinosaur
11706 Orebaugh Ave.
Wheaton, MD 20902

Free brochure.
Cloth dinosaur book kit: pages with stuffed dinosaurs and surprises (baby dinosaurs); screen printed fabric, supplies, accessories.

Dixie's Love and Stuff
2328 Vernor
Lapeer, MI 48446

Brochure, $1.00 and large SASE.
Animal patterns: 20" Bambi, 12" horse, 15" cat; dolls and other animals.

Doll & Craft World, Inc.
125 8th St.
Brooklyn, NY 11215

Catalog, $3.00.
Doll supplies: body patterns, clothes patterns for known dolls. Doll parts. Teddy bear parts, growler voice boxes. Full line of doll shoes, socks. Mama voices. Kid leather. Notions, wigs materials. Extensive books. Has some quantity prices; Mastercard, Visa.

The Doll Lady
Box 121, Homecrest Station
Brooklyn, NY 11229

Catalog and information on discount doll club, $2.00.
Antique reproduction doll kits (with glass-like eyes, molded teeth, dimples, hands, legs; soft body) for boy and girl baby.

The Doll Nook
356 S. Franklin
Seaside, OR 97138

Catalog, $1.00.
Cloth doll patterns: 16" girl, other original designs.

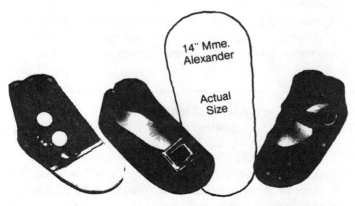

14" Mme. Alexander

Actual Size

© *Doll & Craft World, Inc.*

Dollcraft
245-200 Rivercrest Dr., S.E.
Calgary, Alberta T2C 2X5 Canada

Send SASE for list.
"Candy Family" doll patterns (full size) — 18" girls with yarn hair and clothes. Has quantity specials.

Dolls
P.O. Box 433
Spruce Pine, NC 28777

Send SASE for details.
Soft sculpture doll patterns — 26" size, wears size 3-6 months baby clothes.

Dolls and Things
2902 Rollins
Melbourne, FL 32901

Catalog, $1.00.
Doll patterns: 17" ET, 19" "Annie", pantyhose baby, hot-air balloon mobile, others.

Bonnie Donaldson
9325 Saric Dr.
Highland, IN 46322

Send SASE for list.
Doll type puppet patterns (with moveable mouths) "Baby Bubbles", Gustav Gnome, wrap-around koala, others.

Dorsey Publishing
Box 30084
Corpus Christe, TX 78404

Send SASE for list.
Carole Anderson's **celebrity/characters patterns:** Miss Piggy, Kermit, Bert, Ernie, Cookie Monster, Snoopy, others.

Dragon Lady Designs
219 1st Ave. No.
Seattle, WA 98109

Send SASE for list.
Toy patterns (full sized) including for "magical Dragon" in 21" tall sitting version, 31" long flying version with wing span of 33".

Du Hickies
139 Winthrop St.
Medway, MA 02053

Samples and prices, $1.00.
Pattern sets: stuffed toys and wall hangings, 22" totem pole, ornaments/figures, others.

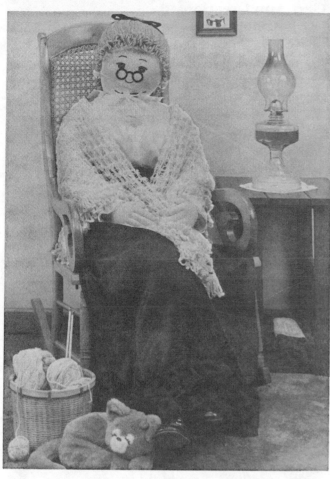

"Aunt Lanta", created by Julie Stephani.
Courtesy of the Society of Craft Designers

Dungan's Rainbow

P.O. Box 865
Bothell, WA 98011
206-485-3634

See your dealer or write for brochure.
Doll and toy kits (20 original printed designs) 80 silkscreen designs in 7 colors. Applique designs.

Era Industries, Inc.

8827 Exposition Blvd.
Culver City, CA 90230

Send SASE for price list.
Cloth doll pattern portfolios and books by Evelyn Ackerman.
(Also sells wholesale to businesses.)

Darlene Erb

P.O. Box 6
Schooly Mt., NJ 07870

Send SASE for prices.
Leather for doll bodies; cork for stuffing.

Ethelby's Doll World

642 Country Oak Rd.
San Dimas, CA 91773

Send SASE for prices.
Cloth baby doll kits and patterns. Has Mastercard, Visa.

Fabrications

P.O. Box 2399
Salt Lake City, UT 84110

Catalog, $1.00.
Soft sculpture goose pattern — 3 sizes in one, plus shawl patterns.

Farm House Crafts

Rt. 4
Huntsville, AK 72740

Catalog, $1.00.
Soft sculpture animal patterns and kits including "Lucy and Liz Goose" gingham.

Suzie Feasel

1121 ECR 1
Tiffin, OH 44883

Catalog, $1.00.
Patterns for "Jelly Beans" **cloth dolls** (7 colors, 20" washable and dryable).

Fluff 'N Stuff

150 Wareham St.
Middleboro, MA 02346

Catalog, $2.00 (refundable).
Supplies: wigs, parts. Trims: beads, feathers, craft fur. Needlecraft pattern books. (And supplies for other crafts.)

Follett and Lehr Publication

1710 6th St.
Moorhead, MN 56560

Send large SASE for list.
Clothing patterns for antique composition, china, and other dolls. Doll baby patterns.

Cut-on Facing: "A favorite jacket pattern had a front facing for button front opening. Save time cutting, layering seam, and pressing, by taping front facing pattern to front pattern, overlapping stitching lines. Sew smart of you! You've changed a sew-on facing to a cut-on facing. This can often be done on blouses, too." — Courtesy of **Phyllis Eifler** of Phyllis Eifler's Sewing Seminars, from *Sewing Is Getting Easier All The Time.*

Jolynn Foster
3747 N.E. 153rd St.
Seattle, WA 98155

Send SASE for prices.
Soft sculpture doll patterns (original) including "Lil-Lumpkins" for child's first doll, with sculpted hands/face, no clothes to make. Girl and boy dolls.

C. P. Fregone
20 Washington St., #32
Methuen, MA 01844

Send SASE for details.
Victorian cloth doll pattern (full size), with complete costume pattern.

Frivals 'N Friends, Inc.
P.O. Box 401101
Dallas, TX 75240

Catalog sheets, $ .45.
"Frivals" animals kits: for "Frillicorn", "Frilligoat", and others. How-to booklets: murals, soft sculpture. (Also sells wholesale by volume, to businesses, professionals, teachers/institutions.)

Frog's House
RR3, Box 25
Franklin, IN 46131

Send SASE for list.
Patterns for doll clothes for "Strawberry Shortcake"; 28 patterns for 5½" dolls, 16 patterns for 4" dolls.

G. K. Creations
21023 Baltic Ave.
Long Beach, CA 90810

Send SASE for details.
Cloth bride doll pattern (16", original, 3-D, with curley hairdo, bridal attire). Allows foreign orders.

Gaillorraine Originals
407 Brentwood
Tehachapi, CA 93561

Catalog, $ .50.
Teddy Bear pattern (for jointed bear) and other animal dolls with clothes — antique replicas. **Dollmaking supplies** including eyes, others.

Louise Gardner
Rt. 2, Box 171
Scottsville, KY 42164

Send SASE for information.
Cloth doll patterns including for "Strawberry Shortcake".

Geri Ann Creations
P.O. Box 8
Cleves, OH 45002

Send SASE for list.
Cloth doll pattern (full size) for 18" country girl, with "toothy smile". Others.

Ginger Designs
Box 3241
Newport Beach, CA 92663

See your dealer or send SASE for information.
Life-size dolls (mannequins) patterns — for sizes 2 to 6 — can wear child's outfits. (See also under children's clothing, for patterns.) Manufacturer.
(Sells wholesale to distributors and retailers.)

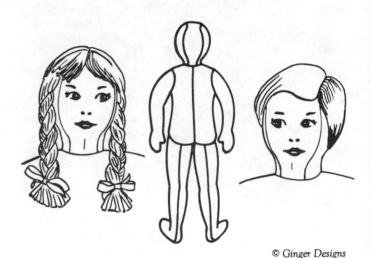

© *Ginger Designs*

Ginger Snap Station
P.O. Box 81086
Atlanta, GA 30366
404-455-6700

Catalog, $ .50.
Whimsical doll kits: 20" Tooth Fairy, 33" girl, reversible sleep/awake. Calico animals (cat, duck family, mouse, bear, lion, others). And full line of quilting/sewing kits/patterns, supplies, see "Quilting".

Golden Fun Kits
P.O. Box 10697
Golden, CO 80401

Catalog, $1.00.
Stuffed toy kits/patterns: Teddy bears (4 sizes), raccoon, fox, koala, squirrel, others. **Doll patterns:** baby, newborn, others. **Supplies:** long pile fur, flesh body cotton, musical movements and turntables. Animal parts, squeakers, voices, criers. Books. Has quantity prices.

Jean Grief
P.O. Box 1638
Weaverville, CA 96093

Catalog, $1.00.
Ceramic bisque dolls including Baby-Bye-Lo (with tears, unpainted, unassembled) with **body pattern;** others.

Susi Groy
141 W. Chocolate
Hershey, PA 17033

Send SASE for list.
Soft sculpture patterns: "Little Rascal on Trap", "Clam". "Seal of Approval", others.

Haan Crafts
625 E. 2nd St.
Otterbein, IN 47970

Catalog, $1.00.
Soft sculpture toy kits: 13" unicorn, other animals, puppets, sports items. Pillow kits. (Also needlecraft kits.)

Happy Hands Shopping Center
4949 Byers
Ft. Worth, TX 76107

Send SASE for list.
Doll/toy patterns: ballerinas (9", 21"), 60" mannequin, American Heritage costumed dolls, wizard, others. Animals (ram, goat, teddy, dinosaurs, dog, elephant).

Heirloom Patterns
38930 Chicago Ave.
Wadsworth, IL 60083

Catalog, $1.50.
Patterns (of 1880 — 1910 era) for child dolls: doll kits (also ready-to-wear).

Hen's Nest Garden Center
6098 150th Ave., No.
Clearwater, FL 33520

Catalog, $1.00.
Over 45 full size **soft sculpture doll patterns:** "Blossom Babies" dolls — variety of sizes and hairdos (long and short curls, others).

Home Spun Enterprises
1847 Wren Cir.
Costa Mesa, CA 92626

Send SASE for price list.
Sock doll kits/patterns: 8" girl and boy with clothing patterns; clown, 9" bunny with clothing patterns, others.

© Sunrise Industries

Homespun Creations
P.O. Box 6125
San Jose, CA 95150

See your dealer or send SASE for list.
Patterns: sock dolls, cloth dolls (boy and girl rabbits, mouse, others); personal accessories.

House Beautiful of Texas, Inc.
33707 Hoff Rd.
Brookshire, TX 77423

Brochure, $1.00.
Teen fashion doll (11½") clothing patterns/kits: folk and western outfits; eastern, European costumes. Wigs.

House of Crafts and Stuff
409 No. Gall Blvd., Hwy. 301
Zephrhills, FL 33599

Catalog, $2.00 (refundable).
Doll parts: hands, bodies, arms, faces, torsos, 20 undressed dolls, Santa faces. Animal parts: eyes — all types; noses, paws, heads, faces, whiskers, others. (See index; other craft and needlecraft supplies.)

"When Making Wooden Dolls apply all finishes before dressing these dolls and be certain all finishes **are thoroughly dry.** If not, they may stain the cloth, or worse, may wick through the fibers and cause irreparable damage." — Courtesy of **R. V. Dankanics,** of The Dollhouse Factory™, from *The Miniatures Catalog.*

House of Gable
425 W. Brookshire Ave.
Orange CA 92665

List, send SASE and $ .75.
Cloth doll kits/patterns: boy and girl dolls (and Oriental, black versions), three foot doll; with clothing patterns. Others.

How Clever
206 Indiana
Elmhurst, IL 60126

Catalog, $1.00.
Soft sculpture patterns (full size): kid's tote bags with small stuffed toys (tent and animals). (And home accessories patterns.)

© Son Rise Puppet Co.

I'm Stuffed
P.O. Box 17582
Tampa, FL 33682

Brochure, $1.00.
Over 25 **doll patterns** including 15" washable baby (doubles as pajama bag), "Sporty" dolls in uniforms, others.

Inhome
P.O. Box 0858
Roswell, GA 30077

Send SASE for prices.
Kits for Softots™ dolls with yarn hair, sculptured body and face.

Ivy Leaf Doll Shop
235 E. 3rd St.
Imlay City, MI 48444

Catalog, $1.00 (refundable).
Doll making supplies: wigs, shoes, accessories. Books.

Jolly Stitchkin's
22492 Forest Hill
El Toro, CA 92630

Catalog, $1.50.
Soft doll patterns — babies, 20" girls, others; clothing patterns. Dollmaking **supplies.**

Joyanna
P.O. Box 32386
Euclind, OH 44132

Send SASE for prices.
Cloth doll patterns (full size): Merlin, ballet dancer, buddies, nun, grandma (in dress, apron, bloomers, shoes, old-time bun), grandpa (in overalls) with pitchfork; others. Has quantity prices.

June Bug Dolls
Box 894
Brentwood, TN 37027

Send SASE for prices.
Doll carrier kit and pattern for 13" to 27" dolls — adjustable, lived.

JV's Creations
Box 4365
Mountain View, CA 94040

Send SASE for list.
Noah's Ark mobile pattern (for felt/fabric), others.

Kado Kits, Inc.
P.O. Box 461
White Plains, NY 10602

Send SASE for price list.
Doll furniture kits (for 12" dolls): 16" cradle (cardboard/fabric, padding, trims), chair and ottoman set (seat and ottoman stores clothing).

C. Kamper Designs
6133 Colchester Place
Charlotte, NC 28210

Send SASE for list.
Teen fashion dollclothes patterns (11½"): halter dress, wrap dress and sun hat, skirts, tops, pantyhose, others.

Kathy's Cousin
P.O. Box 409
Western Springs, IL 60558

Send SASE for prices.
Cloth doll kits/patterns: 18" with yarn hair (2 styles), others.

© By Diane

Kathy's Crafts

RFD 213
Coalville, UT 84017

Send SASE for brochure.
Soft sculpture patterns for: Little Goose, Canadian Goose, nesting hen, calico Kitty, Wild Duck, turkey gobbler, unicorn, others. "Wholesale inquiries welcome".

Katie Kids

P.O. Box 38
Normangee, TX 77871

Send SASE for price list.
Pillow kits (with pocket/toy) — screened on fabric; Jonah with Whale, Kitty with strawberries, chicks with basket; others.

Kay's Klothespin Kreations

1260 Baneberry Dr.
St. George, UT 84770
801-673-5540

Send SASE for details.
"Klothespin Kreations" kits: "strawberry" soft sculpture purse (12") with side door-opening, houses 7" strawberry bonnet doll (clothespin, moveable arms, legs) with cut out clothing and trims; others.

Kermeen, Ltd.

Box 327
St. Albert, Alberta T8N 1N1, Canada

Send SASE for list.
Sock doll patterns for 12" baby, 14" snowman, 9" dough boy, 17" monkey, 13" romper twins, 12" cat; 21" mother cat, and kittens in apron pockets; others.

Jen Kost

Rt. 2, Box 51
Mountainburg, AR 72946

Send SASE for list.
Cloth doll patterns: Elvis, John Wayne, Charlie Chaplin, Mae West, others.

Jan Kruger Creations

7306 Waterline Rd.
Austin, TX 78731
512-346-4941

Send SASE for list.
Cloth armadillo patterns (full size): in several variations.

Kurly Kuddly Kids

1921 Juliet Ave.
St. Paul, MN 55104

Catalog, $1.25.
Patterns/kits: Over 50 dolls (variety of sizes, with stay-in, washable curls) and clothing patterns; body fabric.

Ladybug

4590 Via Vistosa
Santa Barbara, CA 93110

Send SASE with inquiry — specify brand, size.
Doll clothes patterns (for known collector's dolls): Fisher-Price Mandy, Baby Beth; 18" Bigson Kalico Kids, 11" Marx Cindy, Madam Alexander (3 sizes), Chipper, Barbie, others.

Learning Craft

1 Lamalfa Rd.
Randolph, NJ 07869

Send SASE for list.
"Play and Learn" toys patterns: "Shape Train" appliqued clothing, comforters, etc., wall hanging game (Velcro attaches soft cars to items); others.

Ledgewood Studio

6000 Ledgewood Dr.
Forest Park, GA 30050

Catalog, $2.00 and SASE.
Original doll clothing patterns: Authentic antique-to-contemporary fashions. **Trims:** Small-sized ribbons, braids, cords, others.

> **Handkerchiefs in Printed Patterns Make Terrific Doll Clothes, Worked Out with Border Prints, Mini-motifs, etc. ...**

Jennie Lefevre
6400 W. Shady Side Rd.
Shady Side, MD 20867

Send SASE for prices.
Life-size doll patterns: Clothing for man or woman; about 5'6".

Lehman Enterprises
Box 399, R.R. #2
Pound Ridge, NY 10576

Brochure, $1.00.
Soft sculpture kits/patterns: Cockatoo and parrot in hoops, rainbow mobile, unicorn, frog, owl, seahorse, others.

Martha Lichter
629 W. 56th St.
Hinsdale, IL 60521

Send SASE for list.
Doll clothing patterns (for 11½" teen dolls): Wardrobe sets (5 outfits each) winter, summer and sports clothes.

A Little Bit Crafty
13419 Duggan Rd.
Central Point, OR 97502

Catalog, $2.00 (refundable).
Doll parts: Faces, heads, bodies. **Bulk quantity kits** for pajama pillows, dolls, fur animals, art foam items. **Craft fur** (long and short pile, by yard or piece, 36 colors. **Animal parts:** Whiskers, noses, owl eyes, frog eyes, others, cats eyes (with washers). Pom-poms, bells, adhesives, novelties. Plastic bags. (And other craft, needlecraft supplies.)

Little Brown House Patterns
P.O. Box 671
Hillsboro, OR 97123

Send SASE for brochure.
Doll/toy patterns (original designs): Soft sculpture balloons. "Country Cousins" dolls (in folk dresses, aprons, kerchiefs, boots) doll purses (chubby flattened ragdoll with yarn hair, strap handle). Calico stick horses (soft sculpture heads). (And country home accessories — see listing.) Models available readymade.
(Also sells wholesale to retailers.)

Little Lotus
302 Spring St.
Cambridge, WI 53523

Send $1.00 for brochure.
Patterns for soft sculpture dolls (full size): 20" basic doll with faces for Anglo, Afro, Asian dolls; with fingers, toes, set-in eyes technique. **Costume patterns** (Indian, Bavarian, Austrian; sunbonnet; others). Fairy tales dolls patterns: Frog Prince, Fairy Godmother, Puss 'N Boots, Tom Thumb, Thumbelina, Mouse King, others. Old-fashioned girl dolls (8") and their Teddy bear (dolls with moveable arms and legs; with 3 wig styles) and wardrobe trunk; clothing. "Furredy" troll, 26" for craft fur and doubleknit (with fingers and toes or mitts and boots). "Wee Folk" dolls. Sled, bed, cradle board.

Little Sister Studio
P.O. Box 1244
Cottonwood, CA 96022

Send SASE for prices.
Cotton sock doll patterns/kits: "Little Sister", "Little Brother", — one doll per cotton sock with dress or vest; machine washable.

© Loretta Daum Byrne, of Little Lotus

Living Doll Fashions
Box 399
Alliance, NE 69301

Catalog, $1.00 ($1.50 in '85).
Doll clothes patterns booklets: 17 titles, with collections of clothing for fashion (11½") boy and girl dolls (all instruction booklets have separate sheets with full size patterns): Juliette wedding, old fashioned fashions, country-wedding, pinafore — some with varieties of clothing, western, playwear, lingerie, costumes, southern belle styles, contemporary fashions, wedding, holiday costumes. Mix and match outfits, gowns, calendar girls; basic men's clothes. Doll clothing **patterns:** Mermaid, gowns (1800's), Bo Peep, French Queen, basic contemporary fashions, bridal and evening clothes. Clothes for 8" and 12½" dolls, others. Business established in 1974.
(Also sells wholesale to dealers.)

Lodestar Enterprises
1730 S.E. 44th Ave.
Portland, OR 97215

Catalog, $2.50.
Original cloth doll patterns, clothing patterns, animals (dog, cat, others). Washable **craft fur** for wigs (by pieces — 8 colors).

© *Loretta Daum Byrne, of Little Lotus*

Longley-Wilkes
602 Downing
Denver, CO 80218

Catalog, $1.00.
Doll patterns/kits: "Gibson girl" — 18" cloth doll with pompadour; clothed with leg-o-mutton sleeves, bodice, flared skirt. Boy — 18" in t-shirt, jeans, frog-in-his-pocket. Patterns for "Merlin the Magician", exotic belly dancer, gypsy girl, others.

Lorna
P.O. Box 10388
Alameda, NM 87114

Catalog, $1.50.
Over 50 original **fantasy soft sculpture toys patterns** (full size): Unicorn and colt, other creatures; 23" "Terra" doll — of all countries and times, and "Medieval Terra" doll. Others. Has Mastercard, Visa.

Louise's Fabrics & Quiltworks
13972 Riverside Dr.
Sherman Oaks, CA 91423

Send SASE for list.
Teddy Bears patterns: "The Three Bears" — brown bear felt pieces, and 6" needle (for attaching arms and legs); available separately. Has Mastercard, Visa.

Love Me Dolls
Rt. 3, Box 849
Orange, TX 77630

Catalog, $1.00 and SASE.
Soft sculpture dolls/toys patterns (full size) and kits: "Space Baby and friends", Pegasus group, 21" babies (boy, girl) others.

Luv 'N Stuff
P.O. Box 85
Poway, CA 92064

Catalog, $1.25.
Over 30 full-size soft **"Critters"/dolls patterns:** Rabbit and babies, pig and piglets, "Strawberry Delight" mouse, "Crazy Quilter 'N Friends" (cross-stitcher, knitter). "Diet Dolly" adult, overweight gal with box of candy, bag of donuts — wallhanging pattern. Allows overseas orders.

Lyn's Doll House
P.O. Box 8341
Denver, CO 80201

Catalog, $1.50 ($2.00 in '84).
Period style doll clothes patterns for antique or reproduction dolls — adapted from fashion magazines): Gibson girl body pattern (goes with bisque head/parts kits) Gibson girl clothing, layettes, cristening dresses; dresses for all size dolls (Empire, sailor, double-sleeve and smocked styles, others); boy's Russian and sailor suits, others; children's underwear. Hats (sailor, sun, 15 bonnets), 7 shoes (pointed toe, laced, square toe, low and high button boots, strap slipper) leggins. **Book:** *The Doll Dressmaker's Guide To Patternmaking*, by Lyn Alexander. In business since 1977.

Mac Enterprises
P.O. Box 1127
Beaverton, OR 97075

Send SASE for details.
Pattern for 75" long dragon (30" body, 44" tail) —soft sculpture; instructions.

Maid Marion
P.O. Box 842
Marion, OH 43302

Send large SASE for brochure.
Patterns for small toys and bazaar items.

The Mail Pouch
Box 1373
Monrovia, CA 91016
213-358-3728

See your dealer or write for catalog.
Susan Tinker pattern designs for dolls, hoop hangings, others.

Zipping Through Silk: "Lightweight **zippers** for lightweight silks — nylon coil, sewn in by hand, give the softest effect whereas invisible zippers tend to be too rigid." — Courtesy of **G. D. Morgan** of Thai Silks.

Evening dress, © Living Doll Fashions

Molly Malone
461 Goffle Rd.
Wyckoff, NJ 07481

Send SASE for brochure.
Doll/clothes patterns (full size): Girl, babies, boys; 19th century wardrobes, others.

Marie Louise Originals
15802 Springdale St.
Huntington Beach, CA 92649

Catalog, $1.00.
Cloth doll kits/patterns: For 23" — 25" boy and girl dolls, including 25" Katrina (with body pattern printed on fabric, plastic disc arms and legs), others; doll **clothes** patterns. Book.

Marli Originals
629 W. 56th St.
Hinsdale, IL 60521

Brochure, $1.00.
Soft sculpture cloth **doll patterns:** Bride, groom, holiday (angel, Santa, Witch), and others.

Mary Jane Moppets
P.O. Box 7916
Stockton, CA 95207

Catalog, $1.25.
Puppets kits/patterns (full size): 20" mouth-moving people (Biblical and storybook characters, cowboy, Dracula, witch and other holiday people) and animals (rabbit, wolf, dog, cat, others).

McCall Patterns
230 Park Ave.
New York, NY 10169

See your dealer, or write for information.
Doll patterns: Sesame Street™ characters — Big Bird, Cookie Monster, Grover, Grouch, Bert, Ernie; 36" Annie doll and wardrobe, 20" Sandy. Soft sculpture foldable dollhouse and animals. Raggedy Ann and Raggedy Andy — 5 sizes. Doll clothes. Barnyard animals, Teddy Bears (10", 17") elephant, rabbit, lion, others. **"House A Pet"** cat house (triangular), and dog pillow. (And full line of fashions, home and personal accessories patterns.)

Melanie's Workbasket
P.O. Box 2751
Richardson, TX 75080

Send SASE for brochure.
Dolls/clothes patterns: 12½" prizewinning Dutch boy and girl, with wardrobe. Others.

Merrily Supply Co.
8542 Ramchita Ave., TT
Panorama City, CA 91402

Fabric sample card, $2.00.
Teddy bear supplies: Craft fur and mohair fabric, glass eyes, joint sets, washers, long needles, others.

J. R. Meyer Co.
Box 321
East Haddam, CT 06423
203-873-1093

Leaflet, $ .50.
Stuffed toys patterns (adapted from antique folk art designs): animals (cat, pig, horse, dogs, chicken); others. Business established since 1955.
(Also sells wholesale to businesses.)

Middlebury Lane Crafts
2623 Middlebury Lane
Birmingham, MI 48010

Send SASE for information.
Clown doll pattern from man's work socks; 20" size.

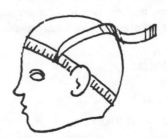

To measure your doll's head, wrap tape around head as shown.
Courtesy, Doll & Craft World, Inc.

The Mini-Magic Carpet
3675 Reed Rd.
Columbus, OH 43220
614-457-3687

Catalog, $1.00.
For miniatures, dolls — full line of fabrics (by yard): Silks (puffed Jacquard, novelty print, stripes, pongee) cottons (tiny dots, plaids, lawn, twill, English shirtings). Hardanger, Evenweave, broadcloth, taffeta, lawn, linens, silk gauze, others. Cotton net for lace. **Trims:** Ribbons (silk, grosgrain, satin, French decorative); 46 laces. **Supplies:** Notions, threads (silks, metallics, chenilles, wools), doll shoe leathers, white cabretta skins, feathers, minibeads; needlepoint kits and graphs for miniature rugs, others (over 60 designs). Has some quantity prices.

Mirabilis
P.O. Box 39139
Redford, MI 48239

Send SASE for list.
Patterns for spaceship pillows: 16" rocket saucer, bat wing cruiser; 11" lion cub, others.

Miss Martha Originals
P.O. Box 5038
Glencoe, AL 35905
205-492-0221

Send SASE for brochure.
Pedigreed Piglets™ **soft sculpture doll patterns** (full size), others including "Preshus", 20" baby with fingers and toes, sculptured facial features; 18" Jamie with clothing. Iron-on eye transfer sheets (for 20", 22" dolls — in green and brown, with various expressions). "Pigskin" fabric, flesh or cocoa body fabrics; 3½" needles. Twin baby dolls kit. **Doll pattern book** (22" dolls, clothes and shoes). Marking pen (disappears). Candlewicking design books.
(Also sells wholesale to businesses.)

Miss Perky Patterns
P.O. Box 116
Wauconda, IL 60084

Brochure, $ .50.
Cloth doll patterns including for 16" clown (for felt).

My-Ty Creations
806 Main
Hays, KS 67601

Brochure, $1.00.
Cloth doll patterns: 16½" Cheerleader, 20" toddler, 19" Nikki in sailor dress, shoes; 22" Tara in bubble suit with hearts, 11" Lollipop and 22" Cupcake dolls (with calico body, lace trim, curley hair). **Body fabrics:** Peach broadcloth, pink velour — by yard. Allows foreign orders.

Nanny M
Box 194
Carson City, NV 89702

Send SASE for list.
Doll Clothes instructions including for one-seam fashions ("fit any size").

National Doll Patterns
P.O. Box 5345
Jacksonville, FL 32207

Send SASE for list.
Patterns for old and new dolls, and clothes with details.

Nayeli Design
10-28 49th Ave.
Long Island City, NY 11101

Send SASE for brochure.
Hand puppet kits/patterns including bunny, others.

Needle In The Haystack
306 S. Lookout Mtn. Rd.
Golden, CO 80401

See your dealer or write for catalog.
Teddy Bear kits mom and baby packaged with plush fabrics and trims.

Needle-In-The-Haystack
P.O. Box 834
McMinnville, OR 97128

Cloth Doll patterns: "Jennifer" and "Tracy" with curly yarn hair, knit fabric body; clothes. Crayon pocketed pinafore kits (size 2-4), Barbeque apron/hot pad kit, others.

A Needle's Touch
P.O. Box 55593
Valencia, CA 91355

Send SASE for list.
Kits/Patterns: Soft Sculptured-stuffed "Mouse House" (two story house, opens, with stuffed furniture — table, bed, dressing table). Barn with double front doors, stuffed farm animals — hen, chicks, pig, horse, sheep.

Needlework-in-the-Box: "Needlepoint [or other needlework — quilted, embroidered, etc.] can be the cover of any box by inverting the lid (as long as it fits flush to the bottom half). Hinge together, and fit needlework into lid — if too deep, prop up with foam or cardboard." — Courtesy of **Dee Davis,** noted decoupateur, of Adventures in Crafts Studio.

Neuhaus Novelties

252 Onyx Court
Redding, CA 96003

Send SASE for details.
Cloth fashion baby doll pattern (freckles, curley hair "Kimmie-Ann") with layette patterns, for nightgown, kimona, booties, overalls, shirt; carry-tote/changing mat with pockets.

Old Time Teddy Bears

304 S.E. 87th
Portland, OR 97216

Send SASE for details.
Old-Time Teddy Bears kits (antique reproduction for 15" size, fully jointed bear) with craft fur, wood joints, eyes, supplies.

Ozark Craft

Box 805
Branson, MO 65616

Brochure, $1.00.
Cloth doll patterns: "Kitchen Witch" duster, Prairie girl, scarecrow, others. **Animal patterns:** dog with puppies, pig with piglets, cat with kittens.

Parradee's

Box 187
Manhattan Beach, CA 90266

Gloveables, $1.00.
How to make doll clothes from knit gloves. (See also under TRIMS.)

Pats' Pals

3739 W. Ramsey
Banning, CA 92220

Send SASE for prices.
Baby doll patterns for 3-6 mos. size (wears baby clothes).

Patch Press, Inc.

4019 Oakman South
Salem, OR 97302
503-363-3480

Write for brochure.
Patch, applique/soft sculpture patterns: Teddy tot (15" bear) with wardrobe, Calico Teddy with wardrobe. 28" Santa, Christmas nativity dolls/hand puppets. Pumpkin basket, other soft box/baskets. Kit'd "Pack-Pals" backpacks in bonnet doll or dog and cat patterns. Others. "Drag Around" 36" girl and boy dolls; soft sculpture trucks. Others. In business since 1978.
(Also sells wholesale to distributors, retailers.)

The Pattern Factory

823 Main, Suite 1B
Sumner, WA 98390

See your dealer, or write for catalog — $1.50 (in '83 — '84) $2.00 (in '85).
Patterns: boy and girl cloth dolls with yarn hair; Santa and mini Santa, toy hare, bear (calico — country). And many designs for home accessories. Allows foreign orders. (Also sells wholesale to businesses — free catalog.)

Pattern Mates

P.O. Box 668, Gracie Station
New York, NY 10028

Catalog, $1.00.
Cloth toymaking patterns: circus animals, others; also potholders (vegetable motifs, others), holiday decorations.

© *Lauretta Daum Byrne, of Little Lotus*

Pattern Pak Originals

P.O. Box 371
Riverdale, MD 20737

Brochure, $1.00 and SASE.
Sewing patterns: Soft dolls, toys, animals; (other patterns).

Pattern Plus

21 Mountain View Ave.
New Milford, CT 06776

Brochure, $1.50.
Cloth doll kits/patterns (full size; some using fabric crayons): 15" teddy bear, 6" Teddy with jointed limbs, bunny babies, 17" Mrs. Mouse, others.

Pattern Tree

112 Moorenand Ave.
Harrodsburg, KY 40330

Catalog, $ .50.
Doll clothes patterns (full size, for 10-12", 14-16" and 18-20" dolls): storybook characters including Bo Peep, Miss Muffet, Mary (lamb), Red Riding Hood, Snow White, Alice in Wonderland, Cinderella, others.

Patterns
116 E. 145th Ave.
Tampa, FL 33612

Catalog, $3.00 (with free pattern).
Over 1000 **out-of-print old patterns** for toys, dolls, animals (most species).

Patterns
410 S. Baltimore
Hastings, NE 68901

13 page list, $1.00.
Doll Clothing Patterns — reprints of old McCalls, Simplicity, Butterick, others.

Patterns
Box 923
Buffalo, NY 14240

Send SASE for list.
Sew toys patterns including circus and vehicle sets, (also home accessories).

Pauliwog
Rt. 1, Box 249
Sand Springs, OK 74063

Send large SASE for brochure.
Soft sculpture patterns/kits: "Buck E. Beaver", Deer in Chimney, 12" Calico cat, 13" dog, Koala bear (momma, baby); man and woman in night clothes, others. Allows foreign orders.

Petronella
1672 Donelwal Dr.
Lexington, KY 40511

Brochure, $ .50.
Sock doll patterns/clothing patterns: 18" clown, 21" scarecrow, 15" angel, girl, others.

The Pig Works
P.O. Box 1305
Woodland Hills, CA 91364

See your dealer or write for brochure.
Toy Patterns: unicorn, rocking horse, witch, pumpkin doll, pillow dolls, others.

Pin Money Patterns
P.O. Box 42
La Mirada, CA 90637

Catalog, $2.00.
Stuffed toys patterns/kits, including "Krazy Kats and kin".

© Buckwheats

The Eyes Have It: "I keep a bottle of thin, clear nail polish handy. I use it to finish edges, treat weak seams, seal almost anything, and to put a real gleam in the button-eye of a doll or animal. I also use a dot of white, type-correction fluid to create a highlight in some cloth doll eyes. Eyes are **very** important to me for expression." — Courtesy of **Loretta Daum Byrne,** pattern designer, of Little Lotus.

LEISURE HOURS.

Platypus
Box 396, Planetarium Station
New York, NY 10024
212-874-0753

Catalog, $1.00.
Cloth doll patterns and booklets: "Country" doll with patchwork clothing, 24" fashion doll and 18th, 19th century wardrobe. Boy and girl dolls (13") with clothing, "Funny People" — 9 dolls from one pattern. Fantasy dolls (mermaid, unicorn, dragon, Sir Gore, jester) 19" girl doll (jointed, 3 yarn hairstyles), period and contemporary clothing. 5" and 8" dolls. Soft sculpture train (engine, caboose, 5 cars). Animals: armadillo platypus, hen and chicks, cat and mouse, lion, penguin, pig, elephant, hippo. Bees, flowers, starfish and crab. Silhouette animals. And pillow kits. **Supplies:** modelling needle, buttons, laces eyelet, craft fur (brown, black), muslin (for dolls, quilts). **Booklets:** *The Fine Art Of Stuffing* $1.50 by Colette Wolff and another, on making faces on cloth dolls. Allows foreign orders. In business since 1970.

Pocket Gallery
P.O. Box 6807
Santa Barbara, CA 93111

Send SASE for price list.
"Country Cradle" soft-sculpture pattern (for dolls) — 3 sizes). Others.

Dorothy Pomaville
209 Walker Ave.
Rockwood, TN 37854

Send SASE for price list.
Doll Patterns: **Raggedy Annie and Andy** for 5 foot model, and 10" through 25" sizes. Orphan Annie and 24" dog Sandy; Others — with clothing patterns.

Beverly Powers
Box 13
South Lyon, MI 48178

Catalog, $2.00.
Over 1000 **doll clothes** patterns, nice out-of-print for old, and new wardrobes. Cloth **dolls and animals** patterns.

Prairie Farm Designs
578 S. Vine
Denver, CO 80209

Country doll pattern — with handpainted faces on muslin for 5" and 7" dolls. Teddy stencil design (on mylar); others.

Present Dreams by Jeanne
19126 Magnolia St., P.O. Box 2710-336
Huntington Beach, CA 92646

Brochure, $1.00.
Cloth Doll patterns for 16" jointed "huggables" — "Sugarplum" and "Peaches" with sculpted hands and feet and clothing. Allows foreign orders.

Puppet Patterns
Box 582
St. Paul, MN 55075

Send SASE for prices.
Animal Puppets patterns (for full size, moving-mouth type): elephant, alligator, bear, dog, cat, others.

Raggedy Joan's Dolls
10436 Midway St.
Billflower, CA 90706

Brochure, $1.00.
Doll patterns including for 18" 3-D "Sweetie" and "tiny friend" with tummy button; and clothes, (includes easy-make curls directions).

Sal's Pals
8622 E. Oak St.
Scottsdale, AZ 85257

Send SASE for price list.
Teddy bear parts: hardwood joints (by pairs or complete sets), glass eyes (variety of colors) others.

San Lou
Box 1380
Marietta, GA 30061

Brochure, $ .50.
Soft-sculpture dolls kits/patterns — Real Children™; 26" and 26" babies (kit includes polyester filling, fabric, hair, pattern, diaper, paint for eyes); two skin tones. Refill kits (no pattern), fabric. Has quantity prices, large order discounts. In business since 1981.

Sandy Creations
5523 Empire Dr.
Pensacola, FL 32505

Send SASE for prices.
Soft doll kits/patterns: "Candy" 16½", "Carissa" jointed, 17½" with yarn hair, clothes; rabbit, others. Allows foreign orders for patterns only.

Sanjean Originals
4665 Norwood Rd.
Columbia, SC 29206

Brochure, $ .50 and SASE.
Cloth doll patterns: 34" girl (for child's button, zip and tie), others.

Savage's Beasts
854 N.E. 58th St.
Seattle, WA 98105

Send SASE for brochure.
Stuffed Animal patterns (full sized): Unicorn, Pegasus, horse, dragons, dinosaurs, dolphins, whale, aardvark and ants, hippo, rhino, armadillo and others; Creature Costumes.
(Also sells wholesale to businesses.)

Jill Schneider
2269 Adela Place
Sidney, B.C., Canada V8L 1R1

Send SASE and $1.00 for sample pattern and list.
Patterns/kits for **ethnic and character doll costumes** — for all size dolls.

Scrap Sack
R.R. #5, Box 90
Warsaw, IN 46580

Send SASE for list.
Fullsize pattern: **"Tote-A-Long" totes** including boy's Fun Village (holds 3 cars, opens flat to show highway design for machine applique) and instructions.

MY DOLLIES

Second Childhood
Rt. 1, Box 75
Deary, ID 83823

Brochure, $ .50.
Ethnic doll patterns: "juniper" 12" for three different dolls — Indian, Oriental, other. Other doll patterns.

Sew-So-Easy
141 Stribling
Charlottesville, VA 22903

Catalog of dolls, $1.00.
Cloth doll kits/patterns: "Strawberry dolls", others; "Sachet fruits" pattern/instructions, Body fabric (knit) quantity prices.

Sew Special
2762 Londonderry Dr.
Sacramento, CA 95827

Catalog, $1.50.
Soft Sculpture doll kits/patterns: 20" gypsy doll with realistic fingers, real eyelashes, gypsy clothing; "Sheriff and Little Nel" old-west dolls, 16½", "thin waisted collectables". Others. Allows foreign orders.

Let Me Impress On You ... "Press the seams open as you sew! While it is annoying to constantly get up from your machine, pressing as you sew gives you a more attractive, professional-looking garment." — Courtesy of **Gail Balego,** of Fashion Blueprints (ethnic clothing patterns).

© Sanlou

The Sewing Centipede
P.O. Box 218
Midway City, CA 92655

Brochure, $ .50.
Cloth doll patterns/kits 24" Clown, Baby doll, (moveable arms and legs) (And see Home Accessories). Allows foreign orders — U.S. funds.

Sheila's Kids
906 Alton St., P.O. Box 75
East Liverpool, OH 43920

Photo and Samples, $1.00 (refundable).
Basic doll body patterns (for 6 different dolls), Clothing patterns. Body fabric (poly/cotton, skin color).

Shurnuff Co.
P.O. Box 2545
Leucadia, CA 92024

Send SASE for list.
Dollups™ color and sew doll/toy kits (with special crayons, fabric pen and transfers for four). (Also has portable show booth instructions.)

Susan Sirkis
11909 Blue Spruce Rd.
Reston, VA 22091

Send SASE for price list.
Heirloom doll/clothes patterns: Cloth dolls of 19th century, French dolls, others. Doll fashions from 18th through 19th century (lady's, men's) children's clothing of early 20th century; others. Has Mastercard, Visa.

Soft Heart Designs
413 Archer
Houston, TX 77009

Send $ .25 and SASE for catalog.
Soft toys including "Baby Bump Branchiosaurus" — kits and patterns.

Softies by Susan
62 Pollock Ave.
Pittsfield, MA 01201

Send SASE for list.
Guardian Angel dolls kits/patterns: "Nutmeg" kitchen angel, "teenie tiny" and tomboy angel; with clothing.

Softstuff
Box 556
Clinton, CT 06143

Brochure, $1.50.
Soft sculpture doll kits/patterns (original designs): 21" ballerina in tutu, baby with dimple-knees, hair; 25" clothed old-time girl, 21" All American boy, girl; angel with wings. Others.
(Also sells wholesale to businesses.)

Son Rise Puppet Co.
P.O. Box 5091
Salem, OR 97304
503-362-0027

Brochure, $ .50.
Furry Cloth puppets and toys patterns/kits: Professional "whole arm" (heads and forelegs) puppets, 18" and 24" size including unicorn, poodle, sophisticated cat, lion, giraffe, spaniel, husky dogs (can also make as stuffed toys). Has quantity prices. In business since 1980.

Standard Doll Co.
23-83 31st St.
Long Island City, NY 11105
212-721-7787

Catalog, $2.00.
Dollmaking kits/supplies (complete line): Over 200 china/porcelain bisque doll kits (with patterns for body and clothing) — all types, sizes. Doll stands, accessories, voices, squeekers, music boxes. **Doll parts:** Heads, arms, legs, sets (bisque, plastic, composition, others). Eyes — all types, sizes. **Doll clothes patterns/books:** All periods, to contemporary: children's, fashion dolls. **Supplies:** trims (laces, pom-poms, cords, metallics), feathers, sequins, buttons, ribbons, threads, zippers, buckles, sequins, pins, eyes, **Fabrics:** Unbleached muslin, denim, felt, satin, nylon net. Cabretta leather skins (white). Aids: stuffing tool, hooks, wood neck buttons, Extensive books. Has quantity prices; American Express, Mastercard, Visa.

Starbuck

Box 587
Ukiah, CA 95482

Send SASE for details.
"Duffy Dragon" Pattern — 22" high soft-sculpture
doll, others.

Stitch 'N Stuff

4900 Winthrop West
Ft. Worth, TX 76116

Send SASE for list.
Doll patterns including for 14" nurse and doctor (with
clothes).

J. Stuff

Drawer D
Hebron, ND 58638

Brochure, $ .25.
Cloth animal patterns (with flat bottoms — sitable):
Teddy bear, dog, cat, elephant.

Stuffed

P.O. Box 17582
Tampa, FL 33682

Brochure, $1.00.
Soft doll patterns (20) including "Pind Princes" on lacy
pillow — 11" sock doll.

Sunrise Industries

395 S. Geneva Rd., Box 1316
Orem, UT 84057
801-224-4207

See your Dealer or write for information.
Daisymae Dolls™ kits/patterns with velour body
fabric, yarn hair; clothing pieces, trims — boy and girl
dolls (sailor outfits, others) infants and babies old-
fashioned boy and girl, others size 14" — 21". Manufacturers, since 1977.
(Also sells wholesale to distributors and retailers.)

Sunshine Dolls

2140 Sunnyside Place
Sarasota, FL 33579

Catalog, $1.00.
**China doll kits (antique reproductions, with cloth
bodies,** clothing patterns): Three-faced baby, 16½" lady,
Byelo baby, others.

T. E. M. of California

1250 Longview, Box 4311
Fullerton, CA 92634

Free literature.
Cloth baby doll pattern (9" size, with complete layette
patterns). Doll **clothes patterns** (for 11½" teen dolls):
Sets of fashion clothing of late 19th century, with instructions and photos.

Take Me Home Creations

P.O. Box 899
Kenosha, WI 53141

Brochure, $1.00.
Pillowpeople With Pockets™ pillows pattern (or as
doorstops, dolls): Variety of characters from one basic
pattern — "Macho Man", lady, gentleman, others.

Tanner Craft

Box 188
Central, AZ 85531
602-428-7227

Free flyers.
Patterns/kits: Puppet dog (stuffed, with manipulatable
mouth, tongue, head and paws). Boxing glove pattern (for
age 2 to 4).
(Also sells wholesale to businesses.)

Biased Undercollars: "When pinning pattern,
change the grain of an undercollar to bias. A bias
undercollar, as used in all quality tailoring, is needed
to maintain a good roll-line for the life of the garment." — Courtesy of **Jane Shaner,** publisher of
The Silver Thimble.

© CR's Crafts

Temptation Products
424 Shortridge
Rochester, MI 48063

Catalog, $ .50.
Cloth doll patterns (full size): Babies, ballerina, clown, liontamer, strong man; other circus dolls.

Timeless Treasures
4794 Norrisville Rd.
White Hall, MD 21161

Send SASE for list.
Pattern for 17" **Little Lulu doll replica** others.

Touch of Craft
P.O. Box 626
Ashville, AL 35953

Send SASE for list.
Soft sculpture doll patterns including for mini (9"); with instructions.

Toylady Press
P.O. Box 503
Dallas, OR 97338
503-623-6001

See your dealer or write for brochure.
Teddy bear patterns — 17" "Beatrice", 10" Bernie.

The Toyworks
Middle Falls, NY 12848

See your dealer or write for prices.
Animal bean bag kits (by Edward Gorey) — cat, frog, pig. (also readymade.) other "ragtop" kits.

Peggy Trauger
20 Wendover Rd.
Rochester, NY 14610

Catalog, $1.25.
Doll clothing patterns (for Collector dolls): 8" Ginny, 16" Sasha, Mandy, 16" Terri Lee ('56), 17" Shirley Temple, 12" Gerber baby, 12" Sasha and Gregor babies. Other patterns: doll bonnets, leather body pattern, 1900 and ethnic costumes, baby doll clothes, 14-16" Jenny Lind body patterns and costume, 5" doll and clothes.

Trudeau's Printing
R.D. 1
Middlebury, VT 05753

Send SASE for price list.
Doll labels: one line (¼") or three lines (½"), white satin
Doll record cards.

Tucker's Music Box
P.O. Box 16274
San Diego, CA 92116

Brochure, $1.00 and SASE.
Musical movements (for toys, etc.), variety of tunes.

Tudor House
Box 56
Coshocton, OH 43812

Send SASE for prices.
China doll reproductions kits — 4 models (12", 15" dolls with china parts, cloth for boy; patterns for body and clothing, instructions.

The Twins Company
1436 E. Broad St.
Columbus, OH 43205

Send SASE for list.
Soft sculpture patterns including for "Sleepy Baby" and his "Quilted Pillow Bed" (pouch/pillow, with patriotic stars/clouds motif); others.

Vea Prints
729 Heinz #2
Berkeley, CA 94710

See your dealer or write for catalog sheets.
Doll Prints handscreened fronts and backs on fabric (15" "Jenny", 8" "Raggedy Ann", 7½" Angel, 17" Cat). And other designs screened on fabric for many uses (patches, trims, potholders, placemats, others.)
(Also sells wholesale to distributors, retailers, professionals, teachers/institutions.)

Vee's
Box 10995
Costa Mesa, CA 92627

Send $1.00 and SASE for list.
Doll patterns, yarn wig maker tool.

Victorian Originals
2830 Payne Rd.
Medford, OR 97501

Send SASE for details.
Victorian doll kits (23" pillow dolls), silkscreened muslin and lace. Allows foreign orders.

Vogue Pattern Service
P.O. Box 549
Altoona, PA 16603

See your dealer or write for information.
Doll patterns: Muppet™ characters — Kermit, Miss Piggy™; Foldable doll tote/house and doll, carry basket and infant. "Beau Brummell" 23" Teddy bear with outfit, 21" hound dog. Stuffed "Safari" rugs/dolls — bear, lion, tiger. Soft sculpture fantasy creatures, Victorian doll sachets. (And full line of fashion clothing home, and baby accessories.)

M. Joel Von Blomberg
2619 Foote Dr.
Phoenix, AZ 85008

Catalog, $1.00.
Doll clothes patterns: Authentically styled French and German period fashions (for 9" to 29" size dolls).

Waverly Lynn
23 Front St., P.O. Box 754
Couperville, WA 98239

Catalog, $ .50 (refundable).
Soft doll patterns — "button nose kids" line (with 3-D toes, ears, bum, belly button) — basket baby (and backpack, wardrobe, quilt, pillow); 18" toddlers, 30" that wears 9 to 18 mo. clothes; boy (anatomically correct —18"). Animals — 3 bears; wrap-around puppets, others.

Whimsey World
P.O. Box 4277
Napa, CA 94558

Brochure, $1.00.
Cloth Doll patterns/kits, including for 16" "Jasper toad", 12" Clown, 16" plump "Sister and brother" baby dolls, others, (kits with precut fabric, floss, ribbon, instructions, etc.).

Lucy White
135 Mark St.
Bristol, CT 06010

Samples, $1.00 plus large SASE.
Mohair (for doll wigs) straight, wavy; variety of hair shades.

Winnie's Handmades
1 Dogwood Lane
Washington, NJ 07882

Send $1.00 and SASE for list, ribbon sample.
Doll clothes patterns: Exclusive designs for 8" Ginny doll. **Ribbons** assortments: mixture of colors and widths for doll clothes.

Wonderful World of Dolls
3755 Ruth Dr.
Brunswick, OH 44212

Doll costume pattern catalogs: Contemporary —
$3.00; Antique — $3.00. Both catalogs, $5.50.
Costume patterns for fashion/dolls (11½" to 18") including all major manufacturers dolls; historical and dated costumes (authentic) — English, American, others; contemporary personalities. Some doll accessory items, sewing supplies.

Wooden Spool
RFD Box 219
Coalville, UT 84017

Send SASE for list.
Toy patterns: 14" Teddy, goose with duster cap and wings. Others.
(Also sell wholesale to businesses.)

Woogam's Originals
Box 68
Centerville, UT 84014

Brochure, $1.00.
Doll patterns/kits (full sized): mouse family, diaper bag baby, witch, others.

Woozleberry Factory
112-10th St.
Wood River, IL 62095

Send SASE for list.
Patterns — including "Lucky Penny", soft-sculptured mouse and clothing, others.

Jenny Wren
8749-34th Ave.
Kenosha, WI 53142

Send SASE for pictures and order information.
Cloth Doll Pattern ("Easy sew") — with natural Shaped heads; clothing; sewing machine directions.

Patty Wyngaard
Rt. 5, Box 556
Golden, CO 80401

Send SASE for list.
Stuffed animals: 10" turtles, frogs; others.

Packing Tip for Travel: Since you have to take along several pairs of panty hose, pull a pair into the sleeves of jackets or dresses to prevent wrinkles."
—Courtesy of **Irene M. James** of I. M. James Enterprises, from her book, *Sewing Specialties.*

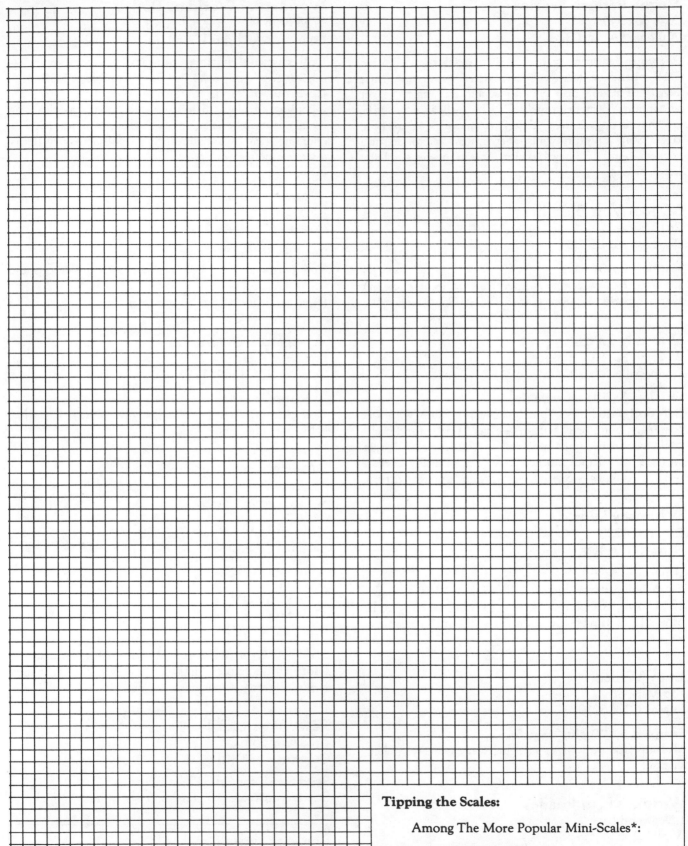

Tipping the Scales:

Among The More Popular Mini-Scales*:

Dollhouse/Miniatures   1" = 1' or ½" = 1'
11" Fashion/Teen Dolls 2" = 1'

*(Scale refers to the relationship between a miniature and an object of actual size.)

B. MINIATURES (1" — 1' SCALE)

Boynton & Associates, Inc.
Clifton House
Clifton, VA 22024

Send SASE for prices.
Plans booklets (for 1" — 1' scale): "Family Affair" Sculpey lifelike dolls and clothing; other needlecraft (and other non-sewing plans).

C. J. Originals
P.O. Box 155
Mendham, NJ 07945

Catalog, $2.50.
Miniature (1" — 1' scale) needlecraft kits (some antique adaptations) for nursery accessories (coverlets, pillowcases, growchart, pictures, playpen pad, others; kitchen (placemats, tablecloths, seat covers, others), living room accessories (seat covers, bellpulls, fire screens, others) in variety of styles; coordinated to other needlecraft kits.

Craft Products Co.
St. Charles, IL 60174

Catalog, $1.50.
Doll house/**Miniatures fabrics** (Velvets, Satins, silks); tiny **trims,** ribbons and lace (and full line of other doll houses and furnishings).

The Crafty Ones
1037 Hyland Circle
Prescott, AZ 86301

Catalog, $2.50.
Miniatures (1" — 1' scale) **kits:** Upholstered furniture, sampler, mini **fabric pleater,** bedding and window treatments, patterns. Supportive miniature **containers;** picture frames. (And extensive line of miniature/dollhouse supplies.)

Create Your Own
R.D. 2, Hickory Corner Rd.
Milford, NJ 08848

Catalog, $1.00.
Miniature (1" — 1' scale) **linens and accessories kits** (fabric screened designs, wool or floss). (Other miniature kits.)
(Also sells wholesale to businesses.)

The Diminutive Dolls' Dressmaking Co.
P.O. Box 414
Mendham, NJ 07945

Catalog, $1.50.
Miniature child and adult doll's dress kits (authentic period costumes): with dress form, materials, trims; adjust up to size 5½" doll. Porcelain doll house dolls (undressed babies, girls, adults).
(Also sells wholesale to businesses.)

The Dollhouse Factory
Box 456, 157 Main St.
Lebanon, NJ 08833

80 page Catalog, $3.50.
Fabrics/18" x 22" pieces (miniature prints — coordinate with miniature wallpaper designs) in checks, cords, florals, houndstooth, Victorian, others; solid fabric pieces. "Bitsy lace" — French and American. Mini **pleater tool** (pleats/shapes fabric for drapes, bed ruffles, chair and sofa skirts) — metal, with instructions; window treatment instructions separately. Dollhouse **doll clothing** kits and patterns. Upholstered furniture kits, drapery rods, magnifiers, measuring tools, others. Books and complete line of dollhouses and all supplies. Has Mastercard, Visa. In business since 1971.
(Also sells wholesale to businesses.)

Dolls by Penny
414 Cessna Ave.
Charleston, SC 29407

Send SASE for list.
Dollhouse doll **clothing patterns:** authentic customer of Colonial, Victorian and turn-of the century fashions; girls and boys, adults.

The Emporium
71 Main St.
Chester, NJ 07930

Samples and brochure, $2.00.
Fabrics: mini-printed designs, variety of styles, colors.

Mini-Illusions Help Scale Down: "I believe the most important thing to remember when sewing for 1" to 1' scale is the fact that no matter how fine a fabric you choose, it will be the equivalent of using a fabric 12 times that thickness, 2 thicknesses will be 24 layers, 4 thicknesses (such as collars) would be 48 thicknesses in real life items — this shows why they appear so bulky unless 'tricks' are used." — Courtesy of **Doreen Sinnett** of Doreen Sinnett Designs, Inc.

Mini-printed fabrics, © The Dollhouse Factory

Favorites From the Past
2951 Harris St.
Kennesaw, GA 30144

Catalog, $1.50.
Scale miniatures (1" — 1') **furniture** kits, Magic-Mini™ **pleater,** iron-on transfers, window cornices, rods, other miniature support items (and extensive line of miniature building components and supplies).

Sharon Gile
R.R. 1, Box 150
Meeker, OK 74855

Catalog, $ .50.
Miniatures **ribbons and trims.**

Harrison Enterprises
1045 Allesandro
Morro Bay, CA 93442

Send SASE for list.
Miniatures (1" — 1' scale) **fabrics** (also dolls and other miniature supplies).

Hobby House Press
900 Frederick St.
Cumberland, MD 21502

Free Catalog.
Over 2000 **books** on miniatures and miniature making (in 1" — 1' scale, others), and doll **clothing patterns** and how-to's (for antique fashions worldwide, others); and non-sewing titles.

The Keshishian Collection
Box 3002
San Clements, CA 92672

Catalog, $1.00 or send SASE with inquiry.
Miniatures (1" — 1' scale) **fringes,** for carpets, lampshades, curtains, others. (And miniature carpets.)

Little Lotus
302 Spring St.
Cambridge, WI 53523

Send $1.00 for complete brochure.
Patterns for "Wee Folk" bendable dollhouse dolls (of cloth, 2" to 8" high): dollhouse family and pets, fairies and winged creatures; elves, gnomes, trolls; unicorn, dragon. (1" — 1' scale) Circus people and animals (elephant, camel, horse, lion, bear, tiger, poodle) with packet of fur fabric.

Maison Mini
3647 44th St., Apt. #1
San Diego, CA 92105

Catalog, $1.00.
Sewing-oriented miniatures: Bolts of fabric, yardstick, button cards, scissors, fabric pieces, pattern envelopes and pieces, (and other miniatures).

Imagine this "translated" into an embroidered carpet for a doll house foyer.

Mary's Attic
2806 Regency Dr.
Winston Salem, NC 27106

Brochure, $ .50.
Miniature crewel embroidery kits: bed spreads, draperies, Victorian lace curtains. (Also readymade.)

Mini Graphics
486 Northland Rd.
Cincinnati, OH 45240
513-742-1400

How-to catalog, $3.00.
Miniature scale printed fabrics (color coordinated with wallpapers): Cottons, silks, damask; in large-size pieces; solids, stripes, prints; pile fabrics, tweed (for carpets, draperies) in traditional and modern designs. Needlecraft projects booklet (for home accessories). Manufacturer, since 1975.
(Also sells wholesale to businesses.)

Mini Majik
P.O. Box 49
Potterville, MI 48876

Price list, $1.00 and large SASE.
Miniature laces, satin ribbons; silk fabric, others. Book: *The Mini-Hatter's Manual* (how-to, on over 25 styles of miniature hats and bonnets of 17th to 20th century), by Alice M. Russell.

Mini Quilts
7765 Eingleberry St.
Gilroy, CA 95020

Price list, $ .50.
Authentic **patch work patterns,** quilts.
(Also sells wholesale to businesses.)

Miniatures by Marty
1857 So. Shore Dr.
Holland, MI 49423

Send $ .25 and SASE for brochure.
Miniature upholstered furniture patterns (also accessories, food, others) "dealers prices".

Muffin's Miniatures
1516 Oakhurst Ave.
Winter Park, FL 32789

Send SASE and $ .25 for list.
Doll: Imported Swiss bastiste and French Val laces; ⅛" silk ribbon. 2mm buttons.

New England Hobby Supply
70 Hillard St.
Manchester, CT 06040

Send SASE for price list (specify interest).
"**Bell**" **stencils** (miniature 1" — 1' scale): set of traditional designs (for fabric, other). And other miniature supplies.

Pab Designs
1301 Brookwood Rd.
Shelby, NC 28150

Catalog, $1.50; SASE for catalog sheets.
Miniature (1" — 1' scale) **kits:** cross stitch, quilting, others. **Equipment:** Wee Helper™ holder frame fabric, magnifier lamp. Manufacturer.
(Also sells wholesale to businesses.)

Alene Padgett
3981 Castleman
Riverside, CA 92503

Send SASE for details.
Porcelain dollhouse dolls, dress patterns (easy-make).

Mark it Down: "To mark a dart, make snip-marks with scissors at cut edge. Then poke pins through dots. Gently pull pin heads through tissue and mark with marking pencil or **soap sliver** (love it!) on wrong sides of fabric where pins poke through. Use a ruler to connect the dots, if necessary." — Courtesy of **Phyllis Eifler** of Phyllis Eifler's Sewing Seminars, from *Sewing Is Getting Easier All The Time.*

*Follow a simple geometric design to create a mini-quilt;
approximately 5" x 7", this size fits most doll house beds.*

Patchwork, Inc.
8106 Croyden Ave.
Los Angeles, CA 90045

Send large SASE and $1.00 for photos and prices.
Miniature patterns, needlecraft kits; 1/144 kits, patterns.

Pinchpenny Miniatures
17 Idaho Lane
Matawan, NJ 07747

Catalog, $ .75.
Miniature: polished brass extension curtain rod with screw eyes (2½" closed, 4½" extended). Other non-sewing scale miniatures. Established in 1975 by three mothers looking for a bargain in miniatures.

The Pixie Shop
5580 Colt Dr.
Longmont, CO 80501

Catalog, $2.00.
Miniatures: Needlework kits, sewing accessories (mini), both accessories and other support items for needlework; others.

Plaid Enterprises, Inc.
P.O. Drawer E
Norcross, GA 30091

See your craft store or write for information (specify "pleater").
"Mini—Magic" metal pleater tool for miniature pleating and shaping fabric (for windows, etc. or bed ruffles, chair and sofa skirts, doll clothes, etc.). Also has stencil and other books.

Susan Ross Designs
442 W. Melrose
Chicago, IL 60657

Catalog sheet and fabric swatches, $ .25.
Miniature sewing kits (1" — 1' scale) — 3 sofas (club, Victorian, Deco), club chair, Victorian chair, upholstered bed (with pillow) — with cutting pattern printed on mini-print fabrics; 4 colors; with pre-cut wood and foam cords, fiberfill, instructions.
(Also sells wholesale.)

Sarah Craft
Box 663
Corte Madera, CA 94925

Send SASE for details.
Needlework pattern booklets (for 1" to 1' scale) — quilt patterns, mini-pillows; others.

Miniature scale (1" = 1') dress, © Doreen Sinnett Designs, Inc.

The Sarah Lee
3433 E. 58th St.
Tulsa, OK 74135

Catalog and supplement, $2.50.
Miniatures including silk ribbons (⅛", 1/12" sizes) hat kits (and Christmas reproductions, others).

Doreen Sinnet Designs
P.O. Box 794
Paso Robles, CA 93446
805-239-2048

Send SASE for details.
Clothing patterns book (for 1" — 1' scale dollhouse ladies): dresses, nightgowns, caps, petticoats, drawers, bustles, others. In business since 1974.
(Also sells wholesale to businesses.)

Keeping Suede Clean: "Use **dry** cornstarch to clean suede. Pat a small amount on spot, let set for eight hours then brush off with a soft cloth and brush with a suede brush. This will usually remove even machine oil spots.

Avoid dry cleaning as long as possible. It removes natural oils.

Wear suede as a second skin. Enjoy it. It gets better with each wearing!" — Courtesy of **Jennifer Morgan** of Jennifer Morgan Designs.

Small Sales Co.
P.O. Box 7803
Boise, ID 83707

Catalog, $3.00 (refundable).
Plaid Enterprises "magic mini-pleater" fabric pleater tool (for window treatments, bed ruffles, sofa skirts, doll clothes, etc.). Bedframes and many other "supportive" miniature items for sewing. Books. Business established in 1964.

Elaine Stewart
P.O. Box 1551
New York, NY 10016

Swatches and price list, $4.00 (refundable).
Textiles (scaled 1" — 1') including multicolored prints in: geometrics, florals, stripes, conversationals; coordinating patterns.

Swallowhill
Box 34
Midland, Ontario L4R 4K6, Canada

Catalog, $1.00.
Dollhouse doll clothes patterns 20 styles (original and custom designs, reproductions). (And full line of porcelain dollhouse doll kits.)

Tiny-Tique
1010 E. Crabtree
Arlington Heights, IL 60004

Catalog, $ .75.
Miniature-printed fabrics (1" — 1' scale) — checks, quilt prints, solids; coordinated to wallpapers. Velvet upholstery and drapery fabric. Miniature ribbons, laces, braids, cordings. (And other non-sewing miniatures.) Manufacturer.
(Also sells wholesale to businesses.)

Venerable Bead
2990 Adeline
Berkeley, CA 94703

Samples and prices, $1.25 and large SASE.
Tiny Victorian glass beads.

XYZZX Creations
5222 Roxanne Ct.
Livermore, CA 94550

Send SASE for catalog.
Miniature needlework kits and supplies.

12
Outdoors & Outwear

Source listings in this section are for outer clothing, camping and outdoor gear, kites, and windsocks, and structures.
(And see the index for specific items throughout the book.)

The Ben Franklin Kite Shop
P.O. Box 392
Mystic, CT 06355

Free catalog.
Kite materials: fiberglass, bamboo, dowels, carps — cotton, nylon (paper). Books. Has Mastercard, Visa. (Also sells wholesale to businesses.)

Country Ways, Inc.
221 Water St.
Excelsior, MN 55331

Catalog, $1.00.
Outdoor equipment kits: insulated sleeping bags, jackets; snowshoes, boats, others.

Daisy Kingdom
217 N.W. Davis
Portland, OR 97209

Catalog, $1.00.
Outerwear patterns/kits: Over 65 skiwear items (jackets, parkas, pants, shirts, vests, gaiters, others), children's wear. **Windsocks patterns.**

Duracote Corp.
350 N. Diamond St.
Ravenna, OH 44266

Send for information.
"Dura Tuff" nylon reinforced vinyl used for outer tipi cover and for liner. Has quantity prices.

Engleman's Tepee
3615 Mt. Pleasant Rd.
Kelso, WA 98626

Send SASE for details.
One pole tipi-making instructions (for 5 sizes).

The Fabric Lady
51 Layle Lane
Doylestown, PA 18901
215-348-1744

Catalog and fabric samples, $3.00.
Kitemaking fabrics: nylon (balloon cloth, taffeta); bargains, closeouts, full line of colors and weights. Parachute threads, tapes, webbing. Kite kits and kite bag kits. Fiberglass tubing, rods. Patterns. Cutting tools.

W. L. Gore and Associates, Inc.
Gore-Tex™ Fabric Division
2401 Singerly Rd., P.O. Box 1130
Elkton, MD 21921
301-392-3700

Contact your dealer or write for information.
Gore-Tex™ fabric: Laminated in single layer bonded to Gor-Tex film; or three layers — fabric bonded on both sides; in 43" and 57" widths, wide range of weaves, weights and colors. Manufacturer.

Canvas Considerations: "Canvas requires a heavy machine needle (size 16 or 18), for seams, sewing with cotton wrapped polyester thread. To prevent raveling overmuch, finish seams immediately by zigzagging or other method. Be prepared for it to be recalcitrant, unweildy, with no give at all; and a very strong material; choose your projects accordingly."
— Courtesy of **Margaret A. Boyd.**

The Green Pepper, Inc.
941 Olive St.
Eugene, OR 97401
503-345-6665

Catalog, $1.00.
Outdoor/sportswear fabrics — quilted, "Polarguard" and others. Patterns: cold outerwear, other clothing; duffles, bicycle saddle bags, others. Allows 10% discounts to teachers/institutions. In business since 1973. They have set up, according to company president, Arlene Haislip, a sportswear program for schools — 6th through 12th grade; ready in Fall, 1983.

Greenhouse Sales
Box 42
Neche, ND 58265

Send 2 stamps for sample, specifications.
Heavy greenhouse (and other uses) plastic — 12 mils; resists cracking. "Discounts". (Also has plastic fasteners, fans).

Margaret Greger
1425 Marshall
Richland, WA 99352

Send SASE for details.
Fabric kitemaking book: Simple Fabric Kites, 6 types (square, diamond, corner, winged square box, flowhorn, "Zephyr"); others.

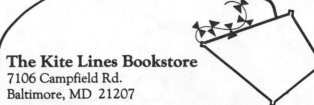

The Kite Lines Bookstore
7106 Campfield Rd.
Baltimore, MD 21207

Send SASE for list, or $1.75 for booklet, *"Mastering Nylon".*
Books: *Designing and Sewing Fabric Kites.* Kite plans packets.

The Kite Site
3101 M St. N.W.
Georgetown, DC 20007
202-965-4230

Free catalog.
Complete line of kitemaking supplies, including nylon fabrics (variety of colors, types) and webbing.

Klein's Archery Haus
Box 941
New Glarus, WI 53574

Write for price information.
Hunting camouflage kits/patterns (for you-sew) — camo fabrics, including blaze orange.

Lodgepole Press
1073 Via Alta
Lafayette, CA 94549

Send SASE for details.
Book: *The Canvas Tipi,* by Jamie Jackson — guide to tipi-making with step-by-step instructions covering the entire process; with techniques given to assure a liveable structure, with proper ventilation.

Mercer Island Fabrics
7811 S.E. 27th St.
Mercer Island, WA 98040

Send SASE for prices.
Windsocks kits (nylon fabric, ring, swivel, nylon line for hanging; instructions) — in rainbow colors, earth colors.

Nantucket Kiteman
Box 508, Marsh Hawk's Way
Nantucket, MA 02554
617-228-2297

Send SASE for prices.
Kitemaking supplies including designer nylon fabrics, others. "Sensible prices".
(Also sells wholesale to businesses.)

Outdoor Wilderness Fabrics

2511 Latham Dr.
Nampa, ID 83651
208-466-1602

Send SASE for price list.
Outdoor fabrics: nylon ripstop and coated ripstop, Oxford, "Taslan Klimate" multi-laminate nylon/Teflon and tricot, taffeta Gortex™ polar fleece. Twill, pack cloth, Cordura (coated), "ballistic" nylon, heavy lock mesh. "Early warning" 60/40. Poly/cottons, downproof double finish materials.

Goose Down Alta vest,
© Timberline Sewing Kits

Patches of Joy

8050 S.W. Wareham Circle
Portland, OR 97223
503-246-6389

Catalog, $1.00.
Kite patterns: five giant fabric models that fly. (And patterns for soft sculptures, wall hangings, pillows, other accessories, sewing aids, clothing kits/patterns.) (Also sells wholesale to businesses.)

R.E.I.

18200 Segale Park Dr.
Tukwila, WA 98188

Free catalog.
Outdoor fabrics: Cordura, Gor-Tex — by yard. **Hardware:** Buckles, others.

The Rain Shed

707 N.W. 11th
Corvallis, OR 97330

Send SASE for price list.
Outdoor fabrics: (variety of weaves, colors, weights —by yard): Gore-Tex™ nylons (lined and unlined "Taslan", taffetas, 3-layer knits, 3-layer Oxford, "tent"; coated nylon, utility, cordura, packcloth. Water repellent/downproof polyester/cottons and nylon/cotton blends. Leno nylon mesh, polyester netting, fiber pile, packcloth; cotton duck, blends. Stretch nylon/Lycra ribbing. **Insulation fabrics:** polyesters "needlepunch", stretch needlepunch, blend with polyolefins — variety of weights. **Insulation fillers:** Polarguard, Dacron "Hollofil", polyester "Quallofil". **Supplies:** YKK zippers (and by inch) snap fasteners, reflective and repair tapes, Velcro, cuffs and ribbing, webbing (flat, tubular), lacing, hardware (grommets and kits, buckles, D-rings, others).

Rainier Rainwear

P.O. Box 69102
Seattle, WA 98168

Free catalog.
Rainparka kits/patterns (hooded parka, in 5 sizes with ready-made waistline, hood drawstring casing, sleeve closures); optional notions pack (zippers, grippers). "Goretex" waterproof fabrics ("breathable" or coated). (Also sells wholesale to businesses.)

Sock-It-Designs

Box 145
Eugene, OR 97440

Send SASE for brochure.
Windsocks kits (for patio, deck, garden) of nylon taffeta, multi-color. (Also readymade.)

Sun Down Kits

14850 N.E. 31 Circle
Redmond, WA 98052

Catalog, $1.00.
Goosedown Outerwear clothing kits: head gear, hooties, long and short jackets; comforters. Has Mastercard, Visa.

Timberline Sewing Kits

Box 126-F2
Pittsfield, NH 03263

Free brochure.
Clothing kits: parka, jacket (arm on, or off), vests, ponchos, gaiters, foot mittend. **Fabrics:** Cordura™, nylon taffeta, ripstop; water repellant fabrics. Insulation, goose down, duck down. Polarguard™. Allows discount to teachers/institutions.

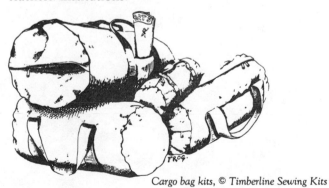

Cargo bag kits, © Timberline Sewing Kits

Sewing Insulating Fabric (For Window Covers, Etc.): Avoid Using Ballpoint Machine Needles — Use Number 12 or 14 Regulars Instead. — Courtesy of **Margaret A. Boyd.**

Allen J. Valero-Designer
RD 1, Box 199
Monroetown, PA 18832

Send SASE for list.
Sheepskin clothing and accessories kits: coats (variety of styles), hats, others; kits include instructions.

Yohan Manufacturing Co.
Box 280
Cornelia, GA 30531

Write for information.
"Shade cloth" — for hobby or commercial greenhouse (and other uses).

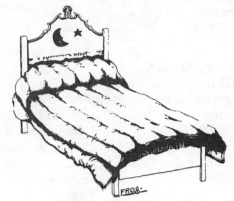

Polarguard® Goose Down Comforter, © Timberline Sewing Kits

13
Supportive Materials

This section presents companies with accessories and aids to design, fabrication, display, sales and related activity. Both products and custom services are included. (Check the index for further supportive materials.)

A. PRODUCTS

Action Bag Co.
846 Eagle Dr.
Bensenville, IL 60106
312-766-2881

See "POLYBAGS PLUS" for consumer mail orders and product details.
Polybags (2" to 12" x 15") including: Floss-A-Way™" and "bolt bags" for fabric. Cloth bags. Manufacturers, in business since 1980.
(Sells wholesale to dealers, distributors — inquire for literature and prices.)

Action Plastics
1460 E. 93rd Lane, N.E.
Minneapolis, MN 55434

Free catalog.
Plastic bags — variety of sizes, plain and ziplock; minimum 25.

Adventures in Crafts
1321 Madison Ave.
New York, NY 10028

Catalog, $1.00.
Boxes, including with recessed lid for inserting needlework (quilt fragments, etc.); others in variety of sizes/shapes/types. Fine-cutting scissors. (And decoupage supplies.) Has Mastercard, Visa. In business since 1971. Company president and designer Dee Davis is considered New York's "Dean of Decoupeurs".

Althor Products
496 Danbury Rd.
Wilton, CT 06897
203-762-0796

Send SASE for price list.
Plastic boxes: (clear, hinged or friction fit types) 1" sq. to 7¼" x 5" x 1¾" sizes; by 100 lots, with/without foam pads. Other plastic boxes (round, square, rectangular). Compartmented hinged stackable boxes. See-through drawer cabinets. Polybags: sizes to 24" x 36" by 1000 piece lots; plain and ziplock. Blank labels (self-adhesive, others), variety of sizes — to 5" x 3".

Associated Bag Co.
160 S. 2nd St.
Milwaukee, WI 53204

Send SASE for prices.
Poly bags, 1000 minimums, variety of sizes.

Bach Label Co.
1212 S. San Pedro St.
Los Angeles, CA 90015

Inquire for prices, specify.
Custom labels, all sizes and colors — printed (satin, cotton, webbing), woven (polyester, rayon-polyester, cotton); minimum 1000 labels.

Charm Woven Labels
Box 14664
Portland, OR 97214

Send SASE for brochure.
Woven labels: with partial inscriptions, custom names added ("Custom made by ...", "Fashioned by ...", and others).

> **Interested In Selling?** Fashion clothes buyers buy for next winter, in the spring; and for spring, in the fall. They work — plan and buy — six months **ahead** of each season.

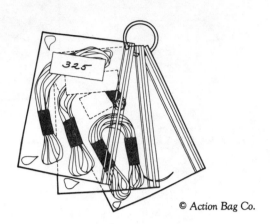

© Action Bag Co.

Chiswick Trading, Inc.
P.O. Box G, 31 Union Ave.
Sudbury, MA 01776

Write for information.
Polybags: plain and ziplock, all sizes (to 14" x 24" by 1000 piece lots); and with Easy-mark™ labeling area, white polybags, others. **Poly-foam** (on rolls). Shrink bags, including furniture sizes. **Packing materials,** tapes, dispensers. Stretch film.

Cotton Clouds
P.O. Box 604
Safford, AZ 85546

Complete supplies Catalog, samples, $2.00 (or send SASE with inquiry — specify interest).
"Cotton" oriented supplies: Hang tags for cotton handmades, 2" sq. with "100% cotton" and floral design. Postcards, fold-a-notes, rubberstamps (baby on cotton boll, "Gift of Cotton" cotton boll-in-hands motif, others), ceramic "cotton boll" buttons. Clothing design and sewing books, and line spinning wheels (and cotton supplies).
(Also sells some supplies wholesale to business, send SASE for details and application.)

The Designery
P.O. Box 2776
Kalamazoo, MI 49003

Send $1.00 for brochure and sample ($ .50 refundable).
Craft **hang tags:** personalized care labels for originals, in over 45 designs.

The Etc Shop
P.O. Box 142
Freeport, NY 11520

See your dealer or send SASE for prices.
Window note **cards** (for needlework, crafted/art work) — window 2½" diameter, 4" x 5", 2-fold — 3 colors. Needle card leaflets.

Frank Eastern Co.
625 Broadway
New York, NY 10012

Catalog, $1.00.
Office supplies: markers, papers, envelopes, filing materials, typewriter supplies and accessories, computer supplies (and furniture), files, storage cabinets, display boards, partitions, others. Office furniture: computer, desk/chairs, organizers, files, others. Small business equipment.

Fibergraphics
P.O. Box 11634
Shorewood, WI 53211

Catalog, $1.00.
Needlecraft/arts oriented bookplates, printed **stationery,** seals, and hang **tags,** etc.

John Franzisko
2 St. James Place, P.O. Box 786
Glen Cove, NY 11542

Send SASE for list.
Woven name tapes (personalized, 1-3 lines of type; 100 piece sets; iron-on or sew-on type).

Glenside Tape and Label
Box 283
Thorndale, PA 19372

Send SASE for information.
Fabric labels (set in script) — one or two lines.

Identify Label Corp.
P.O. Box 204
Brooklyn, NY 11214

Send SASE for price list.
Woven name tapes (by 100 up lots): personalized labels (white cotton, black print, red border) in 3 lines or less including "Fashioned by ...", "Style ..."; with up to 4 lines of copy; others.

Kidbits
15371 Big Mound
Lindenwood, IL 61049

Send $ .25 for list.
Witty **button-badges** for needleworkers.

Koalaty Products, Ltd.
118 S. Elmhurst Ave., Suite 2
Mt. Prospect, IL 60056

Brochure, $ .50.
With craft slogans: T-shirts, aprons, tote bags; (example: "I'm a Designing Woman").

L & L Stitchery
P.O. Box 43821
Atlanta, GA 30336

Send for catalog.
Washable **woven labels** — standard designs with custom imprinting in red; by 20 labels and up lots (including "Merry Christmas", "Hand made by — ", "An Original by — ", and others). Name tapes (1 line, or 2-4 lines; sew or iron-on types).

Messagemaker
Rt. 1
Broadalbin, NY 12025

Send SASE for list.
Merchandise bags (paper): small quantities, variety sizes in assortments.

Modern Store Fixture Mfg. Co.
2505 Stemmons Freeway
Dallas, TX 75207
214-634-2505

Write for information and prices.
Store fixtures: racks (including heavy-duty — variety of sizes, styles). Revolving racks and stands — floor and counter models. Triple mirrors (floor), others. Costumers racks (spiral type, straight arm, crossbar, others). See-through storage units. Shelving items; pegboard racks — full line. Tags, labels, Garment covers (bridal, formals, suit/coat, others); dispenser racks, "Quick-Pack" types, including novelties. Sleeve pads. Apparel steamers. Floodlights. Piece goods holders (for bolts of fabric). Security devices. Mannequins — children through adult, full models, torsos, others. "Easy Pin" shell forms, other forms. Form bases. Wicker forms. Hangers — "Roto-Clip" (to hanging bar), "Ceiling clip", and sock hangers, economy plastic clips.

Pat's Printworks
4424 W. 2nd Ave.
Vancouver, BC V6R 1K5, Canada

Catalog, samples, $1.50.
Fabric labels: personalized and printed, by 100 piece sets.

Patchwork Graphics, Inc.
P.O. Box 304, Old Chelsea Station
New York, NY 10113

Send SASE for brochure.
Greeting cards, photographed from 19th century quilts.

Polybags Plus
44 Grassmere Rd.
Elk Grove Village, IL 60007

Free price list.
Polybags (Action Bag Co.): ziplock (2" to 5" x 8" size, 2-mil and 4-mil) and white panel bags; by 100 piece lots. Bolt bags™ for fabrics. Floss-A-Way™ organizer polybags (5" x 3" size with label, zip-close, on metal ring — for specialty threads). Nickel rings. Minimum order, $15.

Quill Corporation
100 S. Schelter Rd.
Lincolnshire, IL 60069
312-634-4800

Write for prices.
Office equipment/supplies/furniture: Equipment: typewriters (Olivetti), calculators, phones, intercoms, copiers, microfiche, cassettes, scales, others. **Supplies:** for all above equipment, including IBM supplies, others for name brands. Computer supplies, duplicator, printing (paper, envelopes — full line), labels, stationery, packing supplies. Custom printing of stationery, forms. **Furniture:** cabinets, files, storage items, desks, chairs, computer furniture, partitions. Has quantity prices. Runs sales monthly.

Shurnuff Co.
P.O. Box 2545
Leucadia, CA 92024

Send SASE for details.
"Porta Booth" — portable show/display booth, construct-yourself (of pipes, fabric). Instruction book.

South Bound Millworks
P.O. Box 349
Sandwich, MA 02563

Free brochure.
Birch wood brackets, rods (¾" diameter) for wall hangings, curtains, etc. (holds hanging ½" from wall). Wrought iron accessories.

Sterling Name Tape Co.
Depot St.
Winsted, CT 06098

Free samples.
Labels (white or colored polyester tape) with custom logo or styeotk, one or more colors of ink; "our hot knife cutting process makes labels ravelproof to cut down on sewing time. You can have care or content information printed on the back to eliminate the need for additional labels." Has Mastercard, Visa.

Tri-Conn, Inc.
143 Golden Hill St., P.O. Box 190
Bridgeport, CT 06601
203-366-8547

Free brochure or estimate.
Portable (permanent) display booth framework (for up to 10' wide, 10' deep, 7½' high) in aluminum or chrome plated steel.

Unique Ideas
Box 627
North Bellmore, NY 11710

Send SASE for prices.
Woven launder care labels (washable, sew-on) — "Dry Clean Only", and others.

Walden
P.O. Box D
Elma, NY 14059

Send large SASE for samples.
Plastic bags, Most popular sizes (including for dolls, sewing kit/packs, others). Loveables™ **Woven labels:** "Made With Love by ... ("Mother", "Granny", others).

Widby Enterprises, U.S.A.
4321 Crestfield
Knoxville, TN 37921

Send large SASE for prices, samples.
Fabric labels — custom designed, or standard craft labels.

Lois Winston
P.O. Box 29796
Elkin Park, PA 19117

Send SASE for details.
"Needlenotes" note cards/envelopes with needlecrafters' designs.

Woodshop
Box 231
Minden, NE 68959

Send SASE for details.
Pattern for Wood "sewing machine"; "a craft show attention getter".

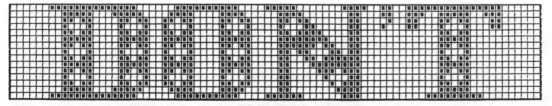

© Rose Clevery

B. SUPPORT SERVICES

These companies provide **custom services** for design, partial fabrication, and finishing.

Alice Prints
107 N.E. 60th
Seattle, WA 98115
206-523-6307

Send SASE with inquiry.
Custom hand printing of textiles (to specifications) by professionals.

Artaids
183 Hagen
N. Tonawanda, NY 14120

Send SASE for complete details.
Pattern enlarging services for: embroidery, dolls, quilts, applique, toys, others.

The Artists Press
P.O. Box 73
Medford, OR 97501
503-779-7270

Information and samples, $2.00.
Service: Reproduction of drawings (pen, ink, pencils) into note and greeting cards (for sewing and other needlework motifs, others). (Also reproduces paintings, for limited editions.)

Color Q Art Reproductions
2835 Springboro, West
Dayton, OH 45439
513-294-0406

Free booklet.
Fine-art reproductions service for greeting cards, postcards, (in your sewing or needlecraft designs, others) 8½" x 11" size, others; in full color, from art work.

Douthat
2504 Kell Rd.
Signal Mountain, Tn 37377

Send SASE for research report.
Coat-of-arms research, for designs for sew-decor (and other uses). Also readymade items.

Rose Clevery
4520 Robertson Ave.
Sacramento, CA 95821

Send $1.50 for samples, prices.
Graphic Service: custom prepared lettering charts (for cross stitch, embroidery, other needle crafts) on order; in 4 alphabet styles/sizes. Produces your names, monograms, quotations, others, or complete alphabets.

The Designing Woman
Lakeville, CT 06039
203-435-9760

Send SASE with inquiry.
Custom needlecraft **designs;** custom monogram services: designs, belt mounting.

Fashion Touches
P.O. Box 804
Bridgeport, CT 06601

Free catalog.
Custom services: professionally covers belts and buttons "from your own fabrics, including suede and leather ... at reasonable prices". Returns most orders "within 24 hours first class mail". Pays postage. "Store inquiries invited".

Grafton Woolen Mill, Inc.
1300 14th Ave.
Grafton, WI 53024

Send SASE for information sheet.
Custom quilt batting (2 weights); custom covering of batting with choice cloth, hand tying of comforters. (Other custom work.)

Hawkins Graphics Studio
Box 503, 501 Fourth Ave., S.E.
White Sulphur Springs, MT 59645

Send SASE for rate sheet.
Custom **Graphic designs** for stationery, business cards, brochures; for craftpeople and artists, at "package prices".

Sally Klein
3305 W. 111th St.
Chicago, IL 60655

Brochure, $ .50.
Service: white on white quilt tops marked.

Constance La Lena Sunflower Studio
2851 Road B½
Grand Junction, CO 81501
303-242-3883

Service: custom weaving, dyeing and garment (and uniforms) making. (See also under FABRICS.)

Panel Prints, Inc.
1001 Moosic Rd.
Old Forge, PA 18518
717-457-8334

Send specific needs inquiry.
Printing services for woven and non-woven fabrics —
unlimited color reproduction (for calendars, ornaments,
hangings, dolls, etc.) and for needleprint and rug designs,
cross-stitch designs; small or large prints, single images up
to 53" x 76" — any size, any quantity.

The Village Studio
Box 16
West Fairlee, VT 05083

Details and sample, $1.00.
Service: enlarging and print photographs onto fabric (for
quilt blocks, pillows, others), or onto artists canvas for
overpainting.

Diane Walker
P.O. Box 461
Alief, TX 77411

Send SASE for price quote.
Your photographs reproduced and enlarged in royal blue
on cotton fabric (for pillows, others).

14
Booksellers

B. R. Artcraft Co.
Baldwin, MD 21013

Catalog, $1.00.
Books (including new, out-of-print): Fabric design, embroidery, leather/fur working, ornamentation, needlecrafts, tapestries, stitchery, costume patterns, clothing, clothing decorating (dyeing, batik, stencilling); other needle and general craft titles.
Allows foreign orders.

Associated Book Sellers
147 McKinley Ave.
Bridgeport, CT 06606

Free list.
"Key" books: sewing, dollmaking, embroidery, fashion design; other needlecrafts; other non-craft titles.

Book Barn
P.O. Box 256
Avon, CT 06001

List, $ .75.
Books (extensive list): embroidery applique, designing, cross-stitch; needlecrafts of other countries; dyeing, textile design; others (needlecraft and general craft titles).

Mary Chapman, Bookseller
P.O. Box 304
College Park, MO 20740

Send SASE for list.
Books: textiles, lace; other needlecrafts. Out-of-print textiles books. Search Service.

Costume and Fashion Bookshop
Queen's Elm Parade, Old Church St.
London SW3 6EJ, England

Write with specific inquiry or for information.
Books: on fashion, tailoring, costumes, textiles; other decorative and applied arts including out-of-print volumes; fashion magazines. Overseas payment (U.S., elsewhere) is on receipt of invoice whereupon books are dispatched by surface-mail at reduced book rate; by International Money Order in Sterling.

Craft Books
P.O. Box 2099
Acworth, GA 30101

Catalog, $2.00.
Craft How-to books, full line in variety of needle and other crafts including: candlewicking, stencilling, cross stitch, embroidery, others.

Craft Books
P.O. Box 42
Northbrook, IL 60062

Catalog, $ .50.
Books (chosen for merit, as best buys): textiles crafts, patchwork, quilting, soft sculpture, leatherworking; ethnic needlecraft titles (Russian, Indian, Guatemalian, Greek, African and other needlecrafts).

Craft Course Publishers
260 So. Paseo Tesoro
Walnut, CA 91789

See your dealer or write for information.
Over 25 Sewing pattern/How-to booklets (fullsize patterns): quilting titles, pillows, stuffed animals, fabric yo-yo's, machine and hand embroidery, kitchen "witches", soft sculpture/quilted boxes, frames, houses designs (for pillows, hangings, bookends, other), holiday accessories, "country" designs, bags and totes, patchwork, applique, dolls and clothes making, novelties, others; (and extensive selections in other crafts, needlecrafts).

The Crewel Elephant
124 E. 13th St.
Silverton, CO 81433

Send SASE for lists.
Books (bargain reprints, closeouts, others): embroidery, crewel, smocking, cross stitch, quilting, patchwork, applique, ethnic clothing and other sewing, miniatures, dollmaking (and other needlecrafts).

Dover Publications, Inc.
180 Varick St.
New York, NY 10014

Free needlecraft catalog.
Hundreds of low-cost books (sewing and fiber/needlecrafts) — designing, how-to techniques, history, copyright-free motifs, others: embroidery, charted and iron-on designs, patchwork, applique, quilting, toy and dollmaking, doll clothes, costumes/fashion designs; fabric printing (stencil, screen, block print, dye, batik), stitchery, smocking, cross stitch, others. Extensive alphabets, designs of all styles and periods, holiday and special occasion accessories/designs, coloring books, textile and related references. (And many other non-needlecraft titles, for crafts and other subjects).

Bette Feinstein
96 Roundwood Rd.
Newton, MA 02164

Catalog, $1.00 (specify interest).
Books: sewing and all related needle/fiber crafts (quilting, dressmaking, costumes, textiles, patchwork, cutwork, stampwork, ethnic/historic clothing, others) books of McCall's Simplicity, Coats and Clark Booklets collections; others; needlecraft/sewing **booklets** (extensive). Old issues of **Needlework** magazines: "The Modern Priscilla", "American Fabrics", others. Has book search service. Buys/sells old needlework books.

The Flying Needle
6290 E. Pinchot
Scottsdale, AZ 85251

Sample, $3.00, or send SASE for information.
Quarterly journal for members of National Standards Council of American Embroiderers. (Has display and classified ads.)

LP Publishing, Inc.
8531 Wellsford Place, Suite J
Santa Fe Springs, CA 90670
213-696-0079

Send SASE for list.
Books (fabric sewing and craft patterns — with full-size patterns) On: photo albums, trimmed baskets, stick and lamp horses/unicorns, soft dolls, mice toys, wallets and purse accessories, handbags and totes, belts and bags, lamp shades; others.

Needlecraft Books
Alanson, MI 49706

Book list, $1.00.
Books: most quilting titles, out-of-print titles; reprints of old pattern books; other titles.

Katherine Ramus
2100 E. Eastman Ave.
Englewood, CO 80110

Send SASE for list (or specific interest).
Books: sewing, dollmaking, miniatures making, embroidery, other needlecrafts (and other crafts and fiber craft titles).

Ross Book Service
Seminary P.O. 12093
Alexandria, VA 22304
703-370-4455

Bookseller, from Feb. '84*.
"Cheap Threads" catalog, $ .50 ('84), $1.00 ('85).
Books (remaindered and other bargains) on all fiber and textile arts/crafts, including: sewing, thread-count, embroidery, soft sculpture, dressmaking, fashion, tapestries design, dyeing processes, laces, textile history, quilting, others.
*Miriam Ross returns to her book business after a stay of several months in Jerusalem accompanying her husband at an institute of archaeological research.

Unicorn
9069 Shady Grove Ct.
Gaithersburg, MD 20877

Catalog, $1.00.
Over 900 needlecraft/fiber craft books: costumes, ethnic/historic clothing and fashion sewing, embroidery techniques, dyeing/batik, toy and dollmaking, general and specific designs, applique, quilting, patchwork, laces, trimming; other how-to, design and informative titles (and in non-sewing categories).
May have closeouts; Mastercard and Visa.

15
Publications

All publications listed below present sewing, needlecrafts and related fiber crafts information — either exclusively, or as among their selections of craft categories.

Please include either the listed sample cost, or a SASE (stamped, self-addressed envelope) with any inquiry regarding the publication, subscription cost, and/or advertising rates.

Note: In the recent survey of publications, where additional information was not received, only the periodical name and address is given.

Ad News Bulletin
555 E. 33rd Pl., #103
Chicago, IL 60616

Sample, $2.00.
Classified bulletin for craftspeople selling crafts and patterns.

American Craft
Membership Department
Box 1308
Ft. Lee, NJ 07024

Send SASE with inquiry.
Bimonthly magazine for members of the American Craft Council; all arts/crafts; textiles, sewing, others.

Arti-Fact Archives
1641 No. Mary Dr.
Santa Maria, CA 93454

Sample, $2.00 ($2.50 in 1985).
Bimonthly newsletter with needlecraft (and other) projects; full size patterns. (has display and classified ads.)

Arts and Crafts Catalyst
5423 New Haven Ave.
Ft. Wayne, IN 46803

Samples, $4.00.
Bimonthly magazine: shows fairs and other events as marketplaces for arts/crafts work (nationwide) with application data. (Has display advertising.)

Better Homes and Gardens
100's of Needlework and Craft Ideas
1716 Locust St.
Des Moines, IA 50336

National magazine guide to **needlecrafts.**

Butterick Sewing World
161 Sixth Ave.
New York, NY 10013

Quarterly national magazine of fashion sewing patterns and other needlecraft projects/patterns by Butterick.

C.H.A.N. Newsletter
Old Economy Village, 14th and Church Sts.
Ambridge, PA 15003
412-266-6440

Send SASE for information.
A quarterly journal of the Center For The History of American Needlework, a nonprofit educational institution; has articles on history, industry, center news, book reviews.

Le Creme of Crepe de Chine: "Handling **Crepe de Chine** fabric (a silk in the natural, or found in polyester blends): Dyes beautifully, is luxurious looking — save it for your most dynamic looks. Use it for feminine, soft clothing, and take great care with this delicate fabric: Use sharp, thin needles; silk pins and sharp shears, and a good quality, all-polyester thread." — Courtesy of **Margaret Fredericks,** publisher of *The Needle People News,* from Vol. 6, No. 4.

Carol's Bits and Pieces
Box 9014
Kansas City, MO 64168

Sample, $1.00 ppd.
Monthly newsletter of sewing tips (illustrated techniques useful to today's fashion sewing).

Canada Quilts
360 Stewart Dr.
Sudberry, Ontario Canada P3E 2R8

Catalog Sources — News and Updates
P.O. Box 6232-SS
Augusta, GA 30906

Sample, $2.50.
Quarterly newsletter, an ongoing sequel to this book, *The Sew & Save Source Book*, and also to *Catalog Sources For Creative People*. Each issue updates the books with listings of address and other changes, new product information and retail/wholesale data. New, detailed sources of supplies, tools, equipment, and resources are presented for all sewing, needlecrafts, and general arts and crafts. (Has display and classified ads.)

The Cloth Doll
P.O. Box 1089
Mt. Shasta, CA 96067

Single issue, $2.75; send SASE for details.
Quarterly magazine devoted to cloth dolls and patterns, How-to's, book reviews, tips; collector's and dollmaking columns, profiles on designers.

Color Compliments Newsletter
P.O. Box 6130
Springfield, IL 62790

Sample issue, $ .50.
This quarterly newsletter is published to keep women informed of the latest news in the color field. It provides data on color forecasting, matching fabric textures to garment style, and on successful color combinations.

Counted Thread
3305 So. Newport St.
Denver, CO 80224

Send SASE with inquiry.
A quarterly magazine for needlecrafters.

The Coupon Letter
P.O. Box 830
Evans, CO 80620

Send SASE for sample.
Monthly newsletter of exclusive discount coupons for home sewing and other fiber and needlecrafts — books, patterns, kits, equipment, supplies; from reputable dealers.

Craft Range
6800 W. Oregon Dr.
Denver, CO 80226

Crafts
News Plaza, P.O. Box 1790
Peoria, IL 61656

Send SASE for details.
Monthly magazine for all crafts/needlecrafts, sewing; with projects, reviews, profiles, products and events.

The Crafts Fair Guide
Box 262
Mill Valley, CA 94941

Crafts 'N Things
Park Ridge, IL 60068

Send SASE with inquiry.
Needle and general crafts projects are covered in this bimonthly magazine.

The Crafts Report
3632 Ashworth North
Seattle, WA 98103

Sample issue, $2.00.
Monthly newspaper of marketing and management topics for professional craftspeople; presents data on how, where and under what circumstances to market all crafts.

Crafts Spectrum
P.O. Box 45
New Carlisle, OH 45344

Send SASE with inquiry.
A newsletter of classified ads for buyers/sellers.

Craftswoman
1153 Oxford
Deerfield, IL 60015

Sample, $3.00.
Quarterly magazine of business and marketing, with information for professionals in all categories of craftsmanship. (Has display and classified ads.)

Craftrade News
Box 279
Mansura, LA 71350

Creative Button Bulletin
26 Meadowbrook Lane
Chalfont, PA 18914

Sample issue, $2.00.
Newsletter for button users, crafters and collectors; with data, history, product news. (Has classified ads.)

Creative Crafts/Miniatures
P.O. Box 700
Newton, NJ 07860

Sample, $1.75.
Magazine with sewing, needlecrafts, crafts and miniature projects. (Has display and classified ads.)

The Creative Express
P.O. Box 4666
Rolling Bay, WA 98061

Year subscription, $1.00 (U.S.), $5.00 (foreign).
A quarterly cooperative catalog newsletter meant to be a source book for needlecrafts, sewing and related areas.

Creative Monthly Newsletter
Box 47-2
New London, WI 54961

The Creative Needle
717 Madison Ave.
New York, NY 10021

Cross Stitch News
2827 Buffalo Court
Arlington, TX 76013

Decorating & Crafts Ideas
P.O. Box 2522
Birmingham, AL 35201

Send SASE with inquiry.
Magazine with sewing, needle and general crafts for home and decorative items. (Has display and classified ads.)

Doll Castle News/Dollmaker
P.O. Box 247
Washington, NJ 07882

Doll Times
P.O. Box 337
Oswego, IL 60543

Send SASE with inquiry.
Monthly magazine for dollmakers, collectors and investors; features data on antique and contemporary styles.

The Fashion/Sewing Newsletter
Suite 509, 320 East 54th St.
New York, NY 10022

Sample issue, $1.00.
Monthly consumer publication, aimed to help readers "sew like a pro"; suggests fabrics and trims with the designer look; how-to's, tricks-of-the-trade, and sources.

Fiber Technic and Marketplace
P.O. Box 518
Paradise, CA 95969

Send SASE with inquiry.
How-to magazine for fibercrafts with free classifieds for materials services.

Fiberarts
50 College St.
Asheville, NC 28801

Bimonthly magazine features on weaving, dyeing, textiles, soft sculpture, clothing; suppliers, news.

Good Ideas for Needlework
79 Madison Ave.
New York, NY 10016

© That Patchwork Place, Inc.

Handmade
50 College St.
Asheville, NC 28801

Send SASE with inquiry.
Bimonthly magazine of sewing, knitting, needlework and crafts topics; with challenging projects with instructions, and full size pattern in every issue. (Has display ads.)

The Handworker Magazine
Rt. 1, Box 349
Wausaukee, WI 54177

Kite Lines
7106 Campfield Rd.
Baltimore, MD 21207

Quarterly internation magazine devoted entirely to kiting, with regular features of making kites from fabrics and other space age materials, and papers.
(Has book reviews, display and classified ads.)

LaPlata Review for Quilters
P.O. Box 830
Evans, CO 80620

Send SASE with inquiry.
This quarterly reviews quiltmaking arts publications; shows and events; and other data of interest to quilting.

The Looming Arts
P.O. Box 233, Jordan Rd.
Sedona, AZ 86336

Sample issue, $2.00.
This publication appears five times yearly, and is geared to beginner and advanced handweavers; provides fabric samples with project directions on weaving.

Make It With Leather
P.O. Box 1386
Ft. Worth, TX 76101

Making It
P.O. Box 286, 300 Sunrise Hwy.
Rockeville Center, NY 11571

Quarterly newspaper, the official publication of custom dressmakers; provides industry overviews, fashion trends and products, news and reviews, current designs. (Has display ads.)

McCall's Needlework and Crafts
825 Seventh Ave., 7th Floor
New York, NY 10019

Send SASE with inquiry.
Bimonthly national magazine for consumers. (Has display ads.)

McCall's Patterns
230 Park Ave.
New York, NY 10169

A quarterly national magazine with overviews of current fashion sewing patterns by McCalls.

The Miniature Magazine (now combined with Creative Crafts)

Miniature World
P.O. Box 337
Seabrook, NH 03874

National Calendar of Indoor/Outdoor Art Fairs
(See Arts and Crafts Catalyst)

National Doll World
Box 337
Seabrook, NH 03874

Bimonthly publication of dolls, patterns, dollhouse patterns and accessoies; exchanges and letters, contests, doll antiques data. (Has display and classified ads.)

National Handicrafter
Commerce Bldg.
Grant Park, IL 60940

Sample issue, $ .50.
Bimonthly publication of plans and patterns on a variety of needles and general crafts; with how-to features. (Has advertising.)

Needle & Thread
4949 Byers
Ft. Worth, TX 76107

Sample, $3.70 ppd.
Bimonthly magazine with sewing and needlecrafts projects, patterns; showcases designers, covers trends and news.

Needle Arts
6 E. 45th St., Rm. 1301
New York, NY 10017

Send SASE with inquiry.
Publication of the Embroiderer's Guild of America, one of the organization benefits to members.

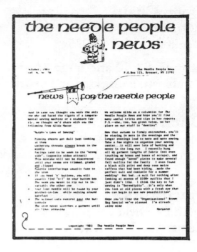

The Needle People News
P.O. Box 115
Syosset, NY 11791

Sample issue, $ .50.
A monthly newsletter of a national sewing club, offering discounts on fabrics, notions, patterns and other sewing essentials; presents information on construction and alterations of garments, etc., with features by professionals. (Has classified ads.)

Needlecraft For Today
4949 Byers
Ft. Worth, TX 76107

Sample, $3.70 ppd.
Bimonthly magazine with needlecraft patterns for each featured project; over-sized pages give added material over standard size.

Needlecraft News
4949 Byers
Ft. Worth, TX 76107

Sample, $1.75.
Bimonthly newsletter, features sewing needlecraft facts, trends; reader exchanges of news and ideas, patterns.

The Needlework Times
P.O. Box 87263
Chicago, IL 60680

Sample issue, $2.00.
This publication features needlecraft people, places, patterns, trends, news, techniques, and home study courses; 6 times yearly.

Nutshell News
Clifton House
Clifton, VA 22024

Publication slanted to scale miniatures and miniature-making.

Open Chain

P.O. Box 2634
Menlo Park, CA 94025

Sample, $1.50 and large SASE.
Combination magazine and newsletter of needlecrafts.

Ontario Craft

346 Dundas St., W.
Toronto, Ontario M5T 1G5 Canada

Patchwork

2418 Deerfield Ct.
Camarillo, CA 93010

Patchwork Patter

P.O. Box 62
Greenbelt, MD 20770

Send SASE with inquiry.
The publication of the National Quilting Association.

Popular Needlework

Box 428
Seabrook, NH 03874

This magazine gives projects for variety of needlecrafts; and doll swap and questions columns, quilting questions; sewing features. (Has display and classified ads.)

The Prairie Wool Companion

126 So. Phillips
Sioux Falls, SD 57102

Send SASE for details.
Semi-annual weaving magazine with projects and technical information; by Xenakis.

The Professional Quilter

917 Lakeview Ave.
St. Paul, MN 55117

Sample, $3.00.
Bimonthly publication for quilting businesswomen. (Has display and classified ads.)

Quilt World

Box 337
Seabrook, NH 03874

This bimonthly magazine features quilt patterns, designs, exchanges, news, contests, photos, features, hints. (Has display and classified ads.)

© *Leman Publications*

Quilter's Newsletter Magazine

6700 W. 44th Ave.
Wheatridge, CO 80033

Sample issue, $1.75 (includes catalog).
This magazine, published ten times yearly, presents applique and patchwork, techniques for quiltmaking, features for beginner and experienced. (Has display and classified ads.)

Quiltmaker

6700 W. 44th Ave.
Wheatridge, CO 80033

Sample, $4.00 (includes free catalog).
A biannual quilting magazine with 15 to 20 new patterns per issue, with directions and illustrations, and on cross stitching applique and machine and hand quilting techniques. (Has display ads.)

Sew News

208 South Main
Seattle, WA 98104

Free sample issue.
Bimonthly tabloid for people who sew; gives tips, fashion, techniques, interviews, news. (Has display and classified ads.)

Sew Smart

1100 Ivywood
New Castle, IN 47362

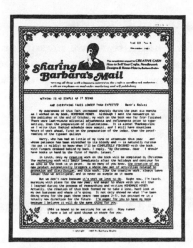

Sharing Barbara's Mail
P.O. Box 10423-SD
Springfield, MO 65808

Sample issue, $2.50 (or a catalog on request).
This is a business-oriented newsletter for everyone involved in the fields of sewing, needlework and crafts, and home businesses in general; heavy emphasis on networking — sharing ideas, resources and marketing data.

Shuttle, Spindle & Dyepot
65 LaSalle Rd., P.O. Box 70374
W. Hartford, CT 06107

A quarterly publication of The Handweavers Guild of America.

The Silver Thimble
311 Valley Brook Rd.
McMurray, PA 15317

Send SASE for details.
This newsletter, published monthly, gives sewing information, how-to's (with diagrams and illustrations), hints and tips on a variety of techniques.

The Smocking Arts
Box 75
Knoxville, TN 37901

Sample, $4.10.
A magazine of The Smocking Arts Guild of America. Provides new designs and smocking and sewing articles.

Simplicity Today
200 Madison Ave.
New York, NY 10016

This is a national quarterly magazine devoted to current Simplicity sewing patterns.

Stitch 'N Sew
P.O. Box 428
Seabrook, NH 03874

This is a national magazine for home sewers; with features, letters, exchanges, projects. (Has display and classified ads.)

Sunshine Artists, U.S.A.
501-503 N. Virginia Ave.
Winter Park, FL 32789

Send SASE for details.
Monthly marketing magazine for professional craftspeople (and fibercrafts people) artists and others who work street and mall shows (gives events, ratings, marketing trends, and data).

The Textile Booklist
Box C-20
Lopez, WA 98261

Sample, $4.00.
Quarterly, reviews over thirty books per issue, on textiles, sewing, needlecrafts, and related; news. Urges self-publishers to submit PR and book copy.

Treadleart
25834 Narbonne Ave. Suite 1
Lomita, CA 90717

Sample issue, $1.50.
This bimonthly magazine is geared to the sewing machine art enthusiast; with machine news and updates, hints, patterns, letters; embroidery techniques and designs.

12 Months of Christmas
Box 130, Willow Point
W. Mystic, CT 06388

Sample issue, $1.00 ($1.50 in '84).
A "Santa's Headstart Program" newsletter, features Christmas projects/original patterns and advice for giftmaking, home decorations, etc. Published by "The Sleigh Belles".

Vogue Patterns
161 Sixth Ave.
New York, NY 10013

A bimonthly national magazine with a rundown of current fashion sewing patterns by Vogue.

The Weavers Journal
P.O. Box 2049
Boulder, CO 80306

Westart
Box 1396
Auburn, CA 95603

Sample, $ .50.
Biweekly newspaper of west coast arts/crafts exhibitions, shows.

Woman's Day Needlework and Handicraft Ideas
Fawcett Blvd.
Greenwich, CT 06830

The Workbasket
4251 Pennsylvania Ave.
Kansas City, MO 64111

Send SASE for details.
This magazine presents needlework and home arts projects, ten times yearly.

Trade Publications

These publications are meant for those in business. Send for further information — use your letterhead, and include a SASE with your inquiry.

Creative Product News
P.O. Box 584
Lake Forest, IL 60045

Gift and Decorative Accessories
51 Madison Ave.
New York, NY 10010

Profitable Craft Merchandising
News Plaza, P.O. Box 1790
Peoria, IL 61656

Sew Business
P.O. Box 1331
Ft. Lee, NJ 07024

Yarn Market News
50 College St.
Asheville, NC 28801

16
Resources

A. ORGANIZATIONS

American Home Sewing Association
(American Home Sewing Guild)
1270 Broadway, Suite 1007
New York, NY 10001

Non-profit organization for all those who sew. Members are entitled to attend workshops, benefits, fashion shows; newsletters. Write above address if interested in starting a guild, or to nearest chapter for more information:
Chapters:
P.O. Box 2818, Kirkland, WA 98033
P.O. Box 35513, Minneapolis, MN 55435
P.O. Box 2523, Denver, CO 80201
P.O. Box 381, Indianapolis, IN 46206
P.O. Box 19346, Houston, TX 77224
P.O. Box 1294, Newport Beach, CA 92663
P.O. Box 8326, Silver Spring, MD 20907

Bishop Method of Clothing Construction Council, Inc.
2522 Upland St.
Arlington, VA 22207

Organization to promote the Bishop Method of Clothing Construction and assure uniformity and high standards in teaching sewing (applying industry techniques to home sewing). Members exchange ideas and conduct programs through adult education. Publishes a newsletter.

Center for the History of American Needlework
Old Economy Village
14th and Church Sts.
Ambridge, PA 15003

A national non-profit organization devoted to all historical aspects of needlework.
Members receive these benefits: A quarterly newsletter, discounts for publications and other material, use of a research library, audio-visual programs, a speaker's bureau presents exhibits on site.

Collector Circle
1313 S. Killian Dr.
Lake Park, FL 33403

An association for thimble collectors and those interested, provides members with seminars, a library collection, quarterly newsletters (The Gazette). They research the hallmarkings of thimbles and sponsor museum collections exhibits.

Counted Thread Society of America
3305 S. Newport St.
Denver, CO 80224

This organization provides a quarterly newsletter.

Custom Sewing Guild
1605 10th St., W.
Kirkland, WA 98033

Non-profit organization of professional designers and manufacturers of fabric clothing and accessories. Encourages worksharing of problems and resourcs among members. Sponsors educational program/seminars.
"Through the guild," said Joni Pascoe, President, "we [can] acknowledge our accomplishments." "Today's dressmaker,"she states, "is often professional, highly trained, with knowledge of fitting and technology and the skills to run her own business."

Turning Pro with a Notebook: "To get the really professional look to clothing that you sew, you must learn to observe the clothing industry. Observe the things that designers are doing to accessorize. Observe the width of various collar designs, width of cuffs, fly fronts, pockets, lapels, etc. These change from season to season much more so than the body portion of a garment. Patterns cannot be relied upon for these changes ... Take a notebook in your purse and jot these important facts down as you shop. Also carry a small piece of tape for measuring." — Courtesy of **Mary J. Wadlington** of Gem Publications, author of *The Custom Touch*.

Hearthside Crafts Quilters' Club

P.O. Box 305, Westview Station
Binghamton, NY 13905
and
P.O. Box 9120, Station E
Edmonton, Alta Canada T5P 4K2

Quilter's Club — **members receive newsletters bimonthly with ideas, patterns, free pattern catalog, discounts. Membership $4.00 yearly.**

National Quilting Association, Inc.

P.O. Box 62
Greenbelt, MD 20770

This non-profit organization publishes *Patchwork Patter*, and provides other benefits for members.

NSCAE (National Standards Council of American Embroiderers)

For Membership Information:
P.O. Box 8578
Northfield, IL 60093

This non-profit educational association (for professionals, beginners through advanced, etc.) is devoted to promotion of high standards in needlework. Among member benefits: A lending volume and slide library with extensive selections on all types of needle work, study portfolios; Needle Expressions (a juried, biennial exhibit of contemporary needlecraft (part of the show becomes a traveling exhibit, through the U.S.), a quarterly journal, and a correspondence school. The Council serves as information for members concerning the organization, and education in the field of fiber arts.

Embroiderer's Guild of America

6 E. 45th St., Room 1501
New York, NY 10017

This non-profit organization provides *NeedleArts* magazine, and has needlework course by mail order.

Handweavers Guild of America, Inc.

65 LaSalle Rd., P.O. Box 7-374
W. Hartford, CT 06107

This non-profit organization publishes annual directories, and a magazine for members, along with other benefits.

The American Sewing Guild at the Minnesota State Fair

Smocking Arts Guild of America

P.O. Box 75
Knoxville, TN 37919
615-637-5456

This organization's purpose is to establish high standards of quality workmanship and to further the appreciation of smocking arts and related handwork through education and communication. Publishes *The Smocking Arts* five times yearly, for members; annual convention includes instructional sessions.

Society of Craft Designers

P.O. Box 2176
Newburg, NY 12550

This organization is composed of creative people: designers, writers, manufacturers, retailers, publishers, distributors, instructors, and demonstrators with an interest in promoting quality in design, professionalism in the marketplace, and education for its members. It conducts seminars and provides a comprehensive referral service/listing (computerized, available to manufacturers, manufacturers' representatives, publishers, and distributors). The annual Fine-Craft Auction and Bazaar provides publicity in the trade and consumer press. The Society gathers references in vital areas of interest. Among them: taxes, insurance, contracts, copyrights, instruction writing, and others. It also publishes a six times yearly newsletter for members.

Thimble Collectors International

P.O. Box 143
Intervale, NH 03845

This is an organization of thimble collectors and enthusiasts; formed to promote historical research, educate members (in display, storage and cataloging of thimbles), standardize designations of thimbles. They conduct workshops, maintain a library of printed material and slides.

B.   HOME STUDY COURSES

Custom Drapery Institute
412 S. Lyon St.
Santa Ana, CA 92705

Free booklet.
Learn **drapery making and interior decorating;** buy fabrics, shades and accessories at wholesale, "no age or educational qualifications".

Hands On!
82 South St.
Milford, NH 03055

Send SASE for information.
Course for **embroidery** needleworker; no projects, but study of variety of materials and techniques; monthly materials, patterns or charts, instructions for experiments; lessons and binder are among materials included.

Jo's Hobby House
413 Maryland Ave.
Bristol, TN 37620

Free details.
Doll Dressing Course — for sewing miniature garments for dolls; step-by-step instructions with illustrations.

Lifetime Career Schools
2251 Barry Ave.
Los Angeles, CA 90064

Free booklet.
Dollmaking and Restoration, designing and creating dollclothes, repairing mechanical dolls, authentication of old dolls. Lessons and free consultation.

Lifetime Career Schools
2251 Barry Ave.
Los Angeles, CA 90064

Free booklet.
Dressmaking Course: professional sewing methods taught — features speed-up methods and factory shortcuts in "easy-learn" format; with how-to assignments and sewing aids; for beginners and old-timers.

Modern Upholstery Institute
802 Field Bldg.
Kansas City, MO 64111

Free book, *Professional Upholstery for Fun and Profit.*
Upholstery course: Complete instructions for upholstering chairs, cushions, seats, footstools, couches; all furniture styles, sizes; develops professional skills, trade techniques from basics to advanced methods.

National School of Dress Design
Division of Career Institute
1500 Cardinal Dr.
Little Falls, NJ 07424

Write for information.
Home study course in **Fashion Design.**

NSCAE Correspondence School (National Standards Council of American Embroiderers)
600 Bell Ave.
Carnegie, PA 15106
Closed July 15 — August 15, Dec. 15 — Jan. 1.

Send SASE for details.
Correspondence school founded to offer comprehensive courses: **Embroidery/Stitchery** for amateurs and professionals. Curriculum includes courses at several levels in a variety of embroidery methods, and in design, color for needlework and contemporary fiber techniques. While students progress at their own pace, each is assigned a counselor certified by NSCAE; most courses are completed in 3 to 5 weeks, extensions are possible. Completed courses are reviewed and graded before exams or certificates.

Quilts by Jeannie May
917 Lakeview Ave.
St. Paul, MN 55117

Send SASE for home study information (specify).
Confidence Quilting Home Study Course: Series of 10 quilting lessons (with full size patterns, instructions) by Jeannie M. Spears (NQA Certified Teacher).

Sewing Center
Rochelle, GA 31079

Free details.
Sewing machine repairing instructions.

South-Western Publishing Co.
925 Spring Rd.
Pelham Manor, NY 10803

Clothing: *Image and Impact* by Jeane G. Johnson — **education kit** on clothing selection and wardrobe planning, with: 6 booklets, activities, personal coloring chart, color families chart. Instructor's manual and key also available.

Kaye M. Wood
4949 Ran Rd.
West Branch, MI 48661

Send SASE for details.
Machine embroidery and applique: Lessons for junior and senior high school sewing classes, 4H and other groups.

C.   GENERAL/MEDIA RESOURCES

American Artist Reprints
1515 Broadway
New York, NY 10036

American Artist Directory of Art Schools and Work-shops, $2.50 (includes schools and colleges, summer schools, private teachers, others) and includes schools with instruction in basic design, fashion design, textile design (and most all art categories).

Artisan Crafts
P.O. Box 10423-SD
Springfield, MO 65808

Free catalog.
Book: *Creative Cash — How to Sell Your Crafts, Needle-work, Designs and Know-How,* by Barbara Brabec (how to successfully start and operate your own business, utilizing your special sewing talents and "know-how", presenting a wide range of opportunities in all areas. **And these reports:** (1) How To Establish and Legally Operate a Cottage Industry, $4.35. (2) Sales Representatives: How to Find Them, Work with Them, or Possibly Become One Yourself, $4.35.

Dick Blick/Horton
P.O. Box 1267
Galesburg, IL 61401

Brochures, flyers and supplements (supplies), $2.00; or inquire with SASE for filmstrip details.
Color filmstrip with cassettes (for classrooms, groups, individuals) on textile techniques: stitchery, Tie-dyeing, Painting Textiles, Silk Screening (and many others on arts, crafts).

Catalog Sources Press
P.O. Box 6232-SS
Augusta, GA 30906

Wholesale Report: *Crafts/Fibercrafts* by Margaret A. Boyd ($4.50).
Presents guidelines and sources for getting wholesale, and near wholesale prices by mail; for professionals, home businesses, retailers, others; with listings of retailers/wholesalers keyed to directory book; helpful periodicals. (Order on letterhead for bonus, wholesalers survey/listings.)

Celebrity Addresses
R.R. 9, Box 79(PB)
Quincy, IL 62301

Send SASE for information.
List of celebrities from whom to get an endorsement to make items in their image.

The Crafts Report/Books
700 Orange St., P.O. Box 1992
Wilmington, DE 19899

Send SASE for details.
Book: *The Crafts Business Encyclopedia* (how-to sell, price, and learn of taxes, insurance, loans, marketing, etc.). Has quantity discounts for schools/organizations.

Crystal Productions
Box 12317
Aspen, CO 81612

Write for catalog.
Sound film strips programs (from American Craft Council slides series) on fibercrafts (and 10 other categories). Programs include film strip, cassette and teachers guide.

Daedalus Publications, Inc.
1153 Oxford Rd.
Deerfield, IL 60015

Send SASE for details.
Book: *How To Have a Successful Craft Show in Your Home* (a guide to planning and publicizing your own holiday boutique), by Anne Patterson Dee — explains the do's and don't's for a well publicized, well run and profitable show.

Empire State Crafts Alliance
9 Vasser St.
Poughkeepsie, NY 12601

Information on format used, list, $1.00 (specify).
Computer Stored lists of craftspeople in New York State, with retrievable references to medium and location.

The Goodfellow Catalog Press
P.O. Box 4520
Berkeley, CA 94704

Send SASE for information on data costs, and jurying for participation in an upcoming edition. *The Goodfellow Catalog of Wonderful Things* (and spin-off publications).

Ivy Crafts Imports
5410 Annapolis Rd.
Bladensburg, MD 20710

Send SASE for information (or $3.00 for complete supplies catalog).
Videotape features David Cress of Rochester Institute of Technology on use of French Colors on fabrics. In Beta, VHS or ¾" Umatic for rental/purchase.

I. M. James Enterprises
P.O. Box 100, 102 Fox Run Cr.
Clarks Summit, PA 18411

Send SASE for details.
Book: *Sewing Specialties,* by Irene M. James (how-to professionally machine-sew special items — panty hose, and with elastic threads, pinless zippers, etc.

Jefferson County Adult Education
10801 W. 44th Ave.
Wheat Ridge, CO 80033

Book: *Threadline: Glossary of Sewing Terms* by Susan GainoRoberts (lists over 1,100 terms, over 100 illustrations, spiral bound), $8.00.

Leather Arts Network
Box 79
South Acworth, NH 03607

Send SASE for details.
The network fosters educational opportunities in leather crafts, promotes its appreciation by the public, and communicates among craftspeople. The next annual international conference is proposed for March of 1984.

McCall Pattern Company
Sewing Power TV Course
230 Park Ave.
New York, NY 10169

Write for information.
Joined with Coast Telecourses of Costa Mesa, CA — a telecourse on clothing construction (for colleges and cooperative T.V. stations, etc.): introduces basics, tools/material and introductory sewing techniques; includes construction of five basic garments.

Mountain Mist Quilters List
117 Williams St.
Cincinnati, OH 45215

Send SASE for Professional Quilters List.
Craftspeople who do quilting on commission.

Museum Books
6 West 37th St.
New York, NY 10018
212-563-2770

Bibliography Books for the Fiber Arts, $ .50 (lists and describes books).

The Needle People
P.O. Box 115, Dept. 34
Syosset, NY 11791

"Tools of the Trade ... A Sewing Supply Inventory" $ .50 ppd., lists basic tools and notions for home sewing projects. Divided into sections: cutting tools, marking tools, pressing tools, and others. (Quantity prices on request.)

Quilt in a Day
3016 Quebrada Circle
Carlsbad, CA 92008

Send SASE for details.
Quilting Teacher's aids: manual by Eleanor Burns — details on store demos, classroom situations, an accounting system, others. Professional advertising material package (announces demos/workshops) and student preparation sheets. Teacher supplies/demonstration package, workshop package — keyed to Quilt in A Day™ and The Sampler™ books for classes.

The Quilt Lady
Box 1166
Grand Island, NE 68802

Send SASE for details.
Color slide programs sets of award winning quilts of Grace McCance Snyder, 1980 Quilter's Hall of Fame inductee. Three slides sets available to clubs or for personal collections; gives full views and closeups in full color, with description sheets included. Slide/cassette program set: inspirational life story of Grace McCance Snyder (professionally produced, script with slide change cues: 13 minute program of 63 slides including 35 quilt slides.

Arthur Murray Rein Furs
32 New York Ave.
Freeport, NY 11520
516-379-6421

Send long SASE with specific inquiry.
Specializes in furs, with access to top experts in the field, will answer any questions about furs, or "get the answers from people who have spent 25 to 50 years in selling, manufacturing, remodeling furs", says Mr. Rein.

(Above) Indy American Sewing Guild Fashion Show

(Top left) Indianapolis Guild demonstration

(Bottom left) Indianapolis Sew Fit program

Courtesy The American Sewing Guild

Sew Easy
P.O. Box 548
Clearwater, FL 33517

Send SASE for details.
Sewing Machine Repair Manual, illustrated guide to easy
—repair, given in problem/solution format.

R. L. Shep
Box C-20
Lopaz Island, WA 98261

Book: *Textile, Costume, and Doll Collections In The United
States and Canada*, edited by Pieter Bach (directory, geo-
graphically arranged; mailing list, travel guide), $4.95
(U.S. funds).

Terry's
P.O. Box 14383
Portland, OR 97214

**Information on beginning a profitable sewing busi-
ness** at home; basic equipment needs, rate suggestions,
helpful insights, $2.20.

The Textile Museum
2320 "S" St.
Washington, DC 20008
202-667-0441

**Write for membership information, or send $1.00
for Shop Catalog.**
Organization sponsors educational programs and exhibits.
**Catalog shows books on textiles, quilting and other
related titles. International t-shirts, dress and other
gift items.**

Elizabeth Thompson
Rt. 6, Box 429
Hartwood, VA 22471

Send SASE for details.
**For teachers: Designs created for teaching embroid-
ery techniques** (beadwork, cutwork, counted thread,
needlelace). Design, plus stitch placement, color schemes,
uses for finished piece, list of materials. Accepts commis-
sions.

D. INSTRUCTORS/LECTURERS

This part of RESOURCES lists those from among the businesspeople in the directory who conduct classes, seminars and workshops (most have a great deal of experience in this area). But this is only a sampling of the traveling lecturers — get further information from a national ORGANIZATION, presented in another part of this section.

The list below is, however, indicative of the talent and professionalism of those in the sewing industry.

When writing for information, or with an inquiry about schedules and fees for workshops in your area, be sure to include a stamped, self-addressed envelope.

Note: The instructors have recommended books in their area of interest, for those who can't attend workshops. Contact a BOOKSELLER (section 14) for copies, or check with local bookstore or library.

Color Analysis

Ruth Zimmerli, of Color Compliments
P.O. Box 6130
Springfield, IL 62790

— With six years experience in color analyzing and application, she has conducted color analysis seminars for art associations, clubs, and special store employee training sessions.

Conducts a three hour color class to give color basics and the confidence to combine and use colors well.

Doll/Toy Making

Loretta Daum Byrne of Little Lotus
302 Spring St.
Cambridge, WI 53523

— Has studied dress design at Layton School of Art; writes regular columns for national magazines and markets her original patterns for ethnic doll designs, "inter-racial" families whose children needed dolls that "looked like them", says Loretta. She's available for workshops in the Madison/Milwaukee area.

Ann Cannon of A. Cannon Originals
P.O. Box 8195
Columbus, GA 31908
404-563-1625

— Teaches at a local college and at Ft. Benning, GA, and would consider holding a workshop.

Andrea W. Warner of Andee's Arti-Facts
1641 North Mary Dr.
Santa Maria, CA 93454

— Designs soft sculpture doll patterns, writes for national publications, teaches dollmaking, quilting and applique and is available for classes day or evenings; at group rates, locally only.

Recommended reading: *Creative Dollmaking*, by Gottilly (for basics), *Dollmaker's Workshop* by Guild (for all 'round use) and *The Quilting Primer*, by Frager.

Embroidery (Machine/Hand)

Joyce Drexler of Speed Stitch
P.O. Box 3472
Port Charlotte, FL 33949

— While merchandising a line of Speed Stitch kits and materials, she provides three-day success seminars for training instructors in the Speed Stitch method of "thread painting", "thread sketching". Seminars are scheduled or can be set up for groups of 8 — 10 students.

Gail Kibiger of Sewcraft
Box 6146
South Bend, IN 46660

— This teacher writes a monthly column for the Needle People News, publishes a newsletter on machine stitchery. Holds classes and workshops, at her place of business.

Recommended books: *Machine Embroidery with Style*, by D. J. Bennett (for basics), *Creative Machine Embroidery*, by Graham (for all 'round use) and *Machine Stitchery*, by Gay Swift (for advanced techniques).

Charlene Miller of Keepsakes Designs
571 N. Madison
Ogden, UT 84404

— Works with machine embroidery and has developed new techniques which have been made into reference books.

Recommended books: *Creative Machine Embroidery*, by Graham and her own book, *Keepsake Cutwork — How To Make Lace*.

Janet Stocker of Treadleart
2458 W. Lomita Blvd.
Lomita, CA 90717
213-833-9407

— Publisher of *Treadleart* magazine, she holds classes and workshops in sewing machine embroidery, applique, monogramming, machine quilting and soft crafts; available in the western states with a Machine embroidery slide show and lecture, all year.

The trapunto technique is one to consider for sections of garments. An area that you would normally quilt, for example...cuffs, shoulder sections, yokes, wide hem bands. For design ideas refer to books with line drawings i.e. stenciling, stained glass pattern books, or even coloring books.

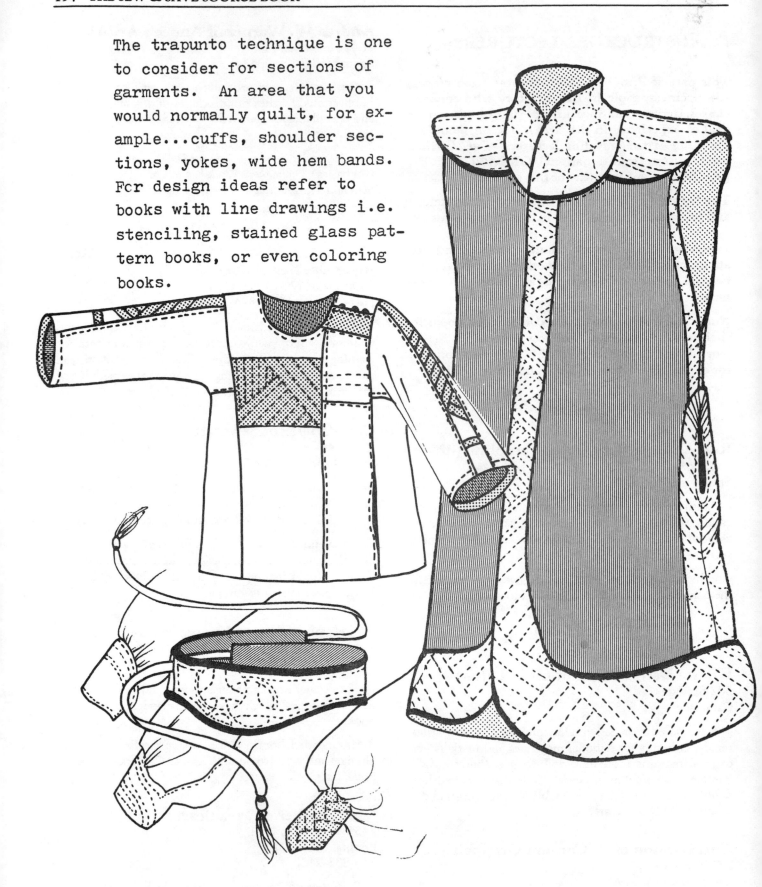

From Design & Sew It Yourself,
© *by Lois Ericson and Diane Ericson Frode,* 1983

Jerry Zarbaugh of Aardvark Adventures In Handicrafts
1191 Bannock St.
Livermore, CA 94550

— Designer/educator/writer/lecturer, winner of numerous awards, noted instructor is available nationwide for two-hour to all day workshops

Fabric Painting/Printing

Linda Durbano of Piira Prints
P.O. Box 1592
Ogden, UT 84402

— Art educator/designer of needlework, fabrics and soft crafts; available for seminars and workshops.

Janet Harlow of Bay Window Designs
201 First, Box 402
Forreston, IL 61030
815-938-3117

— Fabric art designer/instructor; available for workshops or demonstrations on hand-batik fabric with quilting, to give the look of antique woodcuts. Harlow is working on her own book of batik techniques.

Valerie L. Howard of Round Brush Designs
9 Hemlock Rd.
Brunswick, ME 04011

— BS degree in Art Education; available for classes and workshops on stenciling fabric (and other surfaces) for half day, or all day sessions; nationwide.

Recommended reading: *The Art of Decorative Stencilling*, by Bishop.

Diane Tuckman of Ivy Crafts Imports
5410 Annapolis Rd.
Bladensburg, MD 20710

— Noted instructor of silk painting; available for schools, groups, etc., nationwide, on request.

Recommended reading: *Painting on Silk*, by Bruandet, and her own booklet.

General Sewing Techniques

Marilyn Bardsley of Sewing Magic
1612 Glendale Dr.
Marion, IN 46952
317-674-5737

— A certified Sew/Fit Counselor, she presents 2 hour Sewing Magic lectures/demonstrations for stores, teachers, county extension and sewing guilds.

Clotilde of Imports By Clotilde
11 S. Limestone St.
Jamestown, OH 45335

Professional seamstress, formerly with the wardrobe department of 20th Century Fox Film Studios; author of *Sew Smart With Wovens, Knits, and Ultra Suede;* known as a teacher of teachers; available to fabric stores, schools for sessions.

Phyllis Eifler Sewing Seminars
1111 Grape St.
Denver, CO 80220

Home economist, educator, designer presents sewing seminars in Midwest; in cooperation with fabric stores, or independently. Among topics she presents: "Sewing is Getting Easier". "Fit Pants", and others.

Irene M. James of I. M. James Enterprises
P.O. Box 100, 102 Fox Run Cr.
Clarks Summit, PA 18411

— Graduate of Penn State, author of *Sewing Specialties.* Her sewing seminars are available to county extension groups, colleges, workshops or in service training and other homesewing industry groups.

Recommended books: *The New Simplicity Sewing Book* for basics, and *Time-Life Sewing Series,* for all around use.

Peggy D. Layton of Designer Jeans, Inc.
45 E. Gentile St., No. 5
Layton, UT 84041
801-544-3787

— Founder and teacher of copyrighted Designer Jeans Instructor Training Seminars taught throughout the U.S., for professional seamstresses, who become, on completion of the four day sit-and-sew seminars, certified instructors. She is author of *Designer Jeans #1 — The Basics* and others, including on "slip-fit" pattern making, and an instructor training manual.

Bethany Reynolds of Union River Fabrics
125 High St.
Elksworth, ME 04605

— Co-owner of the above store, Reynolds holds classes in English smocking several times a year and in-store demonstrations on sewing techniques about once a month.

Dorothy Stringer of Bishop Method
2633 Woodley Place
Falls Church, VA 22046

— author of *Custom Tailoring*, and home economist, conducts workshops/seminars in sewing basics, designer clothes, tailoring; nationwide.

Handweaving

Mary Pendleton of The Pendleton Shop

P.O. Box 233
Sedona, AZ 86336

—Teacher/lecturer/author on all phases of handweaving and related subjects. Over 30 years in the business, publishes "The Looming Arts", and has been represented in many exhibitions.

Her book, *Navajo and Hopi Weaving Techniques*, is published by Macmillen Publishing Co.

Hatmaking

Denise Dreher

3101 12th Ave. So. #5
Minneapolis, MN 55407
612-722-8951

Send for complete workshop information. A professional milliner/lecturer with T.V. (BBC and others) and Movie credits to her ability*, and tours nationwide giving workshops in hatmaking for universities and organization; can schedule workshops of up to one week. Lectures are given through slide presentations to enhance the overview and methods of hatmaking.
*(including for *The Great Train Robbery*).

Leather Sewing

Jennifer Morgan of Jennifer Morgan Designs

P.O. Box 1073
Sisters, OR 97759

—Degree in interior design, with a custom clothing design business for twelve years. Holds classes and workshops on sewing with suede, available in the northwest and southwestern area of the country.

Recommended book: *Vogue Sewing Book* for sewing basics.

Janet Mysse of Janknits

Box 315
Ingomar, MT 59039

— Sells knitting materials from wool produced on her sheep ranch and her original knitting patterns; offers workshop on furs and leathers combined with knitting. "The knitting is less important," says Janet, "than the sewing together of the garment." Workshops are arranged anywhere, any time.

Marketing, Home Business

Barbara Brabec of Artisan Crafts

P.O. Box 10423
Springfield, MO 65808

— One of the country's leading authorities on crafts marketing and home businesses; author of *Creative Cash* and *Homemade Money*. She gives workshops nationally, and offers private consultation to small business owners. Available as a speaker, nationally.

Pattern Making

Mary Jane McClelland of Fit For You

781 So. Golden Prados Dr.
Diamond Bar, CA 91765

— Certified counselor, teaches by "pivot and slide" method of Sew/Fit, in classes and workshops for stores, clinics, square dance festivals; in southern California.

Mary J. Wadlington of Gem Publications

P.O. Box 2499
Melbourne, FL 32901

— Author of *The Custom Touch*, on pattern making, she has taught pattern making for 15 years; developed the personal pattern for individual fit. Available for four hour seminars to demonstrate her method and the rudiments of pattern making within driving distance of her home, or arranged during her travels.

Quilting and Patchwork

Eleanor A. Burns of Quilt In A Day

3016 Quebrada Circle
Carlsbad, CA 92008

— Author of *Quilt In A Day* and other books, Burns holds classes and workshops in the demonstration of the Log Cabin machine quilting or sampler machine quilting, all day classes at fabric shops, colleges, and quilt shows; available year 'round, nationwide.

Cindy Taylor Clark of Greenhouse Gallery

R.R. 1, Box 6
Alfred, ME 04002

— Quilting artist and designer; holds workshops on applique, design techniques, with emphasis on color theory.

R. V. Dankanics of The Dollhouse Factory
Box 456, 157 Main St.
Lebanon, NJ 08833

— Recommended books for miniature making: *Needlepoint in Miniature*, by Kurten (for basics); *Miniature Needlepoint and Sewing Projects*, by Falk (for all 'round use); and *Needlework in Miniatures*, by Merrill and Jessop (for advanced).

Jane Hill of Hillcraft
P.O. Box 2573
Boca Raton, FL 33427

— Economist/sewing instructor, holds classes in all levels; available for seminars and workshops in the southeast, by arrangement.

Joyce Kelly of Patches of Joy, Inc.
8050 S.W. Wareham Circle
Portland, OR 97223

— Her own original patterns, a McCall's designer and sewing instructor for over 15 years. Gives seminars for stores and conferences nationwide, instructor seminars, workshops and trunk shows.

Recommended book: *Knightsbride* and *Candlewicking*.

Suzy Lawson of Amity Publications
78688 Sears Rd.
Cottage Grove, OR 97424

— Graduate of San Diego College, designer publisher of quilting patterns; available for workshops on Amish quilt designs; or Pictorial quilting of contemporary cloth pictures.

Rosalie Lemontree of The Fashion Sewing Newsletter

Associate in Apparel Design, Fashion Institute of Technology; manager of the Education Dept. of McCall Pattern Co.

Recommends: *Easy, Easier, Easiest Tailoring*, by Palmer/Pletsch for basics; *The Complete Book Of Sewing Shortcuts*, by Shaeffer, for all 'round use; and Fairchild publication for advanced techniques.

Nancy J. Martin of That Patchwork Place, Inc.
P.O. Box 188
Bothell, WA 98011

— Educator/designer with over 50 patterns and 14 booklets to her credit; gives quilted clothing workshops, nationwide, by arrangement.

Jeannie M. Spears of Oliver Press
917 Lakeview Ave.
St. Paul, MN 55117

— an NQA certified teacher, Spears offers a HOME STUDY COURSE and gives classes/workshops for advanced and basic quiltmaking, by arrangement.

Aloyse Yorko of Yorkraft
Box 98
West Redding, CT 06896

— Editor of *Quilt* magazine, quilting teacher and author of quilting books and patterns, she gives classes in her studio, and workshops for quilting groups and seminars throughout the U.S. ... teaching quilting techniques.

Index